Better Late Than Never

For Rene, my link with the past

For Sue, my link with the present

For James, my link with the future

Other Books by Len Goodman

NOTHING!

Better Late Than Never

Len Goodman

with Richard Havers

EBURY
PRESS

3 5 7 9 10 8 6 4 2

Published in 2008 by Ebury Press, an imprint of Ebury Publishing

A Random House Group Company

The Random House Group Limited Reg. No. 954009

Addresses for companies within the Random House Group can be found at www.randomhouse.co.uk

A CIP catalogue record for this book is available from the British Library

The Random House Group Limited supports The Forest Stewardship Council (FSC), the leading international forest certification organisation. All our titles that are printed on Greenpeace approved FSC certified paper carry the FSC logo. Our paper procurement policy can be found at www.rbooks.co.uk/environment

FSC
Mixed Sources
Product group from well-managed forests and other controlled sources
www.fsc.org Cert no. TT-COC-2139
© 1996 Forest Stewardship Council

Printed and bound in the UK by CPI Mackays, Chatham ME5 8TD

ISBN 9780091928025 (hardback)
ISBN 9780091930172 (paperback)

All photos from author's selection except those in second plate section, pages 4 and 5, © BBC Worldwide

Contents

Prologue

Talking the Talk

It was early in 2004. I was 59 years old. I wasn't thinking of retiring, but I was thinking more about getting my life in balance – probably not before time. The dance school was doing well, I was judging and giving lectures, not just in Britain, but also all over the world; however, I was allowing a little more time for golf and the other things that were becoming increasingly important to me. With everything going so well, why was something beginning to get to my wick?

The world of ballroom dancing is certainly not a great big one – it's more like a little village. Six months earlier, in the autumn of the previous year, rumours had begun circulating about a new BBC ballroom dancing show that was to feature celebrities and professional dancers performing together. Every time I went to judge a competition or bumped into mates or acquaintances from the dance world almost everyone asked me the same question.

'Have you auditioned for this new BBC dance show?'

I quickly became tired of finding new ways to say no; of course, I pretended that I couldn't really care less. But the truth was it actually got to the point where it hurt that I hadn't been asked. To be a ballroom dancer you have to be a bit of an egotist. You need to be able to perform in front of thousands of people knowing full well that everyone will be judging you. Dancing is a very competitive world and I don't know anyone that likes losing – me especially. So why wasn't the BBC interested in me?

One morning I had a call from a friend who I'm sure was just trying to rub salt into my wounded pride.

'Ah, Len, I've just been up to the BBC and had a long interview with the people doing this new dance show.' He then proceeded to tell me all about what had happened, before asking, 'So how did you find it? You have been haven't you?'

'Of course I've been! But I don't think it's my cup of tea. So I told them there and then I wasn't interested.' From then on it became my stock answer.

In late March I heard from another friend in the dance world that the programme was going to start on the first Saturday in May. By then the show's name had leaked out – *Strictly Come Dancing*, a lot better than what I later heard they were going to call it – Pro-Celebrity Come Dancing. With time getting along it was obvious that there was no way I was in the running. That evening, unable to control my frustration any longer, I talked to my partner Sue about it.

'I know there's loads of people who've done better as a competitor than me, there are far better coaches that are probably more qualified to do it than me, but I know I'm the best one for the job.'

'And why would that be, Len?' Sue asked, in an as-if-I-don't-know kind of voice.

'Well, they all talk in very technical and boring ways about dancing, their personalities don't come through when they speak. All they will do is baffle people with specialist information.'

I've always known that my biggest asset, my single greatest piece of luck in life and throughout my whole career, has been my personality. There were plenty of others who could dance the dance, but I could talk the talk.

'But Len, you've been saying that you are going to do less teaching and not be so involved in dancing so you can play even more golf. Does it really matter that much?' said Sue, trying to heal my hurt feelings.

'Well, I know I have, but that's not the point! It would still be nice to be asked. Fifty-nine and finished – bloody great!'

'Oh yes, how could I forget it's *that* birthday next month,' said a by now less than sympathetic-sounding Sue.

Within a matter of days I heard that the show's format had leaked out. Pretty soon the names of the judges began to circulate on the grapevine. The producer was someone named Izzie Pick and she and the other executives at the BBC had apparently decided on the four judges: Bruno Tonioli, Arlene Phillips and Craig Revel-Horwood, along with, so it was rumoured, a really nice woman that I knew well from my world of dancing. They had chosen three choreographers from the world of stage dancing and a former world champion Latin dancer. But rumour also had it that Izzie Pick was still not sure if the balance was right amongst the four judges that had been chosen. On paper it seemed perfect, with two men and two women being the obvious way to go.

Besides the judges, they had by this time also chosen the professional dancers. I heard later that Izzie had been chatting with Erin Boag, who along with Anton du Beke, her partner, had been contracted as two of the professionals for the show. Izzie said she was still not convinced they had the best panel of judges and could Erin think of anyone else who might be right for it. Erin ran through a whole host of names and to each one Izzie replied, yes, she'd tried them all. Then, for God knows what reason, Erin said:

'Have you had a go at Len Goodman?'

'Who's he?' Izzie asked.

'Well, he's a bit of a character,' Erin replied.

I'd judged Erin and Anton on numerous occasions. I'd first seen Erin at a little beginners' competition in a small dance school in Southend, although I'd never taught either of them. They had also seen me lecture so I guess all that put together was probably what made Erin mention my name. And so, one evening, the phone rang.

'Hello, is that Len Goodman?'

'Yes.'

'This is Izzie Pick, I'm the producer of a new BBC TV show called *Strictly Come Dancing*, have you heard of it?'

What I said was,'Yes I have.' About bloody time, was what I thought.

'Would you be available to come and have an interview?'

'Yes, I would,' said I, trying not to sound too excited or available.

'When can you come for a bit of a chat and a test?'

'When would you like me?'

'Any chance of tomorrow?'

I said yes, sounding very available and a little excited.

'Do you want a car to pick you up?' asked Izzie.

'No.' I thought it might make me sound expensive if I said yes. 'I'll come on the train, that's fine enough, thank you.'

Saying yes was the simple bit. Deciding what I should wear was much more problematic. I assumed by test that she meant a screen test and not an exam; I hoped so, as I'd never been too swift at exams. For some reason I decided that the English eccentric look was the obvious solution – well, at least to me it was. I thought, having been ignored for so long, that I needed to make an impact, an impression: I just hoped it would be a good one. In any case, what had I got to lose? I'd had a tweed suit that had been made in Dubai that made me look every inch the country gent; best of all it only cost me £150! I'd also bought a pair of two-tone shoes from Crockett and Jones in Jermyn Street; these were more expensive than the suit, but together with a nice shirt and tie they completed the ensemble – perfectly.

The following day, dressed as a slightly off-the-wall Englishman, I arrived at the BBC in Wood Lane where I was met by one of the assistant producers on the show called Matilda: today she's the main producer on *Dancing with the Stars*. She took me to meet Izzie who, when we were introduced, looked at me a little strangely, but covered her apparent shock at my appearance by talking enthusiastically about the show and how glad she was that I could find the time to come in at such short notice. My first impression of her was very positive; I liked her obvious passion for the show and what she thought it would do for ballroom dancing, although I couldn't help thinking she was so young to have such an important role for what could be a huge production. Izzie took me into a tiny room where there was just enough room for a TV monitor, a cameraman and the two of us; we spent the next two hours in there – me talking and the cameraman filming my every twitch.

'So Len, tell me a bit about yourself.' I've never needed any encouragement to talk about myself but tried to keep it as concise as I could, but at the same time I wanted to impress her with what I'd done.

'Well, I've been in dancing since I was 21 so I've been involved in it for close to 40 years. I've taught beginners. I've coached world champions. I've judged every type of competition.' After filling her in with more detail, I said, 'I can teach anyone to dance.'

'What? Even me?' said Izzie, laughing.

'What do you want to learn to do?'

'Salsa,' Izzie replied.

'Stand up and I'll show you.'

So with barely any room to move, I began teaching her to dance.

After this bit of fun we got down to the real business of the interview and Izzie put on a video of a couple doing a waltz and asked me to give a commentary on what they were doing. It was obvious they were not experienced dancers – just beginners' standard.

'Well, his foot work is very good,' said I, before waiting a little while to continue. 'But he just went off time, his left arm is not in the correct position, he lacked rise and fall, there was no sway to the dance, which is one of the characteristics of the waltz.'

'I thought you were really going to enjoy it after your initial reaction,' said Izzie.

'I've always believed that if you're going to criticise someone's dancing then you should always start off with any positives that you can find in what they are doing. I've always done that when I'm teaching.' The truth is I have found that people are more able to accept what's wrong with their dancing if you start by giving them some encouragement. If you accentuate the positive, you tone down the negative.

Izzie next showed me a couple doing the cha-cha-cha.

'His posture is good, with a nice hip action.' Unfortunately it wasn't all good and this time instead of just saying what was wrong I let her have some of my more off-the-wall criticism. 'You know, his arms are a little bit filleted,' followed by another couple of odds and sods.

She showed me two or three other dances on which I commented before we finished.

'Well, Len, thanks very much for all that. It's been lovely to meet you.' She gave me no indication of how it had gone; I left feeling a bit deflated.

I took the Tube back to London Bridge and caught the train home to Dartford.

'So, how did it go?' asked Sue.

'Well, I don't think it could have gone that well because she didn't seem particularly overwhelmed with my personality, knowledge or anything else about me for that matter. I've got a feeling I might be a bit old for them.' Even as I was saying it I was hoping I was wrong. 'She did seem impressed with what I'd done over the years.'

As I talked to Sue it occurred to me that what I could bring to the show was an in-depth knowledge of ballroom dancing that Bruno, Arlene and Craig could not because they shared a background in stage dancing. So maybe, just maybe, I would get the job. However, my realistic side was telling me that my female counterpart had already got it. I also comforted myself with the thought that I'd spent months telling people I didn't want the gig anyway.

Two days later I got another call from Izzie.

'Len, we very much like what we saw of you on the video that we shot when you came in the other day. When I say we, I've shown it to Jane Lush, the Head of Light Entertainment, as well as Alex Rudzinski, the director of the show and we want you to be part of *Strictly Come Dancing*.'

I practically bashed my head on the ceiling.

'Well, that's marvellous. I'd love to do it.'

'We're shooting a kind of pilot show next week, it's not for broadcast, it's designed for us to be able to get the logistics right for the first show that will air a week later. It will, however, be a full dress run.'

'Oh, right.'

'You don't sound so excited all of sudden, Len, is everything all right?

'Oh, oh, yes. I was just thinking of all the things that I'd need to get organised. I'm really excited by the idea and thanks very much for asking me.' After that we talked a little about details and said we'd talk as the week went along to cover off any final arrangements. I found out later that the woman who was also up for the job had pulled out. Apparently her husband, who had also been her dance partner, was about to celebrate a big birthday and she planned to take him to America as a present to celebrate and wouldn't be back in time to do the pilot. She was told that if she wasn't, then she couldn't be in the show. It must have been an agonising decision for her and I would have hated to be in that position myself.

After my conversation with Izzie my head started fizzing with thoughts. Naturally I was flattered that I'd been asked, but suddenly I was also frightened that the show was going to take the rise out of ballroom dancing, which would mean a consequent fall in my reputation. What I loved, what I'd spent all my life doing and trying to achieve for dancing, could be destroyed overnight. The first season was to last 8 weeks and I couldn't help thinking, supposing I'm on this show and it is an absolute mickey take and the whole thing is terrible. Week after week I'd be stuck there on a terrible bloody show. There would be nowhere to go, nowhere to hide; still, if it was that bad they might even pull it off air.

At the back of my mind was the thought that the BBC at one stage did ballroom dancing a great injustice. It wasn't a deliberate injustice, but because of the BBC the general public's concept of a typical ballroom dance teacher was from the show *Hi-De-Hi* – mincing men and women with dresses that looked like an open parachute. Most people's idea of learning to ballroom dance was based on what they saw on that show. Even *Come Dancing* had begun to go downhill the longer it was on air and the worse its slot on the schedules became. I really worried that it could set our little world back and I kept thinking, 'What if *Strictly* is another load of crap?'

I realised, as soon as my head had come down off the ceiling, that there was another more practical problem. The second Saturday of the show was going to clash with the British Ballroom Dancing Championships, which are held in Blackpool every year at the same time. There are certain things in my little world of dance that are very, very important and this is one of them. I had been asked to be a judge, one of 11; given that there's only a pool of 30 in the whole world it was a real dilemma. To be asked is a great honour and it's the absolute pinnacle of our business. I know people in dance who'd literally cut off their leg to be invited to judge. This wouldn't be my first time, but that in no way diminishes the kudos. Over the next two days I called around to speak to a few people asking their advice as to what I should do, and eventually I began to formulate a plan. I'd been told that the second week of the BBC's show was actually going to come from the Tower Ballroom in Blackpool because a lot of the professionals were dancing there on the Friday and the whole show could not have gone ahead without the pros. However, what I was judging at the British Championships would clash with the live television show; I decided I needed to speak to Izzie.

'I know I've told you that I will do it – and, don't get me wrong, I want to do it – but would it be possible to be allowed not to appear on *Strictly Come Dancing* on the second week because I've been asked to be a judge in Blackpool at the British Championships. I would imagine in the 80-odd years that they've been going that no one has ever been asked to judge and turned it down.' I remember kind of laughing a little as I said it to make it seem like a trivial request.

'Oh, no,' said Izzie. 'You either do them all or none at all.'

It was that short and, as far as I was concerned, not very sweet.

I phoned Gill McKenzie, the lady who then ran the British Championships, and told her about the BBC show and how I was hoping that it was going to be a real boost for our business.

I explained that they were going to hold the second week's show in Blackpool and could I be excused from judging for the hour and a half that the BBC show was broadcast on Saturday night.

'Well, a couple of hours at most, Gill, it's only just around the corner to the Tower Ballroom where they will be broadcasting from.'

'Len, absolutely not.'

I was stumped. I went to my closest friends in the ballroom business and explained my predicament. Typical of the replies I got was this fairly blunt assessment of my future from one friend. 'Listen, Len, if you turn down Blackpool you'll never be asked again. You'll be finished in the business.' To a man and woman, that's more or less what they all said.

'Sue, what shall I do? Being asked to judge at Blackpool, although it's flattering, is of no intrinsic value financially other than the fee you get – which isn't a fortune. About all it does is flatter my ego.'

'Len, I think you should do *Strictly Come Dancing*. But maybe you should phone the BBC and find out what they will do if you say you're not going to do their show.'

So I phoned Izzie to ask her.

'We will probably go with just three judges – Bruno, Arlene and Craig, who are all very good in their own fields, but not the most knowledgeable people in ballroom and Latin.'

'Leave it with me, Izzie. I just need to make one more phone call.'

I knew I had to bite the bullet and so I called Gill McKenzie again.

'I am really stuck because you won't let me off judging on Saturday night, neither will the BBC release me. My only wish is to be able to further ballroom and Latin dancing. I think I can serve our interests better by judging the BBC's show than just being one of 11 judges at the Championships. You've got a pool of others that you can pick from who are equally knowledgeable, probably more so than I am. Would you please release me from my contract?'

'I don't like it, Len, a contract is a contract.' I told her that in the past I had been asked to do a demonstration for Butlins at Barry Island in South Wales and a week later I was asked to go to South Africa for three weeks to judge, which was worth 50 times the money, but it never came into my head to cancel Butlins; my word's always been my bond.

'I just think that it's so important for the whole dance world that this show is a success. I'm the only one the BBC has who really knows anything about ballroom and Latin.'

After a bit more chat from me along the same lines Gill said, 'Okay, Len, I'll release you.'

With that our conversation ended, not exactly abruptly, but far from warmly. I fully expected never to be asked again and to be blackballed by my profession. It was one of the hardest decisions I have ever had to make in my professional life. To my surprise, and rather marvellously, after the third week of *Strictly*, I got a letter from Gill. Inside was a compliments slip on which all it said was: 'Len – good decision!' It was really a lovely thing to have received.

Before all that, there was the little matter of the pilot-cum-dress run through on 24 April, the day before my sixtieth birthday – it must have been an omen. Not that I knew anything about it, but Sue had been busy arranging a surprise party at the Ivy in

London for a few of my best friends and closest family. She had also organised a surprise match at my golf club for me and some of my mates. She had wanted to keep it a secret until the Saturday morning, but ended up telling me about it the night before because I was insisting on leaving around lunchtime to be sure to be at Television Centre in good time to film the pilot. She was adamant that there was no need to do that because a car was picking me up from the golf club to get me to the BBC in good time. At first I got a bit shirty about it all. Sue also told me she was taking me to the Ivy for my birthday, just the two of us. What I didn't know at the time was that Sue had called Izzie to see if the pilot could be rearranged for another day. She got the same answer as their original choice of judge: 'If Len doesn't do the pilot, then Len doesn't do the show.' Sue and Izzie had also spoken about getting me over to the Ivy; they agreed it would be tight but I would be all finished by 8 p.m. and a car could then rush me to the restaurant.

I play golf at the London Club, which is in a little tiny village called Ash, not far from Brands Hatch in Kent. My birthday golf game was a real treat and we all had a great time. Sue had arranged prizes and when the golf finished at about half past two we sat out on the terrace, as it was a lovely spring afternoon. Champagne, sandwiches, all my mates laughing and joking, made it a very happy birthday. The BBC had arranged a car to pick me up at four o'clock; by 4.15 there was still no car.

Half past four, still no car. I called Izzie.

'It's going be touch and go for me to get to you by 5.30.'

'It's okay, Len; if the driver gets there in the next few minutes we'll be fine as the programme is due to go up at 6.30 and that should still give you time to get sorted when you arrive.'

'It will, but only if all the traffic lights are going our way.'

Fifteen more minutes went by before Izzie phoned again.

'Len, he can't find the golf club.'

'What a right Herbert!' was what I started out saying, but I'll spare you the rest.

Apparently his instructions said Ash near Sevenoaks, whereas the club is actually ten miles from the town, although it is in the borough of Sevenoaks. Apparently the bloke had been driving around Sevenoaks itself looking for the golf course. He finally got to Ash at 5.30. He was stressed beyond belief, I'm stressed even beyond that and I'm convinced my big break is going to end before it's even started. I jumped in the car and listened to ten minutes of an apology, while he was driving like a ruddy nutcase. We finally arrived at the BBC at ten to seven, the show having started without me, 10 minutes earlier.

Imagine the scene. I'd never really done any television and I walked in – late – and there's Bruce Forsyth and Tess Daly and everyone else. They whisked me on to the set and practically shoved me into my seat. No one had had time to give me any kind of brief and so I was blissfully unaware that there were no professional dancers involved in this pilot. I had no idea what to expect and when a young lad and girl come out who are supposed to be doing a foxtrot I couldn't believe it. As they finished Bruce said:

'We'll go over to our head judge, Len Goodman.'

No one had thought to tell me I'm the head judge: they had just decided I was – I guess it was because I'm the oldest.

'Well, that was pretty good I thought, what do you think of that foxtrot, Len?' says Bruce.

As usual I'm thinking of something positive to say. I was

somewhere between totally confused and in total shock. I was even thinking, maybe this might become the disaster for dance that I had thought it could be. As usual I found something positive to say before giving them a bit of a roasting. Thankfully, while the next couple were dancing, someone came over to tell me that they are just people that work at the BBC; they must have seen the look on my face. I managed to muddle through and we finished at eight o'clock. Izzie and the Director wanted a ten-minute chat and so my leaving for the Ivy was put back. Fortunately, they told us that everything had gone off fine and they were happy with what we'd done on the pilot. Despite all the horrors of my getting to the studio and being late, they said I'd done really well, so at least that put my mind partially at rest. There was plenty to talk over with Sue during dinner was all I kept thinking.

We finally left Wood Lane at 8.25 p.m. to drive over to the West End and as soon as I got in the car I called Sue to say I was going to be late. I was agitated, and upset, that she was having to sit there alone waiting for me, but I was also thinking why the Ivy? I'd been there many times, so for me it was no big deal. At the same time I was excited that the pilot had gone well and things had worked out despite all the earlier dramas, but I couldn't help feeling more than a little frazzled.

When I walked into the Ivy I said, 'Hello, my name is Len Goodman. I'm here to meet my partner, Sue.'

'Oh yes, Mr Goodman, she's upstairs.'

Now I knew that at one time there was a private dining room upstairs, but before I could put my brain into gear Fernando, the maître d', came over.

'Hello, Len, we've turned the function room into a bar, so Sue's waiting for you up there.'

I walked up the stairs and into the room where an absolutely marvellous scene confronted me. My closest friends and family were waiting to greet me; they were all slightly the worse for wear from having to wait for me to turn up. My friend Martin Ling, who's in advertising, was there and he'd done life-size posters of me, including bloody photos from when I was a baby. Besides Martin, there were 11 of my closest friends, my son and my step-mum, the only one of my older family that's still alive. We had a three-piece band – piano, bass and drums – and partied well into the night, singing and dancing. It was a brilliant party and one of the most wonderful nights of my life; the whole thing was just fantastic. The perfect finale to a slightly less than perfect day.

Here I was, 60 years old and starting out on a whole new adventure. Sitting there surrounded by my friends and family, I suddenly thought about something my old dad used to say to me.

'Work is only something you don't like doing.'

Well, I've been blessed because I've had a job I love, one that I would have done even if I hadn't been paid.

Chapter One

Carry On Up the East End

I was very nearly born in Wales. I was also almost born in Whitechapel, within the sound of Bow Bells, but ended up being born in Kent, which will probably come as a bit of a surprise to most people who assume from my accent that I'm a Londoner. Well, I might not have been born one, but I was certainly bred as one. My family were all typical East Enders from a London that was very different from today, although in many respects we were our very own soap opera. My family's world was a two-up and two-down, an overcrowded house, lots of love and laughter, but in the early years there was not a lot of money.

Sixty years before the dress run for *Strictly Come Dancing* and my party at the Ivy, my family could scarcely have dreamed of what would end up happening to me; to them it would have been strictly unbelievable. Although they were Londoners they came from a world that was as far from the glitz and the glamour of television and the West End as is possible to imagine. And while both my mum's and dad's families had lived in London for generations, on Mum's side some of them came from a little further east.

In wartime Britain most people had little or no time to think about what the future might hold; they were too busy getting by, concentrating on the day-to-day. My mother's thoughts, in particular, were on the practical issue of where she was going to have her baby. When she had a pre-natal check-up they found that I was upside down or back to front, I'm not sure which, but whatever it was I wasn't going to be an easy birth. The doctor told Mum that she should go to Swansea to have me. I know Swansea's even further from East London, but in early 1944 Dad and Mum were living in the little village of Felinfoel, about ten miles from RAF Pembrey, which is near Llanelli in South Wales. My father was not serving in the military, but he was an electrician working mostly at airfields, maintaining the lights and other electrical equipment. His was a reserved occupation, one that was considered vital in the war effort, which is why he hadn't been called up into the armed forces.

When Mum arrived at the hospital in Swansea there were no beds available so they decided to send her to London by rail. While she was on the train her waters broke, and so I was very nearly born in a railway carriage. Just as Mum, with me inside her, was leaving Swansea the last major Luftwaffe air-raid on London took place. This was the tail end of what became known as the 'Baby Blitz', Hitler's final attempt to bomb Britain into submission. North-east London took the brunt of the bombing on that raid and I assume because of the fear of more raids, when Mum finally arrived at The London Hospital in Whitechapel it was decided that it was safer to send her to Kent, which is how come I ended up being born in Farnborough on 25 April 1944.

Dad's name was Len Goodman and he was 30 when I was born. My mum's name was Louisa, although everyone called her Lou; she was three years older than my dad. Mum was an Eldridge before she married Dad in 1935. My father had somewhat appropriately met Mum at a dance. Mum was one of five brothers and sisters who were all born in Bethnal Green; not that it was that large a family for the time – my mum told me about her Aunt Emma who had 26 kids. Mum's sisters were Gladys and Ada and her brothers were my uncles, George and Albert. My great-grandfather was of Polish origin and his name was Sosnoski; the family came over to England some time in the early part of the nineteenth century. The only thing I really know about my great Granddad is what my nan told me.

He got the sack from the water works
for smoking his little cherry briar.
The foreman said he'd have to go, Joe,
cos he might set the water works on fire.

His daughter, my nan, Louisa Sosnoski, married my grandfather, Albert Eldridge; he was a costermonger, which is what street traders dealing in fruit and vegetables used to be called. My granddad was a real-life 'barrow boy' and his stall was on Bethnal Green Road.

Granddad Albert was a real character and taught me all sorts of things; he had all sorts of homespun philosophies giving him something of a unique take on life. One day, I must have been about 11 or so, he said to me:

'Your money's like your willie – it only grows if you play with it.'

For Granddad, playing with your money meant pawning his gold watch every Monday morning for a couple of quid. He would then go down to Spitalfields Market to buy whatever he could get. It was always cheap stuff – vegetables or it might be fruit that was not of the best quality – which he'd load on his barrow, a flat thing with two big wheels. They needed those barrows because all round Spitalfields Market there are cobbled streets and they were the only things that could be wheeled around easily. Once he got his barrow back home he'd sort through what he'd managed to buy. Then he'd take his barrow to his pitch in Bethnal Green market where it turned into his stall – his was one of over 200; for six days a week this was his routine.

Come Saturday night he would give my nan the money he had made during the past week to keep the family fed in the coming week. He always kept a little back so he could go down the Beehive, his local, which was on the corner of Harold Street and the Old Roman Road. It was a proper working man's pub – a spit and sawdust – and Granddad never went anywhere else, nor did other people; you stuck to your 'local'. There would always be someone playing the old Joanna (piano) while men hung around the dartboard having a game. Almost everyone smoked, mostly roll-ups, so there was always a fug in the pub. Granddad always kept enough money back to go and get his gold watch from the pawnbrokers for Saturday night and Sunday. On Monday the whole routine would start all over again.

Granddad would rope himself into his barrow, like a horse, and pull it the mile and a half up to Bethnal Green Road from Spitalfields. When I was about four or maybe five, just before I went to school, I would often go with him when he went buying his produce; it seemed like a real adventure to me. He would put me on top of the barrow before pulling us back to his pitch in the market. Every day on the way back from Spitalfields Granddad always stopped at a café called Pellicci's so he could have a cup of tea. It's still there: the café's interior is beautiful, and the marquetry dates from the early twentieth century – it's now a listed building; whenever I'm up that way I pop in for a coffee and to reminisce.

One day a few years later, when I was about 12, Granddad bought a load of celery, which was verging on being rotten – costermongers called it 'melting', don't ask me why. The celery always stuck in my mind because I was given the job of cleaning it. First I had to put it into cold water to 'stiffen it up', then I'd clean it up by cutting off all the brown smelly leaves and then trim off any other rotten bits so we could sell it.

Dad's family came from Walthamstow and his dad's name was James William Goodman. Because we lived with Mum's parents I was much closer to her side of the family and know much more about their family background. It's funny because it's only when you come to do something like this, or when you get older, that you start thinking about your own family history. I've managed to trace my father's family back as far as the early part of the nineteenth century when my great-great-grandfather David Goodman was born in Trowbridge in Wiltshire; ironically, given my love of shoes and dancing, he was a shoemaker. David had moved to Islington by the time my great-grandfather James was born. James married my great-grandmother Sarah in Bedford in 1880 and two years later they had a daughter in Aldershot and then my grandfather James William was born in, of all places, Stirling Castle in Scotland. Not that the family had suddenly shot up in the world, Great-granddad was a gunner in the Royal Artillery and they were based there for a while. By the time the twentieth century came around the family was back in London living in Clifton Buildings in Bethnal Green. Great-grandad was an office messenger and my granddad was a telegraph messenger. Granddad James married Grandma Clara, who was a Spranton before their wedding.

After the war ended Dad, Mum and me lived with her parents in their house in Harold Street, close to Bethnal Green tube station. Recently I found out that Barbara Windsor's grandfather also lived in Harold Street – it was a bit like 'Carry On Up The East End'. Bethnal Green's other claim to fame is that the Kray Twins lived and 'worked' there, but by the time they became infamous we had moved away. The house in Harold Street was a block end, beside a little alleyway that everybody called 'Tight Passage'. You went up this passage, at the side of our house, to our back entrance; unlike the other houses down our street ours had a back yard – although it very definitely wasn't a garden. Off the yard was a door that went straight into the kitchen. From the kitchen there was a room where they used to have the galvanised bath they placed in front of the fire. Once a week my granddad sat in it for his weekly wash. There was also a front room, which was only really used once or twice a week, and that's where the piano stood. The front room faced on to Harold Street; there was a front door that opened straight on to the street. From the hallway you went up the stairs to the three bedrooms. It was the poshest house in Harold Street – which isn't saying a lot.

In the back yard was an outhouse, but to me at five years old it seemed more like a barn – in reality it was just a big shed.

Inside was an outside toilet – the only one we had; the whole family shared it. We didn't have loo paper: we had bits of torn-up newspaper that was kept on a spike. You had a read while you sat doing your business and if you came across an interesting bit that you hadn't finished reading by the time you'd finished, you put it back on the spike but behind loads of other bits so no one else got to use it before you were back in there again. When I say the whole family I mean Nan and Granddad; Mum and Dad; my uncles George and Albert and my Aunt Ada. I never knew my Mum's sister Aunt Gladys because she married Harry, a Canadian soldier, just after the war ended and they went to live in Vancouver.

Years later my dad told me there was a lot of animosity towards Jewish people before the war. My uncles George and Albert were both members of Sir Oswald Mosley's Black Shirts; they used to go off on marches with them and attend rallies. There was a huge one in Bethnal Green in 1936 that they were almost certainly at. By the time war broke out Mosley's party was largely discredited but it didn't stop some people in the East End retaliating against those that had supported his views. On the day war broke out our house in Harold Street was attacked, presumably because of my uncles' involvement with the Black Shirts. It was only the fact that my dad was there at the time that worse things didn't happen; he reckoned my uncles would have been stoned to death. In the event, the air-raid sirens went off and everyone cleared off. Even so every window in Harold Street was broken, because most people in the street were sympathetic to the Black Shirts. When George and Albert were called up they wouldn't go to war: they said they were conscientious objectors. Obviously some people said they were cowards to which their answer was, 'No, you're cowards because you don't want to go to war, but you ain't got the balls to say I'm not fighting.' Whatever the whole truth, because I got all of this second-hand from my dad, this was a big issue around Harold Street; once the war got under way things settled down as it became clear that there was a bigger threat.

Another thing I learned from my dad was about a tragedy that hit Bethnal Green during the war. It was one of those events that probably touched every family living in the area in one way or another. It is known as the Bethnal Green tube disaster and it occurred on 3 March 1943. It's a defining moment in the history of the East End of London and it touched our family. In many ways it represents the complete opposite of what happened at the outbreak of war and the smashing of the windows in Harold Street. This wasn't the East End divided; it was the East End united in sorrow.

Our family's connection to the disaster goes back to before the war when my mum and dad were first married. Mum had two cousins, Harry and Dickie Corbett, who had been boxing champions; Harry was the older of the two, but Dickie the more successful. When Dickie won some money from the fight game he opened a snooker hall in Bethnal Green Road, not far from where Granddad had his stall. He put Harry in charge of the hall even though, or perhaps because, he was a little punch-drunk from having taken too many beatings while he had been fighting. Dickie would sometimes come round to the Harold Street house where Dad and him would spar in the back yard. Now my dad was my size, about 14 stone, six feet tall and he'd done a little bit of boxing, although never professionally. Dickie on the other hand was a bantamweight, who weighed about eight and a half stone; he also had a lisp. According to my dad he packed the punch of a 20-stone man. His fists were lightning fast and when he caught you with a punch you knew all about it.

My dad was mad on snooker so he would also see Dickie sometimes up the hall. One day Dad was playing on a table with a couple of mates when two spivs came in looking for a table. They were big guys and dressed the part in camel coats and trilby hats. Once they started playing they also started taking the mickey out of Harry Corbett, who was small like Dickie. They asked for a cup of tea and because Harry walked a little funny they started telling him not to spill it. As time went along they became even more ugly. Dad said he could see that things could get out of hand but was worried about getting involved because these two geezers looked pretty handy. Harry was obviously getting fed up with it too, and when he was bringing over another cup of tea he spilled some of it on one of the two spivs. This sent them over the edge and they started to really have a go at Harry. One of them said:

'I hear you used to be a fighter, bit effin' pathetic now, ain't yer.'

With that the other spiv stuck up his fists as if to square up to Harry. 'Come on, you stupid worthless git, show us what yer made of.'

In an instant Harry went from being a shambling shadow of a boxer to the real thing; his fists came up and he hit this guy with such force that he literally did a somersault over the snooker table, landing in a heap on the floor on the other side. He was out cold; my dad said it was like something out of a film.

Work began on Bethnal Green tube station in 1936 when the Central line was been extended from Liverpool Street; when war broke out the line was not quite finished. Throughout the Blitz it was used as an air-raid shelter; inside were 5,000 bunks; in all over 7,000 people could be accommodated in it. By March 1943 the bombing of London was not so intense, but after the RAF had bombed Berlin on 1 March there was an expectation that the Nazis would retaliate; when the sirens sounded two days later there was little surprise. As they were wailing three buses stopped and their full loads of passengers began hurrying for the safety of the underground station shelter. Apparently as they did a woman holding a baby fell down the stairs that led to the platforms, a man tripped over her just as there was a shout from the top of the stairs that bombs had started falling. At the same time there was a deafening noise that was not actually a bomb landing at all but a new kind of anti-aircraft gun that was firing from close by. All this led to panic. There was pushing and shoving and, with 300 or more people stuck in the stairwell, the inevitable happened: people started to fall as more and more people crammed into the confined space. When it was all over 101 adults and 62 children were dead from suffocation; 60 more people were taken to hospital. Dickie Corbett was one of the dead. He had been called up during the war and joined the army, but was home in Bethnal Green on leave. He left a wife and three children, one of whom also became a professional boxer – he was known as 'Harry Boy' – who also appeared in a film called *The Square Ring*. Years later I found out from a lady who is helping to raise money for a permanent memorial that Dickie's real name was Richard Coleman, and it's that name that will appear on the memorial.

By the time I was five years old the shed in our back yard also housed a horse for a while. The horse was a sign of Granddad's growing business empire. Soon after getting the horse Granddad moved up in the world from being a costermonger to a real greengrocer when he got a shop on Bethnal Green Road. Not that he got rid of the stall; it was kept and my Aunt Ada and Uncle Albert ran it.

Our back yard was integral to the running of Granddad's business; the shed was always stacked full of potatoes, carrots and beetroot or whatever other vegetables were in season. Besides the shed there was one other thing out in the yard that was vital to the running of the business: the beetroot boiler, which provided me with one of my fondest memories of my early years. My nan was in charge of the boiler. It looked a bit like a cauldron or one of those old coppers that people used for washing their clothes. By the time I was a little kid money was a little easier than it had been before and during the war, and so Granddad was able to buy a sack of beetroot every Monday. It was my nan's chore to cook them in the back yard. Underneath the copper was a large metal ring with eight burners that was connected by a long pipe to the gas supply, somewhere in the house. Besides cooking the beetroot in it Nan also used it for doing the family's washing. As the water was heating up, before she put the beetroot in it, Nan would strip me off and put me in it while it was still tepid. She'd give me a bloody good scrubbing down while I stood in the cauldron – I must have looked a bit like a cannibal's lunch. After I got out, the water was heated some more and then in would go the beetroot for cooking. By then the water would have a kind of scum floating on the top of it after the washing and cooking had finished. I can honestly say I never did pee in it. Customers always commented on how good Granddad's beetroot tasted.

Probably one of the reasons the beetroot water is so imbedded in my memory is because of what Nan used to do while she was washing me – she would sing to me. They were mostly silly little rhymes but they are etched on my mind:

There's a man who came from Norway,
shooting peas up a nanny goat's doorway.

Another one was when she walked her fingers down my little body, going,

Eyes, nose, mouth, chin
walking down to uncle Jim.
Uncle Jim sells lemonade.

As she said this she'd wash my willie and then my bum:

Round the corner sausages are made.

Another like that was when she washed my chest, tummy and willie while saying:

Breast of mutton,
belly of pork,
vinegar bottle without a cork.

If I was naughty or played up, Nan was forever saying. 'You'll have me in the workhouse if you're not careful.' She would say this as a threat to persuade me to be good. By that time the chances of such a thing had long gone but I'm sure that some of my ancestors probably ended up in one. One day my nan taught me a new rhyme.

Mary where art thou,
sitting on a dust pail,
eating mouldy cheese.
Along came a copper,
hit him on the nopper
made him shit brown cheese.

When I sang it to my mum – I was probably four – she said, 'Where did you learn that from?'

'Nan taught it me,' I replied.

That was it: they started on each other with Mum telling her to stop teaching me things; Nan didn't, though.

There was a little boy and his name was Lenny Good.
His mummy gave him sixpence to go and buy some wood.
Instead of buying wood he bought a little toy,
wasn't little Lenny Good a very naughty boy?

Daft but lovely.

Granddad certainly knew his way around a pound note. Besides the beetroot he had another good money-making idea for the business, which was to make their own vinegar. In those days, with no supermarkets, people bought vinegar from their local greengrocer. Vinegar was in far greater use than it is today, as it was an important preservative in the days before every home had a fridge. Every greengrocer had these lovely little barrels with a tap in the side from which they dispensed vinegar into the bottles that customers brought in with them. Sarsons was the main supplier of vinegar and Granddad thought that he could make a bob or two if he could sell vinegar at a price that undercut them. There was only one problem: he would have to make it himself and he didn't have a recipe. From somewhere or another he got hold of a formula for producing it and 'Eldridge Vinegar' went into full-scale production – not quite as catchy as Sarsons, I agree. I seem to remember it involved citric acid and molasses amongst other things. The concoction permanently fermented away in the back yard in a great big barrel, at the bottom of which was a tap from which the smaller barrels were filled and taken to the shop. The tap on the big barrel constantly dripped, which meant that after a few months of making the stuff there was a ruddy great hole in the concrete where the drip landed. God knows what it was doing to people's stomachs, but like the beetroot it seemed to go down very well with the customers. My nan used it at home and it didn't seem to do us any harm either.

There were no such things as sell-by dates and food hygiene regulations in the post-war years. If it looked okay, and when you sniffed it it smelled okay, it probably was okay – so you ate it. After getting in from playing or coming home from school in the afternoon I would usually have a slice of bread and jam, or bread and dripping or, best of all, a sugar sandwich for my tea. If it fell on the floor Mum or Nan would say:

'Go on, eat it up, Lenny, a bit of dirt'll do you no harm.' It helped build your immune system – at least that was their theory, although I'm sure neither of them knew what an immune system was.

When I was a kid there was still rationing in effect even though the war had ended. However, having lived through the war the Eldridge clan, by this time, had become experts at working the system. We were fortunate because there were deals going on between all the traders – the greengrocers, the butchers and the grocers – meaning they used to swap things that were rationed. At the same time Granddad always made sure that anything that was not saleable to the punters came home for us to eat. They called slightly mouldy or damaged fruit and vegetables 'specks', originally costers' slang for a damaged orange that ended up being applied to everything. If an apple or whatever was bad you just cut away the damaged bit and ate the rest; that way you avoided having a maggot.

In the midst of all the costermonger-ing and greengrocer-ing I did go to school, but me and school never did mix that well. My first exposure to education was Cranbrook School, which was a funny place just a couple of streets away from Harold Street. It was a four-storey building and the playground was on the roof – it was all netted and fenced in to stop us falling off. The school's no longer there but the building still is; it's been converted into a block of flats. I first went to school in 1949 and during my first few days there I remember a boy being sent home because he didn't have any shoes to wear. Just like the school, Harold Street is gone and in its place are several blocks of flats.

Having a shop as well as a barrow meant the family's fortune started to improve, due in no small measure to Granddad's business nous. The shop was kitted out with large metal bins into which potatoes, oranges, apples, cabbages and whatever other fruit and vegetables were emptied for display and sale. Potatoes used to come in hundredweight sacks and one day I watched my Granddad hump one into the shop on his shoulders. First of all he emptied half of the potatoes from the sack into one bin and the other half into the next-door bin. He then reached over and took a card on which he wrote 'Selected – one penny-halfpenny/lb' and stuck it on one of the bins. On the next-door bin containing potatoes from the same sack he stuck another card saying 'Regular – one penny/lb'.

'But Granddad, they're all from the same sack...'

'Yes, my son, but you watch – the penny-halfpenny ones will all go before the penny ones do; that's a little lesson you'll learn, Lenny. If you undersell yourself, people sort of don't respect you quite so much.'

And he was right; all the more expensive ones went first. It was another great lesson, one I still think about. While the world's gone logo crazy I still try to think about what's good value for money – whether it's cars or clothes. My runaround car is just a cheap old banger; I don't care if it gets knocked or bashed in the car park when I leave it at the station or wherever. I bought it a few years ago when it had already done 50,000 miles – it cost me 1200 quid. Best of all it never goes wrong.

The variety of shops on Bethnal Green Road and the barrows in the market sold amazing things, especially to a kid. My favourite was a fish and chip shop called Lydons that was run by two old girls; we used to think that their fish was fantastic. One of the old girls did the frying while the other took your money.

'Whaddya want, boys?'

'Rock salmon and chips, please.'

The amazing thing about the one that did the frying was that she always had a dewdrop on the end of her nose. We'd always watch her closely because as often as not it would drop off the end into the batter. Us kids were sure that it gave the batter an extra crispy feel to it.

Another favourite was Kelly's pie and mash shop with the sign in the window saying, 'Kelly's for Jelly' – the jelly meaning jellied eels. There was also a bloke who came round the streets on his bicycle with a large box on the front from which he sold synthetic ice cream. He was called the Okey Dokey Man and he had this little song he'd sing at the top of his voice. 'A halfpenny a half. A penny a large. They're all big pennences and large papers here.' There was another man who came round the streets with a tray round his neck on which there were dozens of little paper objects that he made himself. They were all tiny little things that were made from folded paper. My favourites were the little paper boats he made. They, like everything else he made, he sold for two pins. He'd walk along the street saying this little rhyme. 'Two pins for one, two pins for one, ask your mother to buy you some.' All the kids would run into their house asking their mother for two pins. I've no idea why he wanted pins for payment.

Harold Street was in a rough area: the houses were shabby; no one had a car parked outside their house, because no one owned one. Despite it being a poor street no one's door was locked, so if you wanted to be really secure, you'd shut the door, but the key was always on a bit of string hanging down the inside. All you had to do was to reach through the letterbox and haul out the string and unlock it – everyone did it. As kids we were in and out of each other's houses. If you were round at a friend's home his mum would give you, along with whatever other kids were there, a slice of bread and jam. If my friends were over playing at our house they'd get fed. No one kept score about whose turn it was to do the feeding. One day three friends were at our house and my nan had just given us bread and jam sandwiches when in walked Granddad. I now realise something must have been stressing him because he was normally a really nice easygoing bloke to us kids.

'All you kids get out of here, go on, get off out, and get off home.'

Nan said to him, 'Why are you being like that Albert?'

'Kids are like farts – you only like your own.'

Another of his funny sayings was something he would often say to my nan:

'It's freezing cold out, you'd better wear two hairnets.'

Another time he said:

'Lou' – my nan's name was Louisa, like my mum's – 'this toast is as hard as a beggar boy's arse.' I suppose it's because a beggar boy would sit on the hard cold ground, but whether it was something he made up, or just heard someone else say it, I've no idea. It's a shame I never thought to ask him at the time, but how many of us have those kinds of regrets?

I often think of Granddad Albert when I'm critiquing people's dancing on the television or in beginners' classes because you can't explain to inexperienced dancers what they're doing right or wrong if you try and use technical terms. It's no good saying, 'On that double reverse spin you missed one of your heel leads,' or something similar. It's hard enough for them to learn to dance, let alone know the technical terms.

I once said, 'Dancing is like a garden. You want a lawn, which is the basic requirement, but you also want some flowers. Too much lawn and it's too bland, too many flowers and it just becomes overpowering. A proper dance routine should be some grass and some flowers – some basic stuff and a clever move.'

A lot of what I say is down to Granddad and his queer little anecdotes.

One incident I remember vividly occurred when I must have been five or six. The whole family had been to the pub. I sat outside with the other kids and every now and then Mum or Dad or one of my uncles or my aunt would pop out with a lemonade or maybe a bag of Smith's crisps, the kind that had the little blue packet of salt inside that you sprinkled on your crisps yourself. When it came close to closing time the whole family trooped back up Harold Street with my dad and my uncle George carrying a crate of beer. Once back inside everyone, except Dad, Uncle George and me, was crammed in the front room where Nan and Granddad were playing the piano. We were sat in the kitchen listening to the others singing and carrying on. My Granddad fancied himself – he should have been on the stage or in the music hall; the singer he loved best was Harry Champion and he was always trying to emulate him. While he liked to think he was pretty good, his singing voice was actually rubbish; in fact he had the worst voice in the world. Dad explained to me years later that it turned into a real problem because as soon as he said, 'Right, I'm going to sing,' everyone in the room would look down at their feet or try and avoid Granddad's gaze. It was inevitable that he'd hit a bad note and as soon as he did, if he caught anyone's eye looking at him, he'd say, 'That's your bloody fault, you were looking at me funny like.'

Things would go off, which is what must have happened this particular night because it quickly went from him laying down the law to a full-scale fight! My Uncle George calmly picked the phone up, dialled 999 and said, 'Would you send a police car please to 26 Harold Street. There's a fight broken out.' Just as he said it, there was an enormous crash bang wallop. 'Better make it two.'

Nan and Granddad had only just got a telephone at their house. I'm sure we must have been one of the first families in the street to get one. It gave everyone in the family a good laugh when Granddad had to answer it. He always wore a flat cap known as a cheese cutter. He was never without it; he even slept in it. If the telephone rang he took off his hat before saying, 'Advance 3762, Albert Eldridge speaking.' This was way before telephone numbers became just numbers. Advance covered the area around Bow and the Mile End Road, including Harold Street. I've always wondered why it was Advance and found out recently that it was because the exchange was originally to be called Bethnal Green, but people objected to the down-market name and so Advance was picked; it tells you a lot about where I came from.

As a little kid my favourite day was a Sunday because Mum, Dad and me would go up Petticoat Lane, which was a real experience. The noise, the market traders shouting about their wares was brilliant and the smell of cooking made it seem like a magical place to me. My dad would carry me on his shoulders when I got tired and as I got older and we went down the lane

I was introduced to roll mop herrings, which I still adore, and to salt beef sandwiches. The market was full of stalls and shops selling everything: birds in cages, dogs, cats, household goods – just about everything anyone could need; it was the East End's version of the Bluewater shopping complex in Kent. The geezers that sold stuff had a line in patter that was brilliant, too brilliant in some cases.

One time we went there and Mum said she needed to buy a present for someone whose wedding we were going to; she and Dad settled on a set of china. There was a guy selling the stuff off a lorry with a tarpaulin cover on the back; inside it was crammed with plates, cups, saucers and every other piece of china imaginable.

'C'mon gals, I'm not asking for 18 quid, not even 15, not even 12, nor ten quid, but eight quid for six cups, six saucers, six tea plates, six dinner plates and three serving dishes. I ask yer, is that a bargain or wot?'

At this point a bloke standing near us says he'd have a set. He pushed his way through the crowd, handed over his £8 and walked off with his purchase.

'Now, c'mon ladies and gents, I've sold me first set, anyone for any more? Come on and help make both our days. But I have to tell yer, that bloke was a bit hasty 'cos I was about to drop the price to six quid a set. Have I got any takers?'

With that my mum and several others said they'd have a set. It was one of the oldest tricks in the book, the first customer was a plant, but I didn't understand such things aged seven or eight.

When we got the box of crockery home, and believe me it was heavy as my dad kept saying, Mum said, 'Let's not bother unpacking it,' as it had been wrapped up nicely and packed properly in the box. So they left it and the following week before the wedding they wrapped it in proper wedding paper. After the wedding when all the presents were being opened, to my mum's horror it turned out that the crockery was all odds and bloody sods and some of it was even damaged. The shame!

Other times we would go to Columbia Road market on a Sunday where the array of flowers for sale was astounding. The East End was a mass of markets and streets on which you could buy specific goods. My uncle George, before he started working in the family firm, had a job on Hackney Road, where all the carpenters and joiners had their businesses. Uncle George made ball and claw feet for dressing tables, cabinets and all sorts of things – he got a penny a foot. Wentworth Street, not far from us, was where you went to buy your shoes. There was another Sunday market in Hare Street that specialised in tools and wirelesses – what we called radio. Before the war there had been lots of tailors and clothing companies all around Bethnal Green but when I was growing up these were on the decline.

One of my last memories of when we were still living in Bethnal Green was not about the East End but about the East End moving en masse to Kent. The Eldridge clan plus various other friends and relatives went hop-picking in the county where I was born and would end up living for most of my life. The hop-picking season started in late August and lasted about a month or six weeks, not that we went for that long. I must have been five when we went for a week; I had a brilliant time playing with all the other kids. We'd start out doing some picking but usually our efforts lasted about 20 minutes or so. Then we'd bugger off to play with our mates or other kids we had befriended at the hop fields. In the evening we'd all sit round the campfire where people sang songs and others told stories.

In 1950, shortly after my sixth birthday, we moved permanently to Kent, but it was only my mum and dad and me that went south-east across the River Thames to Blackfen, which is near Welling. Despite having been born in the county, my home, my mates and everything I knew and loved were in the East End so I wasn't best pleased. I'm sure Granddad must have helped them with the money because they bought a greengrocer's in Falconwood Parade and we moved to a small semi-detached house. The parade was a little line of about 15 or so shops that catered for just about all the local area's needs. The houses and shops had not long been built, part of the post-war building programme to make up for what had been lost during the Blitz. Granddad's business must also have been doing really well because around the same time he got another greengrocer's shop on Bethnal Green Road, about 200 yards from the first one – the family was becoming a greengrocer dynasty, not quite Sainsbury's, but still good considering what it all started from. Granddad had stopped pawning his watch a long time ago.

Uncle Albert and Aunt Ada were promoted from the stall on Bethnal Green Road to the other shop, while Granddad and Uncle George took care of the original shop. It was also Uncle George's task to go and buy the fruit and veg. The horse had died by this point; I think he was pretty knackered when we first got him – he was replaced by a lorry. Around four in the morning George would go up to Covent Garden market, the one just north of the Strand in London that has been turned into a tourist attraction, to buy the fruit and veg for all the three shops. He would then head south through the Blackwall Tunnel to deliver the first load to our shop in Blackfen and from there it was back up north to Bethnal Green by eight o'clock to drop off the rest.

From when we first moved to Kent I'd still spend a lot of my school holidays back in Bethnal Green, often staying all week at Nan and Granddad's. To get there I would take the train from Welling to London Bridge and then get on an 8A bus.

'Now, Lenny, tell the conductor you want to get off at the Salmon and Ball,' said Mum. The pub, which is still there and looks much the same, is on Bethnal Green Road, very close to where my granddad had his original shop. And it wasn't just when you went on buses that you asked an adult for help. When I was a boy and wanted to go into a film, one to which you had to be accompanied by an adult, you would stand outside the picture house and ask a man to take you in. 'Mister, will you take us in, mister? We won't sit with you, promise.' This was especially important if he was with his bird.

A few years after we moved I was staying in Bethnal Green when Nan told me there was going to be a street party in Harold Street for the Queen's Coronation. It's difficult probably for anyone who is below 60 to understand just how exciting this all was. In 1953 hardly anyone had television: there was not anything like the kind of entertainment available to kids like there is today. You made your own entertainment. The excitement building up to 2 June was virtually unbearable. I was forever asking my mum or my nan how many days it was until the party.

Every street in Bethnal Green was having a party and each street wanted to outdo every other street. Our street couldn't have been much more than 100 yards long and in every house there were kids. When it finally came it was a beautiful day, there were trestle tables laid out the length of the road, there was bunting hanging from house to house on opposite sides of the street. I'm not sure now what time we all sat down but whatever time it was every seat was filled with an expectant kid.

The first course was a currant bun, which both then and now is one of my favourites; back then not so much the buns as the currants. I carefully ate the bun and made a small pile of currants on the paper tablecloth on one side of my plate; I was saving the best till last. I watched as my pile of currants grew, taking my time, but I also noticed that some kids had wolfed theirs down in a matter of seconds. It was the mums' job to clear the tables after each course and just as I was about to finish my bun and start on my pile of currants one of the mums came clearing the table.

'What? You don't like currants, luv?'

In the blink of an eye my precious pile of currants was brushed into a bin, they were gone. I was devastated and fought hard to hold back the tears. Luckily at that moment the sausages and beans arrived. As they did all the kids started shouting out, 'Yum, yum, pig's bum.' We always said that for some reason before tucking in. What was truly amazing for us kids was that we could have as many sausages as we liked, not just one or two. There were huge frying pans over open fires full of great big fat sausages. For kids who were still used to living in a world of rationing this was nothing short of miraculous.

While we were still eating, a man came along doing conjuring tricks; he was followed by jelly and blancmange. Blancmange was one of my favourites and this time I took no chances and ate that first. All this was washed down with gallons, or so it seemed, of lemonade and cream soda. My granddad provided fruit, which was laid out all along the table; there were apples, oranges, pears and bananas. Some kids had never even seen a banana, let alone eaten one. I had to explain to one boy that you didn't eat the skin.

After our feast was cleared the tables were taken out of the street and games began. There was an egg and spoon race, eating a doughnut on a string and other races along the length of Harold Street. As the day came to an end we were all lined up and given a five-bob bit as a memento. The next day it was back to normality and I went back home to Kent. I took my crown to school, showing it off, but I ended up swapping it, in a fantastic deal as far as I was concerned, for 200 fag cards and a marble with a Union Jack in the middle of it. That evening Mum asked me where I'd put my five-bob bit so she could have a look at it. When I told her what I'd done she went mad and confiscated my cigarette cards and my marble for over a week – an eternity at nine years old. But all in all, the lesson I learned from the Queen's coronation is eat your currants quickly. I'm convinced that's why I eat so fast today; I'm worried about someone nicking my currants!

During the summer holidays, just after the coronation, I was over staying at Harold Street and was out playing with my mates. Much of the East End was still showing the effects of the Blitz and Harold Street was no exception. Halfway along the road a bomb had dropped – this was an area we used to call the glory bumps; kids used to ride their bikes over it, despite us always being told not to in case there were any unexploded bombs. Opposite it was another piece of wasteland that was mostly grass but there was also a large area of tarmac. At one end of the tarmac were two low brick walls that stood slightly above the tarmac and were about nine feet apart. This used to be the entrance to an air-raid shelter. Some of the boys I played with were a bit older than me, maybe 10 or 11, and someone suggested we dig out the entrance to the air-raid shelter that lay between the two brick walls that had been filled in after the war ended.

It was a great idea, but we had nothing to dig with. All of us headed home and got little forks or trowels or whatever we could lay our hands on, so that we could start digging for Britain. This was no easy task given our tools and we spent several days digging out quite a lot of soil until we finally got to expose the whole of a wooden door about eight or ten steps below the surface. The door was pretty manky and while we could easily have broken it down, somehow a little trepidation set in.

'What if there are Germans behind the door?' said one boy.

'Don't be daft, how could there be, we won!' the oldest boy in our gang said.

'They might be dead Germans,' added another.

Before anyone could offer another contribution to the debate a copper came along Harold Street. He probably saw the huge piles of recently excavated earth and wondered what was going on.

'What are you boys up to?'

'Nuffink,' said the oldest boy.

'Well, if it's nothing you better clear off, hadn't you? Go on, be off home.'

We never did find out if there were Germans, either dead or alive, in that old shelter. At around the same time Dad and

George, the man who lived next door to us in Blackfen, demolished the Anderson shelter in our garden. It took a lot of clearing up. War to us seemed so very close.

It was the following summer, when I was ten, that I took a step up in the world as I went from playing my way through the summer holidays to helping the family firm. Besides the two shops there was also money to be made from selling fruit and veg off a stall so I was put to work. I became a part-time barrow boy.

'Hello missus, c'mon girls, I've got some lovely celery, a tanner for two bunches. I've got lover-ley lover-ley tomatoes too.'

Looking back I think it was one of the things that helped me when I became a dance teacher. The ability to talk to people is something that can help get you ahead, and selling off the barrow in Bethnal Green Road gave me some great tips. When I wasn't at my pitch I'd hang around with Granddad Albert at his shop. While I know he liked having me around, he would get on my case for being a pain in the arse at times. I was fascinated by his till, in which they kept the shop's takings. I was forever ringing up the amounts of money that appeared on little tabs in the window on top of the till. Six shillings and 11 pence, two shillings and eight pence, and sometimes I would press too many numbers and jam it, which would really get my Granddad going. 'Len! Len! I've told you, don't keep playing with the Jewish piano.' That was his name for the till because it played the dulcet tones of money being made.

Eventually the Eldridge family bought a third shop in Bethnal Green. I drove by it recently and now it's an estate agents', which probably tells you a lot about how much the East End has changed. But even so, there are still lots of small shops along the road, which continue to ply their trade and make money in much the same way as the Eldridges did.

Life for me with Mum and Dad in Kent was like most kids growing up in the fifties. School, followed by going out to play with my mates in the street or at the local rec – the recreation ground. Dad had given up being an electrician shortly after we moved to Blackfen and started working with Mum in the shop. Life went along relatively smoothly with no great dramas, or so it seemed, but I was becoming increasingly aware that Mum and Dad were arguing more; it got to the point that they were rowing every day. When you're that young you have no idea about relationships and all that kind of thing. Years later I found out just how unhappy together they both were. Dad went to see his doctor, a man named Geddes, who was also a friend of his, and he told him in no uncertain terms that unless he got out of the marriage he could end up killing himself. Dad was so stressed that he lost almost four stone in weight. Soon after seeing the doctor my parents split up – Dad left with a suitcase. I know what he did was right; it's not an environment that anyone wants to be in. It must have been very difficult for everyone involved.

At first I could tell that Mum was really upset; as much as anything it was the shame of it all. In the mid-fifties working-class people just didn't do that sort of thing. There was no one at my school, that I knew of, whose parents were divorced. While we might have been doing well financially our family was still very much working class. As an antidote to the humiliation Mum turned into a workaholic, which is saying something because she was always hard working: everyone in the Eldridge family was. She'd be in the shop from the crack of dawn until ten o'clock at night; it became her release. Even though she got two or three part-time assistants to help her in the shop she took on the responsibility of it all single-handed. She was definitely a chip off my Granddad's block. Looking back I can now see that my mum had no friends, she had no social life and we never ever went abroad on holiday. Ours were usually three- or four-day affairs when we went to Devon at Whitsun or somewhere similar. Mum's whole life was that shop.

When Dad went he left me a little letter saying, 'Please don't think my love for you has changed or anything. It's just that your mum and me can't live together.' Dad eventually met another lady, her name was Rene, and they set up home together in a maisonette in Dartford, just a few miles east of Blackfen. Not too long afterwards I bumped into him in Welling, outside a shop selling furniture. He was buying some things for their new home. Dad gave me a hug and shortly after that he telephoned Mum and they talked for the first time since he left. After that they talked regularly on the phone, especially when I'd been naughty. She'd put me on the phone and get him to tell me off, but it wasn't only Dad dishing out bad stuff. Although initially I didn't see him very much things gradually eased and I started to see him more often – we got on great together and the fact that Mum and him talked made things easier all round.

Just before my eleventh birthday Mum suggested I should do something different.

'Len, the Boys' Brigade is starting up in the church hall up the road. You should go because you'd meet other boys from round here.'

'What's the Boys' Brigade?'

'Well, they do all sorts of things, Len. You'll get a uniform and it'll be fun.'

At six o'clock the following Tuesday I went along for the first night at the new company. I walked in and there was this man; he seemed like an ex-sergeant major. I remember looking up and thinking, 'You look like a giant.' I had arrived at about ten to six, but by a quarter past six no one else had come along – it was just the giant and me.

First of all he explained to me what the Boys' Brigade was all about.

'It's for the advancement of Christ's kingdom among boys and the promotion of habits of obedience, reverence, discipline, self-respect and all that tends towards a true Christian manliness. Have you got that, son?'

'Err, yes...I think so.'

'Well, it looks like no one else is coming, so we'd better make a start. Let's do some marching.'

Next thing I know I'm marching up and down, with him giving orders and pointers as to how to do it better. This must be the discipline part I thought.

'No, no, lad, swing those arms more.' I marched up and down for about ten minutes before he asked me what seemed like a daft question.

'Would you like to play the drum or the bugle?'

'I think I'd like to play the drum.'

'Well, we haven't got any at the moment so you'll just have to pretend and make the noise of a drum while you're marching.'

Next thing I'm marching and mouthing ter-rum, ter-rum and feeling really bloody silly.

'Louder boy! Sound like you mean it.'

The next week two other boys turned up and I think one opted for the trumpet. Like me he just made the noises as we still didn't have the real thing. Not that it would have been any good if we had instruments as none of us had a clue how to play them. Over the next weeks the numbers gradually grew and after about eight weeks the uniforms showed up. I got mine and never went back! Before the Boys' Brigade I'd tried the Cubs but after I got the uniform I never bothered going again. It was the same thing with the Sea Cadets – they came after the Boys' Brigade – although I think it was more the knots that did for me with them. I never could get to grips with knottery.

But school holidays weren't all about being a barrow boy. In the late summer of 1955, when I was 11, and still on school holidays I asked Mum if I could go swimming at the outdoor pool at Danson Park, which was about a mile from our place. I'd been naughty, I guess, so Mum said, 'No! You're not going.' There was no question of my going without telling her because I needed the money to get in. I was so desperate to go that I resorted to stealing, although it was only kind of stealing. Today it's forged £50 notes that everyone's on the look-out for; back then it was forged half-crown coins. The shop was always getting them and, because it was no good trying to take them to the bank, Mum used to chuck them all in an old biscuit tin that she kept at home. I went to the tin and stole a half crown, and soon after I found out that God really does move in mysterious ways.

Having gained admission with my forged half crown, and been given change as well, I changed and went in swimming. I'd been mucking about in the pool for a little while when I got out of the water. As I was running along the side of the pool I slid on the top of an ice-cream tub and over I went, crashing into this little low wall that surrounded the bathing area. I bashed my upper shin on the wall and it really hurt, so much so that I was hopping about yelling in pain. Then, for some unknown reason, I jumped into the pool, maybe hoping the water would ease the pain. Blood was gushing out of the wound and the water around me began turning red. I hobbled out of the pool and by this time it was hurting so much that I was crying. It was literally a bleedin' great gash that clearly needed attention and so I went to the first-aid man, who doubled as the pool attendant. I sat in his little hut and he cleaned it up the best he could.

'You'll need to go to hospital. It'll definitely need stitches. Sit there and don't move,' he ordered.

He then got on the Tannoy, the one they used to tell us to 'stop diving in the shallow end', and said, 'If anybody is leaving the pool and if they're going near to the hospital there's a little boy in need of some stitches. Could they please come to the attendants' hut and see me.'

Almost immediately a man arrived and said, 'I go right by the hospital. I'll take him.'

So off we go, me in this strange man's car, to the War Memorial Hospital in Welling. Can you imagine that happening today? He'd have to have police checks, sign forms and such by which time I would probably have bled to death. Once at the hospital I hobbled in. Obviously there couldn't have been as many people getting ill in those days because there wasn't a queue.

'I'll just wait for you to get stitched up and then I'll run you home,' said the man with the car.

Stitching me up really hurt but once it was done the man carried me into his car and drove me down Shooters Hill to where I lived. 'Do you think you'll be able to walk from the car?' he asked.

'I don't know, mister, I don't think I can.'

So he carried me up the garden path and knocked on our front door.

When Mum opened the door he said, 'I'm sorry, your son has had an accident.'

'Oh?' said Mum. 'You'd better come in.'

He sat down and Mum made him a cup of tea. Eight months later she married him and he became my stepdad.

Chapter Two

Up in the Morning and Off to School

The man who took me home was called Alex Dewdney and pretty soon he was popping round for more cups of tea; before long it was more than just cups of tea. After they got married things in our house changed a bit. To begin with, I think my nose was a bit put out. I never doubted that I was still the apple of my mum's eye, but I was well aware that I was now sharing her affections. At that age you don't really think about your parents having sex or anything like that, but if it did cross your mind you didn't like it very much, at least I didn't. It wasn't that I disliked my new stepdad; it was just that kid thing of pushing the boundaries and trying to get what you wanted by fair means or foul. To be fair, he had a tough time with me. It was all really awkward and if he did give me a wallop, which I probably deserved, I'd quickly say, 'You're not my dad, you can't hit me.' It sometimes led to a bit of friction between Mum and my stepdad. I was from a broken home, in the sense that my parents had split up, but my home wasn't broken in my eyes: it was fine with just Mum and me. I was too young to see it from her perspective; her home was incomplete without a man to share it with, but both my stepdad and I resented each other.

Alex also had a daughter whose name was Adrienne and she was six or seven years older than me – she was a jolly hockey sticks kind of girl. Alex worked for the Pru – the Prudential Assurance Company – he was the 'Man from the Pru'. He used to go round door to door selling penny policies. It seems strange now that this was the way people had insurance: about a third of the population had these little life insurance and endowment policies which they would contribute a few pennies a week towards; the Prudential had an army of these salesmen who collected the money. It was a bit like the Christmas clubs that used to be run at pubs where people would contribute a few pence a week towards the money they spent on presents, food and drink; 36 pounds 18 shillings and 11 pence went a long way in those days. Most people, my mum included, would have nothing to do with HP – hire purchase – and credit cards were something we knew nothing about and it would be years before I had one.

It wasn't just HP that Mum would have nothing to do with. She didn't believe in banks either, nor would she have a mortgage. The greengrocer's shop was all cash in those days. Mum and Alex decided we should move from Blackfen and had a mind to move to Welling, which was a step up in the world. She knew a couple who owned a nice detached house in Marina Drive who were emigrating to Australia. She asked them if they were selling their house. They were, which was great news as it was not just a nice house but it had a good-size garden, too; it was also one of only three detached houses in the road.

'I'll buy it,' said my mum and she did just that – for *cash*. That's how much money the greengrocer's was making. While the new house was nice it had no central heating, and it was just open fires downstairs. Getting ready for bed in the winter was a speedy activity. In the coldest weather I used to get dressed and undressed in bed, I would have all my school clothes by the side of the bed. My rule was that when Mum woke me up to go to school and you could see your breath then I got dressed under the covers.

While the shop was doing well it wasn't just money from the business that bought the new house. In 1957 my nan died; she was only a little over 60. Granddad had died a year or so before and he was only a few years older than that when he died. All the Eldridge kids were left around £3,000 each, a tidy sum back then.

While my mum put her share to good use, my Aunt Ada decided to do just the opposite, or so it seemed at the time. Aunt Ada was the black sheep of the family and she decided that she wasn't going to buy a house; she was going to go on the *Queen Mary* to New York. First of all, though, she needed to look the part and she decked herself out with £500-worth of new clothes, a huge amount to spend.

To put the whole thing into perspective this was a time when more people took the boat across the Atlantic than flew between America and Britain. Taking the boat was a lot more genteel and Aunt Ada had decided this was the way to meet the man of her dreams. She was off to find herself a husband and, having decked herself out like a dog's dinner, she booked her passage to New York on the *Queen Mary*, first class. On the same crossing as Aunt Ada was a gentleman by the name of Albert Wallbanks, every inch the perfect English gentleman, except for one thing.

He was a gentleman's butler, rather than a gentleman. He was butler to Lord Veitch who each winter would holiday in Florida with his wife after having taken the *Queen Mary* to New York and then driven south in the motorcar he kept in America. Albert Wallbanks would be left to close up his lordship's house, which overlooked Regent's Park, before he followed on the next crossing of the liner.

Albert was not someone who wanted to be a gentleman's butler all his life: in truth he was rather partial to the idea of becoming a gentleman in his own right. So there he was, living the high life on board the *Queen Mary*, passage all paid for, on the lookout for a rich widow, when who should he meet on the first day out of Southampton but my Aunt Ada. I would love to have been a fly on the wall listening to the two of them talking with one another about their circumstances. Apparently Aunt Ada had no trouble believing anything Albert said because he was very la-di-da; he even dressed in a white tie for dinner. I can just imagine the two of them giving it large and spinning fantastic tales to one another.

By the time they got to New York they decided they had fallen in love. Albert telegraphed his lordship to say he would not be joining him in Florida and was leaving his employ. The lovebirds then had three or four days in Manhattan before heading back home on the return sailing of the *Queen Mary*. There was just one slight problem: having resigned his position Albert didn't have a return ticket. This was quickly solved when Aunt Ada paid for his passage and the two of them headed homewards to Southampton. As they were approaching home the reality of both their situations must have begun to kick in, but not before they decided to get married. And they weren't going to marry just anywhere: they were going to get married at Caxton Hall in London. This was *the* place to get married. All the society weddings took place there in the fifties and sixties; Ada and Albert were just doing the right thing.

My mum got in a right old tizzy about the wedding. Seeing that it was at Caxton Hall meant we all had to dress up to the nines. She took me to a shop in Bermondsey called Custer's; it was a kids' clothing shop and was *the* place to get kids' suits. Custer's was in Tower Bridge Road and Mum took me to be measured. When they had finished doing that she started looking around the shop where she spotted some nylon shirts.

'Oooo, look Lenny, these are nice.' She turned to the shop manager who had been serving us and said, 'We'll have one of those, thank you.'

The man looked ever so slightly shocked. 'But, Madam, they're four pounds 19 and 11.' Today that would be close to 80 quid and it was clear that the man was implying that Mum couldn't afford it. Mum, without batting an eyelid, said, 'Very reasonable, eh, Lenny? We'll have four.' The following bonfire night I was wearing one of them and waving a sparkler around when I managed to burn a hole in the collar. Mum gave me such a row.

As far as our family was concerned Aunt Ada's marriage to Albert was the wedding of the decade. Before we left home I got a good talking to about behaving myself. I looked like Little Lord bloody Fauntleroy's cousin, although I wasn't alone: everyone else was booted and suited – the East End goes up West!

Their only problem was the money that Ada had got from her inheritance had all but gone. The newlyweds ended up staying in England for just a short period before deciding to go and see my Aunt Gladys and Harry who were living in Vancouver. Albert returned to his former trade and became a butler to one of the richest men in Canada who had made his money in lumber, while Aunt Ada did the cooking and kept house. They must have been pretty good at what they did as they were with him for the rest of their working lives. He, too, must really have appreciated them because when they retired he gave them a fantastic golden handshake, after which they moved back to England. When Albert died, Aunt Ada lived with my mum at Marina Drive for a while. She then got a nice flat in Sidcup and lived there until she couldn't cope on her own. After that she went to an old people's home in Bournemouth, near to where my cousin Martin, my Uncle George's son, lived.

What I love about that story is that it could have all gone pear-shaped so easily after they found out that each of them had been living out a kind of fantasy while on the *Queen Mary*. Instead they really did live happily ever after.

I was far from the best student there's ever been, but what I did love at school was any kind of sport, especially cricket and football, but even that got me into trouble. When I was 11 I moved up to Westwood Secondary Modern; I used to walk to school from our house near Falconwood Parade. It was not very far but it meant crossing the A2, the Rochester Way; you'd have trouble doing that now, as it's one of the busiest roads in Britain, but in the fifties it was a two-lane road. Shortly after I went to Westwood I was picked to play for the under-13s cricket team. The big match of the season was always the one against Chislehurst and Sidcup Grammar School, a team Westwood had not beaten in living memory. They had a boy in their team who was something of a freak of nature. His name was Grover and although he was only 12 he looked about 17. He was head and shoulders above the rest of us, built more like a man than a boy, and was also pretty useful with both bat and ball. We all looked our age and, more to the point, played cricket like we were 12.

Word had gone around that it was almost impossible to bowl him out and he bowled like shit off a shovel; he nearly always took five wickets or more in every game. We would never beat Chislehurst and Sidcup Grammar School with him on the team. In the Westwood team with me was my best pal from school, Peter Dawson – Pete opened the bowling against Chislehurst and Sidcup after they had won the toss and elected to bat. Naturally, more man than boy, Grover was one of their opening batsmen. He and another kid strolled out of the pavilion looking confident and assured; Pete Dawson looked nervous. Pete's first three balls were fended off or let go by Grover who was obviously just getting his eye in. When Pete sent down his fourth ball Grover connected beautifully with it, a certain boundary, and it came flying towards midwicket where I was fielding. I barely had time to see it and just kind of stuck out my right hand, whereupon the ball hit it with such a force that it really stung. Unbelievably I didn't drop the ball: it just seemed to stick to my hand like it was covered in glue. It took a second or so for it to sink in because most of our fielders were looking towards the boundary expecting to see the ball crossing it for four. Suddenly I realised I'd caught him and so did everyone else, although I'm not sure who was the most surprised. Pete looked at me, I looked at Pete, and unlike today where we would have started whooping, hollering and jumping around I just clenched my fist and did a kind of half salute in Pete's direction to show how pleased I was that I'd caught him; Pete did pretty much the same back. With Grover out, there was a collapse in the batting and for the first time since the old king was a boy we'd beaten the Chislehurst and Sidcup Grammar School.

Next morning at our school assembly the headmaster stood on stage. As usual he was wearing his gown, but today he also had a rather stern look on his face, which was, I thought, somewhat surprising given how well we'd done at cricket. He surveyed the whole school before saying, 'Goodman and Dawson, please come here.' The pair of us walked forward smiling, as we knew we were about to be congratulated for our fine performance the previous afternoon.

'Goodman and Dawson, I understand from the sports master that there was disgusting behaviour on the cricket pitch. You both acted in a very unsporting manner and because of this you will take no further part in any cricket for the rest of the season.' And that was it, all for showing some excitement at what we had done. It's one of those enduring memories of my school days that always remind me of how much times have changed.

For the other half of the year we played football and as far as that was concerned there was only one problem – the ball; worst of all heading it on wet, muddy days. Back then they were all made of leather and would get heavier as the game went along. If you were unlucky and the ball connected with your forehead where the lace was located you would walk around for several days with a pattern on your head. But however much it hurt you dared not show that it did; if you did you were a wimp and in real trouble with your mates. There was never any grovelling around on the pitch in bloody agony like you were a big wuss.

One day Pete Dawson and I were having lunch in the school canteen. Although we weren't in the same class we were practically inseparable.

'Len, how do you fancy missing class this afternoon? I've got Rees for science and I hate it.'

'You're lucky,' I said. 'I've got Bishner for history. How about I say that I've got the dentist and my mum forgot to write a note.'

'I could say that my mum's taking me to see my granny who's in hospital,' said Pete.

Despite him being my best mate I was always slightly envious of Pete because he had a bicycle – I didn't. My mum thought they were too dangerous. I had to walk to school because Mum wouldn't let me have one in case I got knocked off it. Having gone to my class and told the teacher about my dental appointment all was fine and he let me go.

'Will you be back afterwards, Goodman?' he said.

'I'll try, sir.' Not likely was what I thought.

With that I was off and heading out of the school grounds when I spotted Pete's bicycle in the bike sheds. No one ever bothered padlocking their bicycle so I thought I'd just take Pete's and wait outside the back gates for him to turn up. He didn't come right away and so I started riding up and down on the pavement. Dawson, unbeknown to me, was not coming because when he had asked the teacher about going to see his poor sick nan, Rees had told him that he wasn't going without a letter from his mother. After about ten minutes, along came a policeman on his bike.

'What are you doing riding up and down on the pavement?' he said.

'I'm just on my way to the dentist.'

'Then why are you riding up and down the pavement?' which with hindsight was not an unreasonable question.

'I was just warming my legs up.' I could feel myself beginning to get nervous, but when he asked his next question I was petrified.

'Is this your bike, lad?'

'Err...no.'

'Then whose is it?' asked the policeman who had by this time propped his own bike up against the school fence.

'My mate's from school. His name's Peter Dawson.'

'I think we had better go back into school and see the headmaster.'

Part of me wanted to make a dash for it but I knew it was pointless. So the two of us started walking back towards the school building with me pushing the bike. Standing outside the headmaster's room with the policeman made me feel queasy. As we walked into his study, he looked at me and said, 'What have you been doing, Goodman?'

Instead of coming clean I kept up the pretence. 'I was going to the dentist.'

As I said it he looked at me and I looked at him – I knew that he knew. The policeman explained what had happened.

'Why have you got Dawson's bike?' asked the headmaster. 'Actually, don't bother answering, Goodman, I'll just send for Dawson.'

Five minutes later in walks Pete, not knowing any of what had gone on.

'Where's your bicycle, Dawson?' asks the headmaster.

'It's in the bike rack, sir.'

'So, Goodman, not only have you lied about going to the dentist – which you do know is playing truant – you've also stolen another boy's bicycle.'

At this point I tried to protest at least partial innocence. 'But sir, you don't understand, I was going to put it back.'

'I understand perfectly well, Goodman. So well, that I'm going to give you 12 strokes of the cane, something I've never ever done before. There's six for the truancy and six for stealing.'

God, did it hurt. Afterwards he sent me back to my history class.

'You're back quickly, Goodman, well done.'

'Well, sir, I told a bit of a lie.'

After telling him what had gone on he decided to punish me too. 'Goodman, stand outside the door for the rest of the afternoon.'

I'm sure everyone has someone from their school days that they remember looking up to. Someone who achieved things that mere school kids could not; boys or girls who were just a cut above the rest of you; kids who are forever etched on your mind for what they achieved – your hero or heroine. Well, mine was Ben Catlow who possessed three exceptional talents. For one he could yodel, and if that wasn't enough he was also able to curly whistle – the technique that makes your whistle warble.

We had a music teacher named Mr Perrin; he was one of the few teachers that you were able to get away with things. In our music room was an upright piano that Mr Perrin would play while we sang along; songs like 'Cherry Ripe' or 'Nymphs and Shepherds'. One day we were all waiting for him to arrive in the classroom when I had an idea. I went over to a cupboard in the corner of the classroom where all the lost property was kept. I picked up every old jumper, coat, old pairs of plimsolls, some football boots, and even a few bags, and loaded them into the top of the piano. Having done so I sat back down with the rest of the class. When Perrin walked into the class, all of us, well most of us, attempted to hold back our sniggers.

'Okay boys, today it's "Nymphs and Shepherds" for our first song. You all remember how it goes, don't you?' At that point he started to sing.

'Nymphs and shepherds, come away.
In the groves let's sport and play,
For this is Flora's holiday.'

He then added. 'You should all put the emphasis on the last part of each line. It's on page 11 of your songbook.'

With that he sat down at the piano and went to play the first chord; nothing happened. He stood up, lifted the lid to see why there was nothing coming from his piano. Nobody could hold back any longer and we all started laughing. This sent Perrin into a rage, like none of us had ever seen before. 'Who did this?' he screamed.

Now I said Catlow was a hero and he was, but he was also something of a timid lad. We all liked him but there was no getting away from the fact that he was a wimp. Perrin, possibly instinctively, went straight over to Catlow's desk where he towered over him.

'Who put the slippers in the piano?' he asked him.

'Go, Go, Good, Good, Goodman, sir,' said Catlow.

'Goodman, come out here.'

As I got up from my desk to walk to the front of the class Perrin began pulling all the things out of the top of the piano that we'd put in there – including a very large white plimsoll.

'Goodman, I rarely give any boy a thrashing but I'm afraid in your case I shall make an exception. I'm absolutely appalled by what you did so I'm going to give you the slipper. Bend over.'

Part of me was thinking, bloody Nora this is going to hurt, but being 13, the other part was thinking I've got to maintain my image. Instead of bending over so he could whack me I bent over with my arse pressed hard against the wall. This was a big mistake.

As I'm bent over, the rest of the class start laughing, but stopped abruptly as the headmaster, who had been standing outside watching the whole episode, burst into the classroom. He was bright red in the face, and came in more like a storm trooper than a teacher.

'What's been going on here?' asked the headmaster.

After Perrin finished explaining, Mr Daniels looked at me and said, 'Goodman, you're pathetic. Go and stand outside my door.'

As I stood waiting for the head to come back to his study I wasn't feeling queasy: I was actually quaking. When he did he just waved me in through the door and made me stand in front of his desk. Having been here before I knew that I was about to get a lecture. And true to form he laid into me, telling me how rude I was, how inconsiderate, finishing with a short synopsis of my future.

'Of course, it's obvious you're never going to amount to anything, Goodman. You're a failure at school. You'll be a failure in life. Your attitude is totally wrong; you have no aptitude for anything. If you think you're only in this world to have a laugh and enjoy yourself you will be in for a big shock when you have to get a job.'

As he finished, silence filled the room. I stood there thinking Blimey is that it, maybe I've got away with it. Then he uttered the immortal words, 'Fetch me my wand.'

I went over to the corner of his study where he kept his cane propped against the wall; it was like Charlie Chaplin's little walking stick although it was a lot less funny in the hands of the headmaster. This time it was only six but his timing was perfect and it hurt like hell. When I got home I looked at my bum in the mirror; it was covered in wheals. There was no way I was going to say anything about it to my mum. She wouldn't have been up the school complaining about why they had caned her poor little Lenny; she would have been so angry at what I'd done that she would have given me another good hiding.

It was like the time my friend and I had decided we would see who could say 'bugger' the loudest during a French lesson. We'd been experimenting for about 15 minutes with the master walking up and down the class reading from his text book. We'd tried it once too often and he just hit us both around the head with his book. As far as I know it did neither one of us permanent damage. When I stupidly told Mum about it she cuffed me round the ear with her hand.

Ben Catlow's third amazing talent? He was the weeing-up-the-wall king! He could pee higher up a wall than anyone in our year and maybe every other year too. The reason for this skill was not just pressure: it was because God had blessed Catlow with an extremely long foreskin. He would pull on it and hold it and then proceed to let fly with a huge jet that could shoot 20 feet or more.

When I was 14 some of my schoolfriends started going to the Court School of Dancing in Welling. I never fancied it much, being more interested in playing football and running. Pete Dawson was always on my case about it. 'Len, you'll love it, you really will. You'll learn how to dance.'

'Well, I suppose so,' was how I reluctantly agreed to go the next week.

Having plucked up the courage it was the start of a ritual. Close to where I lived was a hairdresser's called Maison Maurice, the place where all the lads went for a cut, friction and blow-dry, and even my dad went; not quite Mr Teazie Weazie but close enough for us. I would go on a Wednesday night for mine, having walked straight there from school. Barry was the man to have cut your hair as he did the best 'Boston', the straight across cut at the back. Once Barry had finished the cut he would massage this stuff into your hair – the friction bit – and then he would blow it into shape. It cost two bob, or maybe two and sixpence, but it was money well spent because you looked the bee's knees.

Then it was home for a bath. We didn't have a shower – that was far too fancy. I'd get myself dressed up in my best bib and tucker and meet up with Pete and some of the other lads before heading off to the Court School of Dancing, which was next to the Granada cinema in the High Street, Welling. Being mid-week and as we were still young teenagers it wasn't a late night: we started at seven o'clock and it finished at nine. It was called a 'teen and 20 single mingle', but there was no one as old as 20. It was all school kids from about 13 to maybe 16 years old.

On the first week I made my way gingerly up the stairs into the room. It didn't attract huge numbers but it was a good mix of boys and girls. It wasn't like nowadays with 50 girls and three blokes. That evening we started off with a bit of instruction for about half an hour in which we learned to do the quickstep. All the boys were one side of the room and all the girls over the other side learning their own steps. Next week it might be a waltz that you learnt after which you'd have to partner up, which was the worst bit for me. I found the whole thing very nerve-racking. When I was with my mates I was a bit of a lad but this was not my cup of tea at all. The problem was I was very shy and I had not really been in contact with girls, apart for my cousin Marilyn who I'd seen naked, but that was in 1950 when I was six.

Learning the quickstep with the instructor going, 'Forward on your right foot, side close side, back on your right foot, side close side, forward on your right foot, side close side, back on your right foot, side close side,' was a lot to take in.

'Okay, now find yourself a partner.' Having not been before I hung back which meant the choice wasn't that great. When you're 14 going on 15, who you're dancing with matters to you. Everyone had paired up and there were a few more girls than boys, and before I could get my act together a girl came over and got hold of me. Next thing I knew we were dancing around doing the quickstep – well, after a fashion we did. For the rest of the evening it was more of a free dance but to begin with I was a bit stuck, as I had to wait until a quickstep came on, as it was the only dance I vaguely knew.

As the weeks went by and I got to grips with more of the dances things improved. I sort of learned the basics of the waltz, the foxtrot, the cha-cha-cha and the jive. But even so I was still slow to ask girls to dance on account of being very shy. Eventually my confidence grew and I plucked up the courage to start asking different girls to dance. I went from being a shy little boy to a confident, cocky little bugger. I even started to invent dances to amuse my mates. My best one was the Douglas Bader quickstep. I made my mates all dance with two stiff legs; they all enjoyed that one. I discovered a substitute for conkers, Dinky toys and marbles – it was girls.

One of the highlights of the night was an 'excuse-me' dance. This was when your partner and you danced together and a boy could come over and tap you on the shoulder and say 'excuse me' and take over your girl. It also worked where the girl could be tapped on the shoulder and you got a new partner. If you were left partnerless you had to go and excuse someone else. Every couple or three weeks they would have an excuse-me where you had to kiss your partner goodbye. Naturally this was called a 'kiss-me excuse-me'. The girl we all wanted to kiss was called Sally, but if you went and asked her for a dance on a kiss-me excuse-me she would hardly ever say yes. She'd just sit it out.

Who could blame her; the class cracker didn't want a load of young blokes kissing her. The fact that she said no virtually every time meant that people gradually stopped asking her. Our little gang from my school, there were six or eight of us usually, were always larking about, having bets on whose turn it was to ask Sally to dance. Our master plan was simple: if she said yes to anyone in our gang then every one of us would take it in turns to 'excuse me', and claim their kiss. For reasons I've long since forgotten I was the first one to go over and ask her to dance; I think I probably lost a bet.

'Hello, would you like to dance?' I could feel their eyes burning into the back of my head.

'Yes,' she said; no one was more surprised than I was.

We began our dance together and as we were gliding around the floor I was all eager anticipation. I think they even dimmed the lights a little, which had the effect of making my hormone count rise. The plan was for Pete Dawson to come over and tap me on the shoulder, whereupon I would claim my kiss from Sally. Now there's one thing you should know about the Court School of Dancing. It had quite a low ceiling which meant, with all these teenage bodies dancing around in close proximity to members of the opposite sex, it tended to make you hot. Trying to remain cool was a challenge. Suddenly, out of the corner of my eye, I saw Pete approaching. I felt the tap on my shoulder and I was about to kiss the girl of my, and everyone else's, dreams. Then Pete utters the immortal words, 'Excuse me.' As I'm about to kiss Sally, by some as yet unknown law of physics, my shirt collar turns upwards and comes between our lips. Instead of kissing each other's lips we both kiss my shirt collar. I was totally humiliated. This was my first ever real kiss with the gorgeous Sally; why hadn't I worn a button-down shirt? Fifty years later and I still feel myself beginning to pink up as I write this. The shame, the embarrassment, the ignominy. There was me, thinking that I was about to have a full, what we called a film-star kiss, heads moving in unison, and she and I kiss my bloody collar. Naturally I didn't go to the Court School of Dancing, Welling High Street, for quite a few weeks after that. I was sure people there were talking about little else than how Len Goodman had kissed his own shirt.

Eventually I decided I could face the people at the Court once again. Pete kept on asking me when I was coming back. It was back to my old routine – Maison Maurice for the usual and home for a bath. When I got to the dance school I almost crept up the stairs, not wishing to be noticed. As I got to the top, who was the first person I saw coming out the ladies' loo but Sally! How would she react – would she brush me aside or, worse still, laugh at me? I think I smiled as she approached me.

'Hello, Len, where have you been? I've had no one to dance with.'

My heart soared and before I could really answer her I, in a moment of absolute gay abandonment, said, 'Hello, Sally, would you like to go to the pictures on Saturday?' This was not just asking the girl of your dreams, this was the first time I'd ever had the nerve to ask *any* girl out.

'I'll have to ask my mum. If she says yes it's okay, I'll call you after school tomorrow. You'd better give me your phone number.'

I went home that night with wings on my heels; my heart was fluttering. I, Len Goodman, had actually asked a girl out on a date. In bed that night I lay thinking of Sally when suddenly I got into a cold sweat. Supposing she didn't phone? Worse still, what if she phoned and my mum answered the phone?

Next day at school I couldn't concentrate. All I could think of was Sally. Will she phone? Won't she phone? As soon as school finished I ran home, desperate for her to call.

Normally after school I would be in the front room playing records on our Grundig radiogram, one of those large pieces of furniture with a cocktail cabinet on one side and the radio and record player on the other; I was absolutely fascinated by the radio's dial. It had Radio Warsaw, Radio Lithuania and all these other strange places I'd never really heard of. Right down at the bottom of the dial was Radio Luxembourg, which didn't start broadcasting until 6 p.m. when it was, rather appropriately, time for the Six O'Clock Record Show. Later there was David Jacobs, Sam Costa, Jack Jackson and Alan Freeman amongst the DJs. So before it was time to listen to Luxembourg I played records. Jerry Lee Lewis, Buddy Holly and The Everly Brothers were amongst my favourites. I would stand in front of the mirror miming to 'Rave On', 'Heartbeat', 'Great Balls of Fire', 'All I Have To Do Is Dream' and Chuck Berry's 'School Days'; I was word perfect.

But not that night. I was too nervous to do anything but stand right next to the telephone at the bottom of the stairs in our hall. After a while I got tired of just standing so I sat on the stairs and just stared at it. Ten minutes, 20 minutes, 30 minutes and then at 4.40, 40 minutes after I'd got home, the phone rang. Such was the momentousness of this event in my life I can still recall every detail.

'Hello, Bexley 237.'

'Hello Len, I've spoken to me mum and dad and they said as long as I get home by 7.30 I can come out with you.'

Life would never be the same again. Up to that point my life had been like most young boys'. We lived our lives by an unwritten set of rules that mapped out the whole year. In September and October it was the conker season. Then, for some inexplicable reason, came fag cards – the cards that came free in cigarette packets and later with tea. Next up was miniature cricket using a marble. We used to have a small bat and we'd draw a little set of stumps on a wall. Anyway, all this was no more; girls had entered my life.

Sally and I agreed to meet on Saturday at half past three at Welling Corner as we were going to the Granada, the cinema next to the Court School of Dancing. It was a double feature at four o'clock, which finished at seven, allowing us enough time to get Sally home by 7.30. In the flicks we sat side by side watching the film, neither of us moving. Now, you'll have to trust me when I tell you that I'm not sure how this happened because suddenly we were holding hands. It was magic. It must have been hot in the pictures, either that or nerves were playing a part, because our hands were both wet with sweat by the end of the first film. During the interval I nipped down the front, because we were naturally sat at the back in the stalls, to where the usherette was selling ice creams and bought us a tub of Wall's vanilla ice cream. I hated the taste of the lid having licked it once and thereafter always thought people that licked the lid of a tub were a bit odd. Luckily Sally didn't lick hers. The second film was barely past the opening credits when I put my arm around her and Sally's head rested on my shoulder. It was like Anthony and Cleopatra. There was only one problem: her hair was so highly lacquered it was like having a Brillo pad rubbing against my face. And it smelled; it was like sniffing glue, which I think added to my feeling that I was getting high. Despite everything, I knew that this was the best thing that had ever happened to me in my life.

After the pictures finished Sally said she had time for a coffee. Just along from the cinema was a coffee bar where we both had a frothy coffee – the very latest craze to hit north-east Kent.

There were some kids from my school in the coffee bar and they started pointing at us and making snide remarks, but I didn't care: I was with Sally. When we finished our coffees we left so that Sally could get the bus home. She lived in Plumstead and under normal circumstances I would have got on the bus with her but having paid for the pictures I didn't have enough left for the bus fare, so I waited with her at Welling Corner for the 696 trolleybus. These were as far away from bendy buses as you can get. They were great big double-decker buses that ran on electricity by being attached to overhead wires, and they had great big fat tyres. As the bus arrived Sally turned to me and kissed me goodbye. It was bloody wonderful and I still remember how marvellous it was and how fantastic it made me feel. If you could bottle that feeling it would sell for millions. I walked home with the greatest feeling of euphoria I've probably ever felt before or since. I was in love.

Following this first date Sally, who was a little older than me, and I were courting. She went to Elsa Road School in Welling and so after school I'd run down the hill from Westwood to where she caught the 696 trolleybus and we would stand and wait for the bus together. If there weren't too many people around we held hands. On Wednesdays we'd meet at the Court School of Dancing and sometimes on a Saturday we went to the cinema. This went on until well into December. No conkers, no fag cards, no miniature cricket, just Sally. Then something very odd happened. I spotted another girl at the Court School who was also very pretty. And there was something else: Sally had become a little spotty. Obviously, at that age kids do get spotty but I didn't really understand all this, nor did I like it. But there was something even worse.

'Len, my Mum and Dad would really like to meet you. Can you come around for tea on Sunday?'

Oh no, this was too much. I was 14¾ almost, and here they were, lining me up as a prospective son-in-law. Of course, that was all rubbish, and they probably just wanted to check me out, but that's how I imagined it.

'I can't on Sunday, Sally. I'm sorry, it's my mum's brother's boy's christening.' It was the first thing that came into my head.

Having got myself out of that that, agreed to go to the Embassy ballroom on the coming Saturday. We'd done this a couple of times despite the fact that you needed to be 16 to get in. 'No One Under 16 Allowed, by order of the Management' read the large sign on the window of the booth where you paid to get in. When I queued up to pay I would break out into a sweat worrying about what the lady who took the money would say. It was a pending catastrophe because you were with a girl!

'Are you sure you're 16 son?'

''Course I am. I've been an apprentice for a year.'

'Okay, this time I'll believe you. It's 1/6 each, so that's three bob for the two of you.'

I'd always managed to get in; thankfully this was way before anyone had thought of ID cards for teenagers.

Once inside the Embassy a whole new world opened up. Compared to the Court School of Dancing, which was about the size of someone's very large front room, this was like Buckingham Palace. The Embassy held maybe 300 people on the dance floor, it had a chrome and glass foyer, flock wallpaper, even a silhouette of a lady's head and one of a man's head on the doors of the toilets. The urinals were the poshest I'd ever been in. Added to which the Embassy had a dance band, a kind of poor man's Joe Loss, but it was a hell of a lot better than the records we danced to at the Court. Most important of all it had a glitter ball. Not that we had too long to enjoy all this as Sally still had to be home by ten o'clock. When it was time to leave I said, 'I'm flush this week so I'll come home on the bus with you to Plumstead.'

'Oh Lenny, you're so nice.'

Despite my waning feelings for Sally we held hands on the bus back to Plumstead. I had fourpence, which was just enough to get us both to her place but it would mean me walking all the way back to Falconwood Parade. But first we walked the short route to her home, which was actually a flat above the shoe shop that her mum and dad owned.

The shop was a double-fronted affair with the door set back about ten feet so that the shoes could be displayed in the windows. Men's shoes were on one side, women's shoes in the other window. We walked to the shop's door where we stood huddled against the cold and had a bit of a snog; actually it was hardly a snog, more like a kiss goodnight. The whole thing was rather farcical. I was wearing a mac and as I went to kiss her the lapel of my coat went up her nose. How cool is that? First it was my shirt, now my coat. Things got a little better and I was just beginning to get into the swing of it when suddenly the lights of the shop flashed on and off three times.

'Oh Len, that's my dad. He knows we're down here. He'll be wanting me to go indoors now.'

After one more lingering kiss I turned around to go, but just then Sally said, 'Len, I've dropped my glove.'

The pair of us began feeling around on the floor in the pitch black looking for it, when suddenly she said, 'Found it.' At that precise moment my hand came into contact with a dog turd. As we kissed, one more romantic embrace, I rubbed my hand on the back of her coat. With that, Lenny left Sally and walked home. I didn't go back to the Embassy in Welling for a few weeks. At that age I had no concept of cruelty, and little understanding of another person's feelings.

I should point out here that I hadn't gone to the Court School of Dancing or the Embassy ballroom because of any real love of dancing: there was no desire on my part to take it seriously. I went because that's where you met girls and that was my mission. To be honest it was the same for all my mates; it could have been dancing, bowling or even flower arranging if that's how you met girls and got to go out with them. I was doing what hundreds of thousands of kids across the country were doing. As more old-fashioned forms of dancing seemed to be giving way to rock and roll in a big way, our lives were a little different from what our parents got up to, although it's funny how dancing has been a constant in the whole process of getting to know the opposite sex. I was about to get to know the opposite sex a whole lot better, and naturally dancing played a part, but first there was the small matter of my employment.

Chapter Three

Tradesman

In July 1959 it finally came time for school and me to take leave of one another – there was certainly no sense of loss on their side and I have to say the feeling was mutual. As one of my last school reports said, '*Leonard has, as always, worked hard throughout the year and has made steady progress. Unfortunately he has still not managed to curb his anxiety to be the first one to finish. He must concentrate on carefully finishing work next term.*' All my life I have done everything fast. When I play golf all my mates tell me to slow down. 'Len you're the only person I play golf with, where I end up getting the stitch,' is how John Knight so tactfully put it. On the other hand if I hadn't reacted as quickly when the BBC telephoned about the *Strictly* interview, maybe things would have worked out differently. Life is sometimes like two sides of the same coin, that's how close your strengths and weaknesses are. It's difficult to curb one facet of your character, one that might need a little taming, without adversely affecting something that's a really positive trait.

One thing I wasn't fast about was actually starting work. I had a job lined up but it wasn't to start until September, which meant I had the whole of the summer off. The strange thing is that one day you're a schoolboy, then a couple of days later you're a man. No more conkers, French cricket, fag cards, five-a-side football in the playground with a tennis ball, marbles or British Bulldog. 'Son, you're a man now.' I was 15 and a bit.

Peter Dawson and I decided that because we were now men we should go for a week's holiday to Brighton before we started our respective jobs. First of all, to prove we were real men we had to persuade both our mothers that this was indeed a good idea – no easy task. We were helped in this because Pete's mum and dad liked to go to Brighton on holiday and always stayed in the same bed and breakfast; somehow this seemed to give everyone a degree of confidence and comfort. Pete's mum spoke to the landlady who agreed to keep an eye on us; his mum also sent a cheque to the woman to pay for our digs, breakfast and an evening meal. Mum still didn't believe in banks and so she paid my share to Pete's mum in cash. Once the finances were sorted they probably tried to put each other's mind at rest. 'What possible trouble could those boys get into?'

To cover everything else Pete and I had a fiver each, which was to last us the week. Nowadays that doesn't sound a lot, but as the fifties were ending it was the equivalent of about £200; we were well set up.

'We can spend our days on the beach lying in the sun, watching birds and having an ice cream, can't we, Pete?' Although the ice creams bit sounded a little less manly than I meant it to.

'Yeah! Then in the evenings we can have a beer.' Although how Pete thought we would suddenly look old enough to go into a pub and order a beer, having never done so in our lives before, I'm not too sure. Still, we had it sussed and it made us sound a bit more like real men out on the razzle.

When we got on the train at East Croydon it was a lovely sunny day and all the way down to the coast it remained that way. 'Can't wait to get on the beach, can you, Pete?' However, as we came out of the tunnel just to the north of Brighton that goes under the South Downs, it was raining and it was still tipping it down as we pulled into the station; it would carry on like that for days. I'm not talking showers; I'm talking stair-rods. Spending long lazy days on the beach and soaking up the sun went straight out the window. But not to worry, we had another plan: the penny slots and the amusement arcades on the pier would be our entertainment. After about three days we realised that we had a looming problem. We were shelling out money way too fast. One afternoon, having tired of the pier, the slots, cafés and frothy coffees, as well as hot dogs, we started to rather aimlessly walk around Brighton's famous lanes.

We'd been wandering about for close to an hour, looking more like a couple of drowned rats than the Jack-the-lads we fancied ourselves to be, when suddenly Pete stopped and pointed across the road.

'Len, look!' At the end of Pete's finger was a tattoo parlour.

'Not likely mate, my bloody mum'll kill me.'

'Not if you have it done where she can't see it she won't.'

With that, Pete started across the road to the shop's front door; Pete strode through it with confidence while I followed in his wake. My mum would have killed me, of that there was no doubt, but I was also thinking how much having a tattoo done was going to hurt. The problem is not my low-pain threshold; it's the fact that I have no pain threshold!

Once inside, Pete stood admiring the vast array of designs that adorned the shop's walls. 'What do you think, Len?' Next he pointed to a tattoo with the words 'Mum' and 'Dad' entwined around a decorative staff.

'I'll have that one on my arm, just here.' Pete indicated his right forearm. 'What are you going to have, Len?'

'I'll just have a look while you're having yours done,' I replied, trying to buy myself some time.

Meanwhile Pete followed the tattoo artist through a curtain into the back of the shop so he could begin working on the design. Every now and then I heard a groan, which did nothing to help me concentrate on finding something for myself, one that was both small...and quick.

Finally Pete emerged, grinning from ear to ear.

'Sounds like it hurt, Pete, did it?'

'Nah, not really,' he said.

I wanted to ask him why then had he actually screamed at one point, but decided I might come over as a bit of a wuss.

'So, young fellow me lad, have you decided what you want?' asked the tattoo man.

'Err, yes, I'll have that one.' I was pointing to what was the smallest design in the shop. Tattoo man had to put on his glasses to see what I was pointing at.

'Ah, you want the Saint,' he said. It was a little matchstick man with a halo over his head, no more than half an inch from the tip of his matchstick leg to the top of the halo.

'How much is it?'

'It's half a crown.'

'Okay, that'll be fine.'

Tattoo man and I went behind the curtain into his operating

theatre. Once inside I sat down, and before he could begin I said quietly so that Pete couldn't hear me:

'I've gotta be honest, if it starts hurting at all I'm not having it.'

'You're not going to feel a thing.' And with that he started. The needle had barely touched the skin on my right shoulder.

'Oh no,' I said through clenched teeth, 'I can't. Get off.' It bloody hurt like hell.

'Don't worry, lad, we've all got a strong side and a weak side, this must be your weak side.'

With that he switched to my left shoulder where exactly the same thing happened, except my left side is obviously my weak side because it hurt even more than the right side. I was out of the chair in a flash and back in the front of the shop.

'No, no, I'm not having it, here's your half crown but I cannot go through with it. C'mon, Pete, let's go.'

I was not hanging around, in case he should try to convince me to have it.

The following day we decided to give up on our holiday and head for home – we'd lasted just four days. There was no sun, no beach, no birds and by the fourth day there was also no money – it had completely run out. It was a good job that we'd bought a return ticket. The legacy of that first holiday on my own is two tiny tattoo full stops – one on each shoulder.

After spending the rest of the summer at home messing around, it came time for me to face up to the reality of the rest of my life. Those six weeks actually felt very little different from being on school holidays, except that I knew I wasn't going back to classes. My life was now mapped out for me. It's true that while there would still be plenty of opportunity for football, nights out and having a laugh, there was now the little matter of earning a living. During my last year at school, whenever the subject of me getting a job came up, I'd say to my mum, 'I'd like to work in the shop.'

'Len, don't be daft,' she'd reply. 'It's far too much like hard work. Up at the crack of dawn and even earlier sometimes. What you need to do is to get yourself a trade.' Getting a trade was all the rage in the post-war years, a time when Britain had 'never had it so good'. Especially if, like me, you left school with no O-levels or qualifications of any kind. 'You need to get an apprenticeship,' said Mum. And like many thousands of other school leavers in 1959 that's exactly what I did, although it took a little help from my dad.

Dad worked for a firm called ICT – International Computers and Tabulators – who made the 1950s version of computers; later they became ICL – International Computers Ltd. These computers were as big as houses, so big that if you'd described a laptop or even a PC to anyone working in the factory when I joined the firm they'd have thought it was the stuff of science fiction. Their computers worked off cards with holes in them that all flew out of machines, along with big things that went whizzing round; it was like something out of *Dr. Strangelove*. From my description you can see the technicalities of it all somewhat passed me by. With my in-depth knowledge of the computing and tabulating business, I was clearly going to be a major asset to this rapidly expanding industry.

Mum, having decided that a trade was what I needed, spoke to my dad. He was a manager at ICT so he was able to put in a good word for me and I was taken into the firm's apprentice scheme. I was to be an apprentice engineer fitter and turner; at least that's what it said on the forms I signed on my first day at work. While this sounds all well and good it takes no account of the fact that I am someone who is just not cut out for a job in a factory. They had no idea what they were letting themselves in for – and neither did I.

I brought a similar level of talent to being an engineering apprentice as Peter Schmeichel brought to ballroom dancing; I was just not cut out for it. For me the best thing about the job was my new dark blue boiler suit that looked really smart; all it needed was a hankie in the left-hand top pocket and it would have finished it off lovely.

I was still living at home in Marina Drive with my mum and my stepdad so I would take the train from Welling station to Dartford every workday; from there it was just a short walk to the factory.

Ironically there was no escaping the classroom because for the first six months we spent our time in the apprentice school, plus one day each week we went to college to complete a City and Guilds course. In the ICT classrooms we learned practical skills that included operating lathes and capstans. Our primary task was to make our very own tool kit, one that had four different screwdrivers – I've still got one of them – a shaver thing, a scribe and a number of different 'g' clamps. We were required to make everything to very tight tolerances: no shoddy work was acceptable, so naturally I came unstuck.

It wasn't that I didn't try, it was just I had no aptitude for tool making. I, like probably many others, both before me and since, found that as I showed less and less grasp of what needed to be done, and thc more the others forged ahead of me, I seemed to go further backwards. From being Speedy Gonzales I'd turned into the real slowcoach of the apprentice intake. Those doing the teaching got fed up with me being a poor learner and tended to concentrate their efforts on those who showed more promise; I can hardly blame them. If I'm honest I was more interested in being the all-round class joker; although my fellow apprentices found it funny, those doing the teaching did not. And while I did try and get to grips with things I usually made a complete hash of everything.

Despite my being absolutely useless there were a few little things that did occur that were of a more positive nature, that have stuck with me ever since. Dad said something to me when I first started that did me a lot of good.

'If somebody asks you if you know something and you do, then say you don't, because maybe they'll teach you how to do it in a better way than you've been taught before.' One day exactly that happened. The regular teacher had taught us how to grind a drill that had become blunt so that it was resharpened. It was something I just couldn't seem to get to grips with until on one occasion a man came in to teach us who was a specialist in grinding drills. He asked, 'Are there any of you who don't know how to grind a drill?'

No one said a word except me. 'I'm not really too sure.'

'Okay, son, you stay behind and I'll show you.'

All the others went off but his method was miles better than the way we'd been shown. Since then I've never said I can do something unless I'm absolutely certain that I can, because there's always the chance you might find there's a better way.

When I first went to the BBC to work on *Strictly Come Dancing* I said to the director, 'This isn't my job so please never feel that I'll be annoyed or upset if you tell me how I can do it better. I want to know what I do wrong; I want to learn and improve.' Whenever I start working with a new director I say the same thing. In 2007 I did a new show that was related to *Strictly*, a kind of Eurovision *Strictly Come Dancing*. Before we started filming I said, 'I want guidance because this is not my job, I'm just a dance teacher from Dartford who got lucky.'

This has meant that I've had loads of good advice during my television career that has helped me immeasurably. It's all thanks to a few words of advice from my old dad.

Despite the drill-grinding tips, I was still way off where I needed to be to complete my course; all the other apprentices got their toolkits made in six months, well before I was even close to finishing; they were immediately off and on to the next part of their training, while yours truly was left behind. The other apprentices went and did their three-month stints in all the various parts of the factory, doing such things as unit assembly, final assembly, the drilling section and the grinding section, all part of their apprenticeship to become fully fledged engineers of some description, but I was still in apprentice school trying desperately to get my tool kit finished. I was so useless that I never did get it quite right and eventually, after 14 months, the management took pity, or more likely just gave up on me, and let me loose on the shop floor. Working with the other men at the factory was okay, but it also introduced me for the first time to the world of unions and shop stewards. Ours was a man named Mick, who was a bit of a bully when it came to getting people to tow the union's line. Soon after I left the apprentice school, there was some dispute or another between the union and the management and we were ordered to walk out by Mick. One of the guys I worked with said he didn't want to and didn't agree with it. Mick took the cigarette he was smoking out of his mouth and stubbed the lighted end on the bloke's face. It made me question what the unions were trying to do.

Just before I left the apprentice school, I got another one of those little life lessons that's held me in good stead ever since. It was abundantly clear to everyone that I was lousy at just about everything I attempted; I was the Quentin Wilson of the engineering trade. My ineptitude may or may not have been behind the fact that Bernie Vernon, the man in charge of the apprentices, went from being kind and helpful towards me to the point where he became so exasperated that he turned ultra-nasty. The upshot of all this meant that any filthy rotten chore that came along he gave to me; one in particular I hated. Next to the apprentice's building was the main toilet block for the whole factory; there must have been 30 or 40 traps in this large building.

'Goodman.'

'Yes, Mr Vernon.'

'Boggy, the toilet orderly, has not come in and so I need you to go and report to Jack Smith, the man in charge of factory cleaning. He's got a very special job for you.'

So over I went to see the factory foreman.

'I want you to sweep out and clean all the toilets.' He then added something I've never forgotten, something that I've used throughout my career – both as a dancer and as a teacher. 'But I'd rather you swept out and cleaned one beautifully than swept out the whole lot in the hour and didn't do the job at all properly.'

Concentrate on getting things right one bit at a time so that it's perfect: don't try and rush it so it all just about looks passable.

Six months after I made my escape from the apprentice school ICT decided to close their Dartford factory – everyone was made redundant. The closure of the Dartford factory presented the company with a bit of a problem. We were indentured apprentices, which meant they had to find us new employment in order for us to continue our training and complete our apprenticeships. This was no problem as far as the smartest of the boys – the clever-dicks – were concerned; just about all of them were snapped up by another Dartford firm called Halls. Some of the others, who were also good, but not the best, went to Burroughs and Wellcome, the chemical company; they're now called GlaxoSmithKline. The handful that were still left were farmed out to Vickers in Crayford; everyone, that is, but Leonard Goodman. Given my apparent – make that total – lack of any suitable skills I was the last to get a placement. I ended up at Simms Motor Units in Finchley, a company making injectors for diesel engines. They couldn't have found a more difficult place for me to travel to from where I lived; I don't think it was a punishment but it certainly felt like one. I had to be in Finchley every morning at half past seven which meant getting the train from Welling to London Bridge and the Northern line to East Finchley from where it was a short walk to the Simms factory.

I'd probably been there no more than two days when they realised that they had got one of England's least talented apprentices. The truth was talent didn't come into it; I was total crap. However, whether it was someone at Simms recognising that I might have some useful part to play in their company's future or just out of sheer luck, I'm not sure, but I was put to work with a man named Ralph Phillips. I was lucky because he was not only a lovely man, he was also the Simms' odd-job man, although officially we were called the Maintenance Department. If things needed doing around the factory, like a leaking roof, something that had conked out, a drain pipe that had fallen down or a broken window needed mending, then Odd Job and me were called for – no job was too small for us.

Odd Job's real skill lay in welding and he would fix all sorts of things that came into our little area in the factory; pretty soon he was passing on his skills to me. For someone who had so far been useless at just about everything they had tried to teach me I found that I was a natural welder – well, possibly an exaggeration, but compared to everything else I'd attempted I was a natural. Having discovered I had a knack for it Simms decided I might be more use to them if I were properly trained so they sent me on a three-month welding course at BOC – the British Oxygen Corporation – in Cricklewood on the North Circular Road. Why couldn't it have been Hollywood? Not only had I found something I was reasonably good at, I also enjoyed it. I may not have been the world's greatest welder but following my course I was a match for most people.

After completing my welding course, travelling to and from work sometimes got a little easier, at least in one respect. A lad named Dave Hutton, who was also an apprentice at Simms, lived not far from me in Swanley. He and I were not really best mates, but he would sometimes offer me a lift home on his scooter. It was okay if the weather was reasonable but in winter, on a bad night, it was horrible. It was freezing bloody cold like you cannot believe, added to which, most often as not, I wasn't dressed for travelling on the back of a Lambretta. I'd usually gone to work on the train, dressed in my normal clobber. In those days you didn't have to wear crash helmets and you just hung on the back of the scooter as best you could. It was nothing like those scenes you see from 1960s movies where glamorous Italians ride their Vespas or Lambrettas in the sunshine of Rome; we just looked like a right couple of Herberts.

There was another problem. Dave was not the most savoury looking character on account of his spot problem – not that I want anyone to think I have a phobia after what happened with Sally, but he was covered in blackheads, pimples and worse still. I was prepared to put up with my rather too close proximity to him on account of the fact that the journey took under an hour on the scooter, much less than the tube and train. One night we were haring down the Old Kent Road, getting closer to Welling by the minute, when Dave suddenly turned around.

'You okay, Len?'

As he said this, a load of unmentionable flew out of his nose and covered my face in snot and mucus. It was a bloody nightmare scenario, like a scene out of *Ghostbusters*. To this day it still haunts me. I've never really got over it.

The commute, even with the occasional lift home from Dave the Spot, was a grind. If I took the tube and train I arrived home at seven at night and on many occasions, after about an hour or so at home, I'd say to Mum, 'I've gotta go to bed because I'm getting up again at half past five.'

Finally, enough was enough. I told my mum I was leaving Simms. I'd done my best but this was no life; I had to find something different. Luckily I had one thing working in my favour.

I'd come to realise that maybe my welding skills could be put to better use nearer to home. Most welders are not trained as welders: they are usually employed as something else and they just sort of pick it up as they go along. I, on the other hand, was highly trained! One day I was telling a mate of mine, who was also a West Ham supporter, who worked for Harland and Wolf at the Royal Docks in North Woolwich, how fed up I was with commuting to Finchley. He suggested getting in touch with his firm as they were always in need of trained welders. I did, had an interview and the next thing I knew I was working with a gang of East End blokes – much more my cuppa tea. I couldn't have landed a better little number if I'd have gone looking for it.

Initially I worked in the factory welding up the gantries – the kind that hold the overhead cables for electric trains; we did thousands of the things. When that job was all finished the work became much more varied and as often as not I'd be out welding in the docks themselves, working on a ship. In the days before I started working at the docks it was a very different process, one that was far more labour intensive. To rivet a ship it needed a gang of five men. One to heat up the rivet, another guy, called the catcher, who took the hot rivet and pushed it in the hole. Then you had a guy on the inside of the steel panel, who would bash the rivet into place. Then there was the 'fire guy'; he was needed because the rivets were red hot and therefore it was his responsibility to deal with any emergency. The fifth guy was the one in charge of the gang.

When welding came along the ship-building companies told the rivet gangs that they could get by with a two-man crew. Naturally the union would have none of it, insisting that there should be at least four men on every gang. This meant that for every single electric arc-welding gun there were two welders, so when one of you was welding the other one wouldn't be welding. To operate the machine that created the electricity to drive the welding gun, it needed a man to look after it; this was the plant minder. He sat on his bum all day long watching the machine go round and round. Naturally we still needed the fire guy and that's how I ended up on a crew with three great blokes.

The whole thing was like something out of *I'm All Right Jack*, the film in which Peter Sellers plays a union official who refuses to cooperate with the 'time and motion' people. Like those guys we were up to every trick in the book. On Monday I would clock myself in as well as clocking the other welder in. Next day he would go in and do the same for me; this meant we only worked half a week most of the time. There was another nice little earner that everyone was involved in and that was overtime. The company was keen to get ships in and out of the docks as quickly as possible, so there was never any question of leaving early. In reality, if a job went on after 5 p.m., our normal knocking-off time, we were paid up until 7 p.m. It was amazing just how many jobs actually finished at 5.15 – an extra 15 minutes' work for which we were paid two hours. Similarly, on bigger projects, where we had to go past 7 p.m. meant that we were paid until 9 p.m.; once again a lot of jobs finished at a quarter past seven. The real big bonus was when things went on until after 9 p.m. That would mean you were paid right around until the next morning – no matter what time you clocked off. It's no wonder we don't build too many ships in Britain today.

Obviously working at the docks meant I was earning a packet, a far cry from apprentice wages, although staying at

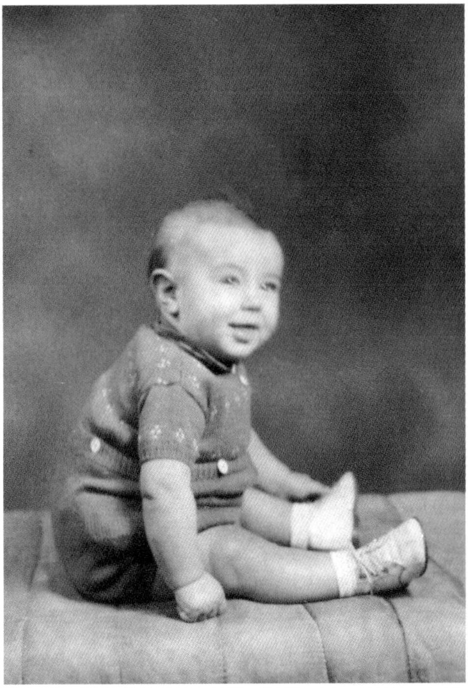

'Our little Lennie' – Me at 18 months, although my dad always said I looked Chinese.

On my 11th birthday; each April my nan knitted me a new jumper.

My first car, with Bubba Miller and his sister. The outside WC is behind us and the beetroot boiler on the right.

Mummy's boy.

Dad and Mum on their wedding day.

Run, run as fast as you can, you can't catch me, I'm the Gingerbread Man! I'm on the right in the front row.

Dad (left) and Uncle Jim with my nan on her 100th birthday.

Coronation day 1953, the day of our street party.

My apprenticeship workmates and me in our football team (I'm 3rd from right at the back).

Going with Dad and Rene to my first dance in my sharp Mod suit.

This is what happens when you drink too much water!

Pete Dawson and Speedo Man.

Four pints and a hat – Brighton boys 1962.

Tripping the light fantastic.

Linda, the girl that started my dancing career.

Henry Kingston, to whom I owe so much, Cherry and me at our first competition.

My second competition,
and first time dancing Latin.

At last, a certificate
for something.

PONTINS

PONTIN CERTIFICATE

This is to certify that Leonard G. Goodman
was placed 1st in the Grand Finals of the
Pontin Novice (Modern Two Dance Trophy) Competition
at Pontin's Grand Reunion Dance, Royal Albert Hall, London
on Saturday, 19th November, 1966

The happy couple,
Cherry and me on
our wedding day.

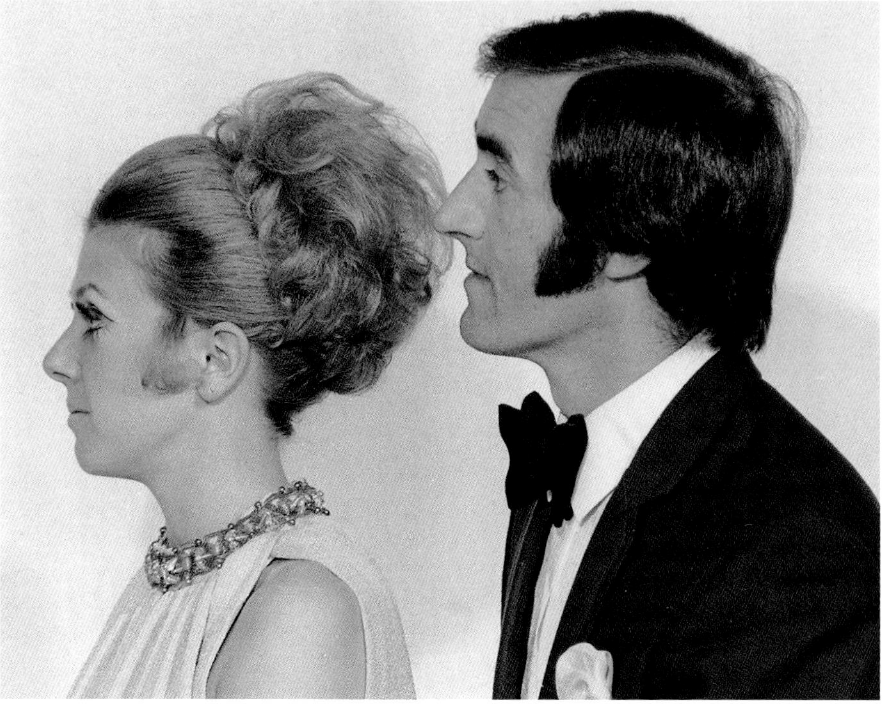

Aphrodite and the man
with the sideburns....

The good news? We came third in the
Kent Championships, the bad news
was there were only three entries!

home, and Mum's natural inclination to spoil me, meant that I always had enough money to go out and enjoy myself. I was also getting more into clothes and with the changes in Britain that were taking place it was a great time to be a teenager. Music was changing too and I, like most kids of 16 and 17 in the early sixties, was excited by what I was hearing. It made me want to spend less time at places like the Court School of Dancing: I wanted to rock and roll. However, for whatever reason, Dad never gave up on me when it came to trying to get me into ballroom dancing.

Dad and my stepmum were regulars at the Erith Dance Studios, which I later learned was owned by Henry Kingston and Joy Tolhurst, a husband and wife who were former world champion dancers. Dad was always pestering the life out of me to go there with them.

'Len, you'll love it, I know you will, you should come.'

'Not on your life, I'm not doing all that old-fogey dancing. I like doing my jiving and there's only one Saturday night a week and I'm not wasting it on a load of old fuddy duddies doing ballroom dancing.'

Nevertheless Dad never stopped badgering me. One week he told me they were having what they called a party dance where a professional couple came along to demonstrate, which was followed by everyone having a bit of a dance. I was probably about 16 or so and thought this all sounded like a pretty daft idea.

'Look, we've got Bill and Bobbie Irvine who are the world champions demonstrating, they are fantastic, Len. You really should come.'

Just to shut him up I went. On the way I told Dad that there was no way that I was going to dance. When we got inside I sat in the far corner at a table with Dad and a couple of other people; it's amazing how old 40-something is when you're pushing 17. I tried not to upset him and when he asked me how I was enjoying myself I said something about it being all very lovely. The guy who ran the club then came out to introduce Bill and Bobbie Irvine. He was in evening dress and, while he looked the part, he made me think they were even older and out of touch. However, even a surly 16-year-old could see the Irvines were fantastic. It must have rung a little bell in my head somewhere because it made me realise how fantastic ballroom could actually be.

Chapter Four

Len the Mod

Having been sneaking into the Embassy in Welling since before I was 16 I wasted no time, once I was old enough, in becoming a regular. They had great dances on a Sunday, but this wasn't ballroom dancing, it was more pop dancing, a bit of pre-Beatles jiving – this was rock and roll. I also went there sometimes on a Friday and my ritual was pretty much as it had been when I was at school; naturally Maison Maurice still figured, but now that I was working meant that cleaning myself up took a little longer. I'd take the train from Dartford and once I was home it was straight into the bath. My biggest problem was that my nails were always black, despite using the Swarfega that was in giant bottles at the factory. I'd scrub them, I'd rub bleach in them, anything I could think of to make them look presentable, because it didn't look too good holding a girl's hands with filthy nails.

The Embassy is now long gone but it will always have a special place in my heart. I was pretty good at the jive as I had a natural rhythm that always allowed me to busk my way through whatever song was played, whether I knew it or not. I'd get hold of any pretty girl in those days just for the fun of being able to jive. To be able to dance you have to have the confidence to just get up and grab someone; you need to just do it and not feel bad if you go wrong. I would practise in our front room using the standard lamp, not as a dance partner but to cast a shadow on the wall so that I could see my hip action! I soon met lots of other people just like me who were there for a good time; some I knew from school, but lots were just people who loved to dance. The trouble was there were always some older guys who it was all too easy to upset. If you looked at their 'bird', their 'bint' or them in the wrong way you were in trouble. 'I'll punch your bloody lights out if you look at her again,' was their typical way of warning you off. I got into a few scrapes but nothing very major, as I'm not really the aggressive sort. Always better to make yourself scarce than be a martyr was the way I saw it. In any event, by the following week they'd forgotten all about you and were probably going out with someone different anyway. The Embassy was always full of top talent.

It was through the Embassy that I indirectly had my very first meeting, of sorts, with Bruce Forsyth. It was not in the flesh, so to speak, but 40 years later, when I did meet him on the pilot for *Strictly Come Dancing*, it reminded me of one of the most embarrassing things that have ever happened to me.

I'd dance with lots of different girls at the Embassy but ended up going out with a girl named Mandy Sawyer. Her dad had a tobacconist and confectionery shop in the same Falconwood Parade of shops as Mum's greengrocer's; the Sawyers lived in a house in Hook Lane. Mandy's mum shopped in our shop and we shopped in their shop, so while our families were not friends we were on speaking terms, which is what ultimately made my relationship a problem. Whereas Sally was a school days' romance, Mandy was a step up; being at work changed the whole business of going out with girls. However, to begin with it nearly never started.

Mandy, like many other girls at that time, had a beehive hairdo and wore black eye make-up and white lipstick; she was very much in the Dusty Springfield mould. She was a skinny girl who loved to jive and she was really good at it too, which was what attracted me to her in the first place. The more we danced the more she grew on me. From just casually meeting up at the Embassy we began to arrange to meet up there and sometimes we went to the pictures – she'd become my girlfriend.

'Shall we go down the Embassy on Sunday?' I asked Mandy. We had been going out together for about three months at this point.

'I can't, Len.' She sounded genuinely sorry. 'I've got to babysit for my uncle who's going out with my mum and dad. How about I ask my mum if you can come round and we can stay in and we'll play some records?'

This sounded pretty good to me, and next day she said her mum was happy for me to go round to their house. I'd been before, but always when Mandy's parents were at home. We would sit in their front room listening to records; her musical taste was more mature than mine and I have her to thank for introducing me to Frank Sinatra, Ella Fitzgerald, Tony Bennett and Sammy Davis Jr. I really loved their style and their voices and have done so ever since. I'm not saying we hadn't had the odd kiss and a bit of a snog, but we always kept one eye on the living-room door so we could instantly move apart if it started to open.

'Hello, Mrs Sawyer,' I'd say, trying to sound very polite and innocent.

'Are you two enjoying yourself?'

'Oh yes, Mrs Sawyer, just listening to records.'

Come Sunday I arrived at seven o'clock and Mandy's mum and dad were still there.

'Everything should be very quiet, Mandy, the two little kids are fast asleep in bed. You two just enjoy yourselves.' Off they went and we decided to watch the telly. It was *Sunday Night at the London Palladium* starring Brucie. As the music started up it acted as a fanfare or an overture, I'm not quite sure which, to my starting some serious snogging with Mandy – heavy petting used to be the technical term. Pretty soon one thing led to another, as it sometimes does, which meant that Mandy, suddenly and inexplicably, had no clothes on. I should point out that I was a virgin and in all honesty I'd never actually got this close to sex. I think I'd touched Mandy's breast once before, but I made out it was an accident – although she didn't seem to object. Not only did she have no clothes on, but I was also naked – well, not quite, I still had my socks on! We were lying on the carpet, fiddling about, fondling and generally rummaging and, unlike before when we kept one eye on the door, we were totally engrossed – neither of us heard it open.

To say it was unexpected would be an understatement. Mandy's mum and dad, her uncle and aunt – whose kids were upstairs – and another brother, along with his wife and their eight-year-old son were all in the room; there were seven pairs of eyes and they were all trained on us. I found out later that the other brother and his wife had unexpectedly decided to join them on their night out and had brought their eight-year-old round for us to babysit. After what seemed like an eternity pandemonium broke out.

'You bastard! Get out!'

I didn't take a second telling: the bastard was obviously me. I jumped up, grabbed as many clothes as I could and ran for it. I was out of the door in a millisecond, closely followed by one of my shoes that flew past my head; next thing my other shoe hit me on the back. As I bent down and grabbed both of them, the last words I heard were, 'And don't bother coming back, you dirty little bastard.'

Was he serious? I had no intention of going back. My only thoughts were how an earth was I going to get out of this predicament.

Their house was in a street where buses ran up and down; I was still naked but rapidly trying to dress myself before another one came along. Once I'd got dressed I suddenly remembered to be petrified. What was Mr Sawyer going to say to my mum? His shop was only a few along from ours. I knew I was in the wrong and I knew what would happen if Mum found out; the embarrassment of being caught was nothing compared to facing her retribution. Imagine if Mandy's mother popped into our shop and, while she was paying for her five pounds of King Edwards, told Mum what I'd done.

'And you know what, your Len had no clothes on.' Topping myself would have been the only option. For weeks I lived in a state of perpetual fear; I've never been so scared, before or since. It's another memory that still haunts me.

After about a month nothing had been said and I began to think – Len, you've got away with it. Having thought about it constantly after it had first happened I suddenly realised that I hadn't thought about it at all for a couple of days. It was then that the phone rang.

'Hello, Len.' It was Mandy Sawyer. 'My dad's forgiven you and he wants to meet you at Welling Corner. He says he'd like to have a man-to-man chat. Tomorrow evening about seven o'clock, can you be there?'

'Okay, Mandy,' was about as much as I could manage to say. I'm sure I turned pale.

The following evening I'd like to say I strolled nonchalantly down to Welling Corner, but the truth is I was too bloody scared to stroll. It was the nervous walk of someone wondering what the hell a man-to-man chat was like. As I got closer I could see Mr Sawyer waiting for me.

'Hello, Len...'

Before he could say another word I was off. 'Mr Sawyer, I don't know what happened. It was a moment of madness. Really I don't.' The words came out in a torrent. 'Nothing like that had ever happened before. One thing led to another, you know, we were just sitting quietly watching Bruce Forsyth on *Sunday Night at the London Palladium* and we kissed each other and I've no idea how we arrived at that situation. How we ended up without any clothes on is still a mystery to me. I've never done anything like that before in my life. I'm so relieved that you came back when you did, because we could have got into all kinds of trouble. I'm not that kind of person and I know your Mandy's not that kind of girl'

I think that last sentence clinched it for me.

'Well, Len, I know that things do happen and I'm prepared to let bygones be bygones. We love our Mandy and we only want to see her happy. The fact is she still carries a candle for you, so we are happy for you to start seeing her again.'

Oh bugger! is what I thought. By now I'd lost interest in Mandy Sawyer, as there was a girl at the Embassy who was an even better jiver. What I thought bore no relation to what I said. 'Oh, thank you Mr Sawyer. I feel the same way about Mandy.'

What a bloody coward! I knew if I said or did anything else he'd be straight round to see my mum. I spent the next six months going out with MS, all the while trying my hardest to get her to hate me. Eventually I succeeded.

Shortly after finishing with Mandy I turned 17. Being an only child has its downsides, but it also had some big upsides as far as I was concerned. None more so than my present this particular year, which will give you an idea of how much my mum spoiled me. She bought me a car, and not just any old car, but a brand-new, 2.4-litre Mk2 Jaguar, the kind that Inspector Morse drove on his TV series. She paid 1400 quid for it from Richard's showrooms in Bexley Heath. My mum was really daft because it would be another eight months before I could drive it, having not passed my test or even had any lessons. God knows what the insurance was, but it must have been huge. Not that I even thought about it because I wasn't the one paying it. That was Mum as well. Her justification for buying such an expensive car, daft as it sounds, was, 'Len, I'm petrified that you might have an accident and kill yourself...or worse.' I'm not sure what was worse than killing yourself but there you are. 'The thing is, Len, you've got to have something that's sturdy, something with good doors.'

Now my mum's yardstick by which she judged cars were ones that had doors that closed with a nice clunk. Never mind the chassis, just as long as the doors were good clunkers. I was more interested in the fact that it had so many buttons and great-looking dials with a fascia of walnut veneer. I know I was spoiled, but at that age who wouldn't love it?

After I'd passed my test I enjoyed being out and about with my Jag. One evening, a month or so shy of my eighteenth birthday, I had a little accident in the car park of the Black Prince pub in Bexley, just off the A2. I was backing out of a parking spot when a car came along and bashed into the back of my Jag. I'm not sure whether it was my fault or his – it was probably 50–50. When I got home I told Mum, who despite the fact that it was the slightest of knocks, said, 'That's it, Len. You can't drive that car any more. It might have knocked the wheels out of place.'

What that meant I'm not sure but she promptly said we'd have to sell it.

'Don't worry, Len, we'll just get you another.'

This time it was a 3.8 litre Mk2 Jaguar. From memory the doors didn't clunk shut any better.

That little greengrocer's was a goldmine; there were often queues of people outside waiting to be served. This was before the supermarkets took hold and people started shopping once a week. Back then everyone bought their fruit and vegetables every day, or perhaps every other day or so. Most people didn't have fridges, although we had one for the shop. It was one of those big walk-in butcher's fridges in which we kept the more perishable produce. What's interesting is that shops didn't open up and then disappear after a few months; there were certainly no charity shops. Along Falconwood Parade were two butchers', an independent and Dewhurst's which was a big chain of butcher's shops. There was Burford's the baker, where old Jack Burford baked all his own stuff, there was a barber, two newsagents' and tobacconists' and a Co-op. Mum got all her other groceries from there as well as the divi – the dividend. When the Co-op started trading in the nineteenth century they made all their customers members of the 'Co-operative Society'. Everyone received an annual dividend in proportion to their purchases. Shortly after we moved to Falconwood Parade, we had been followed there by my Uncle John and Aunt Ruby, my dad's sister. They had a crockery shop called John Petty's in which they sold tableware, glasses, some hardware and little porcelain knick-knacks. John had been in the Navy, where he was Petty Officer Petty.

By the spring of 1962 I was going out with a girl who I had met at the Embassy. We only went out together a few times but she was a really good dancer. One night I asked her if she'd like to go to the pictures during the week.

'Only if we can go and see *West Side Story*,' she said.

Now I've always enjoyed musicals and so she got no argument from me. From the opening sequence, which features the Sharks and the Jets, I was hooked and have continued to be. Nothing could compare with the dancing in that film: for me it's one of the greatest films of all time and I've watched it umpteen times. I love the songs too – 'Somewhere', 'Something's Coming', 'Tonight', 'Maria' and 'America' take me back to that first time I saw the film at the Granada in Welling.

Around the same time I saw *West Side Story* for the first time, a fantastic event took place in Welling – Lorraine's coffee bar opened; this was the place where the in-crowd met. This was shortly before I started work at the docks and so I was still on apprentice's wages of two pound 50 a week.

In the late fifties Welling High Street was a mass of small shops, like a slightly bigger version of Falconwood Parade; Dixon's furniture store had closed down and for about two years it had stood empty. Its windows were covered with stickers saying 'Bill Posters will be Prosecuted'; I never could work out who Bill Posters was. One day a sign had gone up in the window saying 'Opening Soon: Lorraine's'. Bugger me, I thought, another ladies' dress shop. One Saturday afternoon I'd been having a kick-around on Shoulder of Mutton Green with a load of mates when we decided we'd had enough and so we headed off down the High Street to go to the pictures. For some reason the 20 or so of us were walking along, one behind each other like a snake. We'd just passed Marzell's, men's outfitters, where they sold cutaway-collared shirts, when all of a sudden we ground to a halt. We were stunned. The new shop opening up was not for ladies' clothes – it was a coffee shop. Blimey, not even Bexley Heath had a coffee shop and here was Welling with its very own 2i's! We all piled in where the owners, whose names we later found out were Mike and Lorraine, must have thought all their Christmases had come at once, as we all had a couple of coffees each at two shillings a cup. It had the very latest in plastic-moulded chairs, Formica-topped tables, glass cups filled with coffee and froth, and machines with levers and knobs. It may have been a far cry from Starbucks, but it was worth mega bucks to us.

On most weekday nights I would be in Lorraine's or sometimes at the Embassy or the Savoy in Catford, another dance hall I used to frequent. It wasn't long before I started going up to London with some of my mates. Sundays were the best days for going up town because there was an afternoon dance at the Lyceum in the Strand. I went with some lads that Pete Dawson and I met at Lorraine's – it was our regular hang-out. One evening a group of blokes came in who neither of us knew; they'd pulled up outside on their scooters before coming to sit at the adjoining table to ours. The four of them were all drinking frothy coffees and I had the feeling if we were not careful trouble could start; they all looked a bit hard to us and were a couple of years older. I decided to speak up.

'Hello, I love the scooters. Are they Vespas?' knowing full well the answer was yes.

One of them nodded.

'Mind if I take a look?'

Another nodded his approval. Out I went to find they were not just Vespas, they were Vespa GS models, the top of the range. After a few minutes I went back in and sat down, saying how much I liked them. We started having a chat, with Pete and I quick to say how much we would like to have a scooter – it was our way of letting them know that we looked up to them. They introduced themselves as Tommy, Tony, Kenny and Ray; next thing Pete and I were roaring up and down Welling High Street, riding pillion on their Vespa GSs. They all came from Kidbrooke and were a bit more worldly than either Pete or me.

I bought another round of coffees and we started chatting about how to be a Mod. Pete and I had been aware for a little while that this was the thing to be, but were unsure what you had to do to become one. They explained how you had to wear certain clothes, but just as important you had to walk and act in a certain way. We arranged to meet them that coming

Saturday night and go down to the Embassy. From then on Pete and I began slowly to become Mods. You couldn't rush these things, as it cost quite a bit of money for one thing. To be a proper Mod you had to wear a Fred Perry shirt, you had to wear Levi's jeans, which you could only buy at one shop – Moray Marks in Whitechapel. Levi's were one pound 19 and 11 a pair, a penny under two quid; it was not much less than a week's wages, but you had to wear them if you wanted to be a proper Mod. You also had to wear a certain type of jacket, one worn very short, known as a matador jacket. You also had to wear special shoes called short points, which were quite different from those big long winkle-pickers – they were for the guys that drove motorbikes. You couldn't buy short points in any old Freeman, Hardy and Willis shop; you had to have them made.

It was coming up to my birthday and I asked Mum if I could have some money to buy my Mod clothes, although I didn't actually mention to her that they were Mod clothes.

'How much do you need?'

'About £25.'

'How much?' said Mum, obviously not quite believing what she was hearing.

'Well, I could get by with 20 quid at a push,' said I, not wishing to put her off the idea altogether.

'Well, Len, I know you think I'm a bank, but I think I need something in return.' The something was helping her every Friday evening after I got home from work with the orders that needed to be delivered. The deal having been agreed, the money was handed over a few weeks later. First port of call was Moray Marks where I bought my Levi's; although buying them was just the start. The trouble was they were stiff like cardboard and your first task was to loosen them up and the best way to do that was to kick them around. I took them out the bag and kicked them all the way up Whitechapel High Street – one of the Kidbrooke four had given me this vital tip. As soon as I got my Levi's home it was straight in the washing machine with them.

Next stop was Terry's of Homerton; this was the shop that made the short points. It was the start of a pain that persists until today. Here I was told to take off my shoe so they could draw around my foot to create a template for the shoemaker. No one had tipped me off to this important point of detail and I had a hole in my right sock, which meant I could only take off my left shoe – my smaller foot. This resulted in my right shoe being half a size too small, which gave me a corn that still gives me gyp. But never mind the pain, the shoes were just beautiful. They were green leather with a fabulous lace that went up the side. These laces had to be tied so that the bow was at the bottom, don't ask me why, all I can tell you is that it was part of the Mods' dress code. Then it was Harry Lee, the tailor, on Plumstead Bridge where I had a jacket made in tweed: it was cut away, with one button, and a half belt at the back. I also had an overcoat made that came to my ankles; it was topped, or rather bottomed off, with a two-inch vent.

Vital to being a real Mod was being able to walk like one. For this you had to put both hands in the pockets of your Levi's, which then held your overcoat back and open – it was essential in creating that all-important look. God help you if you had to blow your nose and your coat fell shut!

I was now a Mod, I was in with the in-crowd and I went where the in-crowd went, which created a whole new set of unwritten rules to be learned and obeyed. Not quite right, I was *almost* a Mod; I just needed one more thing. A lad, who was slightly older than us, who I knew as 'Knackers', was so named because when going down to Torquay with a group of other Mods on their scooters he wore only shorts. The wind had blown up his shorts the whole way to the West Country and burnt his testicles. Somehow the cold air had anaesthetised him but on arrival he found he had third-degree burns on his bollocks. I heard Knackers was selling his Vespa for 75 quid and after pestering and promising to do anything she wanted, my mum gave in and I became a fully fledged Mod.

Being a Mod was truly great from Easter to August bank holiday; most Saturday mornings we left Kent for our base at the Skylark, a pub just off Brighton beach. We had a bell tent which Bert the landlord stored for us and we used to go and camp up on Black Rock – I loved it. Up the road from the Skylark was the Fortune of War, which was the Rockers' pub – we had our pub and they had their pub. It was in the Skylark that I first heard the Beatles on their jukebox; it stopped me in my tracks. From that day on I became a fan, although I never did get to see them. I'd seen Buddy Holly at the Granada, Woolwich, Ray Charles at the Gaumont, Lewisham, Cliff Richard and Marty Wilde at the Granada, Dartford – but never the Beatles.

The only downside of being a Mod were Rockers; if a Mod was caught by 'them' you knew you were going to get a good hiding, a punch up the bracket at the very least. Nearly every Saturday someone or another would be in fight; either a Rocker would come too near our pub, or one of us would go too near theirs. Strangely I can never remember it raining; we used to lie on the beach all day topping up our tan. Tommy had a special concoction of olive oil and vinegar – and it was Sarsons, not the Eldridge own make – he assured us was the perfect tanning agent. You needed to lie stretched out because you would burn quicker that way, although lying on those bloody pebbles nearly killed you.

Every Saturday night it was off to the Montpelier Club, and then it was back to sleep in the bell tent – anything up to 12 guys and girls. Sun, sex and NSU we called it; we all got non-specific urethritis at one time or another. To keep us up and going we took Purple Hearts, which were uppers or pep pills. Such was our lack of real knowledge of these drugs that no one gave it a second's thought of what they might do to us. I was lucky that it led to nothing more serious or potentially damaging. I had a Brighton girlfriend called Sunny. She and her sister Nikki were Swedish and Nikki ended up going out with my mate, Tommy.

One time when we were all in the tent we had a bit of a run-in with the law. It all started because we'd been using the ladies' lavatory to get ready before we went out on the Saturday night. Some of the others were using the gents' loo and so Tommy, Tony and I were in the ladies' while Kenny was supposed to be standing guard. Just as Tommy was giving his old gentleman a bit of a wash a woman walked in and immediately let out a scream and rushed out – 'There's a man in the ladies' ablutions!' Next thing, her husband came in and gave us all a bit of a mouthful before he too cleared off. We thought no more about it and went off down the Montpelier Club for our usual night out.

We arrived back at the tent at some ungodly hour, me with Sunny, and some of the other guys had girls along with them.

We were totally unaware that the police had been staking out the tent after the distraught woman's husband had complained. Ray had the wind and a discussion started about lightning farts, which prompted Ray and Kenny to leave the tent in order to see if it was possible. We were all in the tent, listening to the sound of endless matches being struck as Ray farted, when suddenly there was the sound of voices.

'And what do you think you're doing?' said a voice none of us recognised; it was the police. We were told to pack up and leave for disturbing the peace, and the police car followed us for five or six miles until we were out of the centre of Brighton. After driving a little further we stopped at a nice open area and had the tent erected in minutes, despite it being pitch black. A few hours later we were woken again by the police for erecting a tent on a pitch and putt course near Rottingdean. On every other occasion we kept out of trouble and spent an idyllic summer. For a 19-year-old it was like a dream come true. The following summer was very different.

Perhaps it was because a year at that age makes a lot of difference in how you see things, but it could also have something to do with the fact that Brighton, the police and the authorities in general were none too keen on the reputation that the Mods and the Rockers were now getting. On our first trip to Brighton early in the summer of '64 we found that the police had set up roadblocks on the A23 near to the two stone columns that signified the entry to the resort. Anyone on a scooter or motorbike was turned away. It was no good trying to sneak in via Worthing or anywhere else along the coast as they had that covered too. We went to Eastbourne instead, but that proved less than exciting. One of my mates said it was like the place where elephants went to die!

The following week I came up with a cunning plan, one which involved my mum's delivery van. I borrowed it for the weekend and, with all my mates crammed in the back, we headed for the coast. However, we didn't get too far before the police stopped us again and escorted us back out of Brighton with police motorbikes at the front and rear. That finished me off with Brighton and scooters; from then on I didn't ride it any more and ended up selling it. Pete and I went back to playing football on a Saturday and enjoying ourselves around home. We went to Tommy's wedding – he married a girl named Joan – and that was the last time that I saw them until 2005. I had an email from Joan after she had seen me on *Strictly Come Dancing*, and I managed to get tickets for ten people – all my old mates from the Brighton days came to see the show. I hadn't seen any of them for 40 years, and we all met up after the show, laughing and reminiscing about when we were Mods.

Chapter Five

Going Up in the World

My dad's philosophy on life was simple: 'Len, we are all just like a leaf in a stream, with little or no control over where we go. It's the flow and the eddies of the stream that take us in one or another direction.' Way before it became popular to say it, Dad's idea was to 'go with the flow.'

That philosophy certainly summed me up in the five or six years after I left school. Work was something I did but didn't enjoy very much. Going out with my mates or sometimes taking a girl to the pictures, a night at the pub, or going dancing was just about having a laugh. There was also football. I hadn't stopped playing just because I'd left school. I was football crazy and played as often as I could. I was in a five-a-side team, a Saturday side and a Sunday side. I also used to train three times a week so my life was going to work, playing football and a Saturday and Sunday out with a girl.

Now, I did enjoy dancing, but it was the having-a-laugh kind of dancing. More than that it was about meeting girls. Then again, maybe some of my love of dancing was genetic. My mum and dad were very keen ballroom dancers before the war, but then so were many people. People have always loved dancing – it's probably man's earliest form of entertainment. I'm fairly sure that in the 1930s and 1940s many more people went dancing on a regular basis than they do now; there was far less choice of alternative forms of entertainment. It was the same with football. Many more people went to watch football on a Saturday in the 1930s than they do now. In those days every town, every village, every church hall had dancing going on; in London and the big cities there were huge places to go dancing, like the Hammersmith Palais, the Locarno in Streatham and the Royal in Tottenham, where thousands danced nearly every night of the week. Hammersmith Palais, which recently closed down, was a huge draw for dancers. In its heyday it could accommodate several thousand on the dance floor; now it's going to be an office and shopping complex.

People were encouraged to go dancing by the BBC broadcasting live shows practically every night of the week from a dance hall somewhere around the country.

Dancing in the pre-TV days was how many people met their future husband or wife. When my mum and dad went dancing before they were married they invariably entered the competitions that took place most nights of the week. Apparently they often got to the final dance-off and either won or came pretty close to winning. Once I came along all that went out of the window, but when I was a little older they told me what it was like to go up the Palais. Once Mum and Dad had split up, Mum was not the sort to go dancing; she was far too busy running the shop. For my dad and stepmum that wasn't quite the case and they used to go ballroom dancing at Erith.

Dad continued to pester me about going back to the Erith

Dance Studio with them. 'You'd like it, Len, I know you would. Why don't you come?'

'Oh, shut up, Dad. I don't fancy it. Once was enough.'

One Monday evening I was on my way home from work when I met a mate I used to knock around with. After we'd been chatting for a while, I asked, 'Do you fancy going down the pub tomorrow night?'

'No, I can't, Len. I go out on a Tuesday.'

'That's bloody queer, you're always out on a Tuesday night. Where do you go?' I asked.

'Well, to be honest with you, Len, and I'll bloody kill you if you let the others know, I go ballroom dancing.'

'You what?'

'No, Len, it's bloody great. Hardly any blokes go at all.'

'I'm not bloody surprised! I'd feel a right bloody pillock,' I said.

'Yeah, but *loads* of girls go. You can dance with whoever you want. Because so few blokes go they all think you're a hero. It's brilliant.'

'Where do you go?' I asked.

'I go to a dance school in Erith.'

I thought to myself that must be the same place Dad goes to, the one I'd been to once to see Billy and Bobbie Irvine dance. It put me off until I remembered that they went on a Saturday night. Although despite the attraction of meeting girls, ballroom dancing didn't really appeal.

It was shortly after this that disaster struck. I broke a metatarsal bone in my foot – the same one that Wayne Rooney broke a few years back. I was playing for Slade Green United on

Hackney Marshes when it happened. I kicked the ball north while at the same time the biggest centre half in the world – well, that's my story and I'm sticking to it – tried to kick the ball south. The outcome was my foot went west and I was in agony for weeks. It was not only black and blue and nasty-looking, but was also the size of a Chinese wrestler's crotch. All the doctor said was, 'Try to keep off of it as much as possible.' This was ludicrous, as I still had to go to work at the docks. I spent my life hobbling around which certainly put paid to any thoughts of going dancing.

The foot was incredibly slow to heal and I went back to my doctor to see what else I could do; I was anxious to get back to playing football. My usual doctor wasn't there and the locum was an old Scottish doctor. He told me in no uncertain terms that I could put football right out of my mind.

'You'll need to build your foot up a lot more before you can play again. Why not go swimming?' he suggested.

Well, that wasn't really an option as the nearest pool was outdoors at Danson Park where I'd cut myself ten years earlier, added to which it was February.

'Well, laddie, you could try dancing.'

'Dancing?' I couldn't believe it.

'Aye Lad, you need to keep that foot working, you need to exercise it and so dancing is my recommendation.'

Despite my interest in possibly meeting some other girls, at the time I was going out with a girl named Linda Baker and later that evening I told her of what the doctor had said. I also told her what my mate had told me a few weeks earlier, although I was careful to leave out the bit about how many unattached girls there were at the dance school.

'Well, Len, it might help your foot, so it's worth a try. You said your dad and stepmum go and they're always on at you about going. So why not?' Linda said this as she drove me home from the doctor; my foot was too swollen to drive.

'Linda, I'd feel like a plonker going ballroom dancing.'

As a cure-all for this great big fat foot it seemed like a bloody silly idea to me.

However, later that day Linda drove me round to my dad's place and told them what the doctor had said.

'That's lucky, there's a new beginners' class starting next Tuesday,' said Dad.

I just thought how was that lucky?

'Not on your bleedin' Nellie. I'm not going.'

I should have been quicker to realise that when Linda offered to pick me up and take me to the pub the following Tuesday, she had other plans. We stopped in Pier Road, which led down to the River Thames, parked, and it wasn't until I'd got out of the car and begun walking along the road that I suddenly twigged, helped by seeing the sign – Erith Dance Studio.

'We're going dancing,' said Linda

'We're not,' I replied.

After we spent ten minutes arguing on the steps of the studio, while people negotiated their way around us so they could go dancing, I finally gave in, as much for a quiet life as for any other reason. I made my way up the stairs to the studio where everyone was sitting around waiting for it to start. I sat there trying to melt into the wallpaper. We looked like we were waiting to see a doctor, not waiting to have fun. I had a face like a slapped arse and it didn't help either my image or my confidence in that on my left foot I had a winkle-picker and on my right foot I had one of my dad's carpet slippers. We were the youngest couple and not by just a little bit. The expectant dancers all seemed ancient; the men in suits, the ladies in dresses and me in a pair of jeans, a Fred Perry shirt and my odd footwear.

As we sat there everyone seemed to be eyeing each other up. Talk was in whispers, with just the odd cough to break the silence. Suddenly I felt a bead of perspiration on my forehead: I was gripped with a sudden fear and an overpowering urge to use the toilet. Maybe I could make my escape through the window – then I remembered that climbing through a window in a winkle-picker and a slipper might cause me to break my good foot. I was shaken from my thoughts when suddenly all hell broke loose as a smartly dressed lady and a girl burst into the room.

'Now then, everyone, up on your feet and gather round. We're going to learn to dance!'

With that, the 30 or so of us got to our feet and stood there waiting for what was to happen next; my slippered foot was throbbing.

'I'm Miss Tolhurst and this is my assistant Pauline and we're here to teach you.'

I found out later that Joy Tolhurst was a former world champion, although if anyone had told me at this point I'm sure I'd have been underwhelmed. As we all stood around them in a circle all I could think was – fat chance. Linda kept looking at me as if to say, please don't embarrass us, Len.

First we were shown how to hold our partner – the five points of contact for the perfect ballroom hold. Maybe it was just me, but I got very confused because it was two ladies showing us. Which lady was the man and which was the lady? Eventually I got the gist of the grip and the ladies came around adjusting our arms and our body positions. As I was determined not to enjoy the evening I did everything in my power to appear to be the most uncoordinated person in the world in the hope that Linda would give up after just one week. Having grasped the hold, at least partially, we were taught some steps, starting with the waltz.

'Left foot forward, side and close, right foot forward, side and close,' Miss Tolhurst called out.

This was simple, even for someone wearing a slipper and a shoe, as we all moved around the floor like a chain of elephants one behind the other.

'Come on now, young man,' I heard Miss Tolhurst saying. I realised that she must be talking to me. 'You need to stand closer to your partner. Body contact is one of the most important elements of dancing properly.'

Keeping my distance from Linda was nothing to do with my feelings towards her: actually I quite liked her. I was just frightened of having my foot stood on by her elegant four-inch stiletto heels. Pauline came over to where we were dancing and as she looked down at my foot encased in Dad's slipper a look of horror crept over her face.

'Look, I'll show you how to get nearer.' With that, she took hold of me and pulled me closer. Oh, the embarrassment! Not only am I hobbling around, I've got the teacher's assistant practically hugging me to her bosom. Because we had stopped, the line of elephants had turned into a traffic jam, while some tried to negotiate their way around us.

Having loosely mastered the hold and the step, next came the rise and fall. The waltz should have a gentle rise and fall. Well, my left leg was no problem – it had a lovely rise and fall – but my right leg was all fall and no rise. I looked like a man trying to dance with one leg in the gutter and the other on the pavement. I was bobbing up and down on one foot and the other was as flat as a pancake.

The class was scheduled to last for two hours with a break in the middle for a cup of tea. As we queued up, a man who introduced himself as Bill said, 'You've been in the wars, son.'

'Yes,' I said, 'I hurt my foot playing football.'

'I'm struggling as well because I've got a withered calf and only one testicle.' A little too much information for a first meeting.

The girl behind the bar serving tea asked what I wanted.

'Two teas, please love,' I said, little knowing that the pimply-faced 15-year-old would one day be my dance partner and later still my wife. After finishing our cup of tea we started the next session with much more of the same, although I totally lost concentration.

'Len, try and keep up,' said Linda.

'I can't stop looking at Bill and thinking about his withered calf and his one bollock.'

At the end of the teaching session there was always a 30-minute free practice session, but by that time I'd had enough and so had my foot. I explained to Pauline, who seemed more approachable than Miss Tolhurst, that my foot was playing up but even so I had still enjoyed the evening.

'I won't be staying for the practice but we'll see you next week,' I said, thinking it was less awful than I'd imagined but mostly that if this will fix my foot then I must keep at it.

On the way home in the car Linda said, 'Well, that wasn't so bad was it?'

'Well, I've done a lot worse on a Tuesday night in the middle of February.'

My dad phoned me the next day. How was it? Did you like it? Are you going again? I had to admit it was okay and I would be going back the next week. In fact, I was quite looking forward to the next Tuesday's lesson.

Week two and we continued to develop the technique of the waltz, learning about sway of the body, the swing of the shoulders. It was all a far cry from my time some six years earlier at the Court School of Dancing where we just learnt to shuffle round, looking forward to the kiss-me excuse-me. Tuesday became the highlight of my week, and soon we were learning slightly more complex moves, like natural and reverse turns; I was actually getting to grips with it all. One thing that I also learned in those first few classes, something that remained true once I started my own classes, is the fact that you get a real cross-section of society learning to dance. There are fat ones, thin ones, tall ones, the short, the quiet, the noisy and, of course, there's always the class joker. Ours was a man called Tommy, a true cockney, who by day was a plasterer. He was always making us laugh. One day Miss Tolhurst said, 'Commence with your left foot.'

'Which foot?' shouts Tommy.

'Your left foot,' said our teacher.

'Is it the same side as your left ear, Miss Tolhurst?'

One of his favourite catchphrases was, 'I'm confused – one of my legs are both alike.'

The Erith Dance Studio was on two floors right above Burton's, the gentleman's tailor. Our classes were on the first floor and on the floor above that was where Henry Kingston used to teach. I say 'teach', but in actual fact he was a coach, not a teacher. In dancing a coach is well above a teacher. And he was not just any old coach, he was a top coach. Henry and Joy Tolhurst had been dance partners and were also married. They had been one of the top couples in the dance world for many years. Despite having seen them years before I hadn't taken that much notice and didn't connect them with the couple I had watched dancing when I had gone to the Erith with my dad and stepmum. I was soon to learn that Henry was an even better coach than he was a dancer.

Amongst those he coached were Bill and Bobbie Irvine who were world champions at the time, Richard Gleave and Janet Wade, who became amateur world champions, and Anthony Hurley and Fay Sexton who would also go on to become professional champions. While we were busy learning the rudiments in our beginners' class these people would troop through our studio on their way to Henry's inner sanctum. Not that anyone in our class had any idea who they were. All I knew was that Henry Kingston was a cut above, which naturally meant that anyone he taught was likewise. At the end of his coaching sessions he would come downstairs to our studio to check out his diary that he kept behind the tea bar in the corner. As soon as he came in everyone tried to dance a little better. It was like a silent voice had called out, 'Henry Kingston's in the house!' We would all suddenly stand a little straighter and try our hardest not to make a mistake. It was not that he ever said anything or was unpleasant; far from it, he was a charming man. As a former world champion he just had an aura about him.

About halfway through the evening of our third week of learning the waltz Henry Kingston appeared in the room along with two couples. Naturally everyone's elbows got a little straighter; I certainly tried standing a little taller with my head more erect.

'I'd like to introduce Bill and Bobbie Irvine.' He went on to explain their many achievements and then said, 'Billy and Bobbie are going to show you a quickstep.' He nodded to Pauline who put the needle on the record of the big record player in the opposite corner of the studio from the tea bar – they began dancing beautifully to a Victor Silvester record.

I, and probably everyone else, was captivated. I recalled seeing them before but this time I had an appreciation of just how brilliant they were. After the quickstep they stopped and Bill Irvine spoke to us. He was a Scotsman and had a lovely lilt to his voice.

'Good evening, ladies and gentleman. That, of course, was the quickstep and now we would like to demonstrate the tango.'

Bobbie stood beside him, the most elegant and sophisticated-looking woman I had ever seen in the flesh. I later found out that she was South African, while Bill had been a milkman before he became a professional dancer – perhaps he worked with Sean Connery.

After the Irvines finished, Henry Kingston introduced the other couple as amateur champions Bill and Sylvia Mitchell, who were going to show us the foxtrot.

'It's a dance that takes its name from its originator, vaudeville actor Henry Fox,' Henry informed us. After they had finished, a waltz was put on and the Mitchells carried on dancing.

Halfway through they split and Bill Mitchell went and invited a lady to dance with him. Sylvia, with her raven-black hair shining, headed in my direction.

'Shall we?' she asked ever so nicely.

'No!' I didn't say, no thank you, just no! I was petrified of making a fool of myself, despite having been learning nothing else but the waltz for three weeks. I clung to my seat as if I was about to be taken into a torture chamber or worse.

'Oh, come on, I know you know how to waltz.' I figured there couldn't be more than eight bars left, so up I stood and danced for the few remaining seconds. Years later I got to know Sylvia very well and she and I would often laugh about how scared I was that first time she asked me to dance.

After four weeks of learning the waltz we were told that we would be learning the quickstep. A sharp intake of breath came from all 30 couples.

'Gentlemen, right foot forward,' said Miss Tolhurst, and so we began learning our second dance. By the end of the evening we were positively flying around the floor. But just as most of the couples were getting the hang of it, disaster struck. The larger-than-life Mr and Mrs Rose fell over, and I'm sure that this measured several points at least, on the Richter scale. Mr Rose was back up on his feet like a shot, but Mrs Rose was a different kettle of fish: she was like a beached whale. No matter what we all tried we couldn't get her up; in fact, the more we tried to pull her up by her arms the more she slid across the ballroom floor on her arse. Eventually her legs hit the wall and that was the purchase we needed to get her back on her feet. Learning to dance is never dull.

I was sure that they wouldn't show up the following week because of the humiliation of what had happened, but come next Tuesday, there they were. Before the class started Mr Rose announced that it was their wedding anniversary. What none of us knew was that Mr Rose was the manager of the off-licence at the Co-op in Dartford.

'Miss Tolhurst, I've brought two bottles of Liebfraumilch with me and I was wondering if instead of tea, in the tea break, perhaps we might all partake of a glass of wine?'

'Certainly not, Mr Rose. We're non-licenced premises and we don't encourage people to drink alcohol while learning to dance at our school.'

I remember thinking, bloody posh business this ballroom dancing when you can turn down a glass of Liebfraumilch. Despite another week of mortification the Roses kept coming back for more.

At the beginning of April, after about six weeks of the class, it was announced that in a further six weeks we would be able to take our bronze medal in the waltz and quickstep – that's if we wanted to. It was all a far cry from how dancing classes are today – you would never spend four weeks learning just the waltz because people would be bored rigid. Instead we now teach a little bit about a lot in the first three or four weeks; you do a little bit of cha-cha, some jive, quickstep, waltz and foxtrot. They taught no Latin American dancing at all to begin with; it's probably a reflection on how these days people just want to get on with it. Back then, especially for those who wanted to become true ballroom experts, you were taught every nuance of a dance.

By this point I was no longer dancing under doctor's orders, as my foot was well on the way to total recovery; I'd given Dad back his slipper and I was back into a pair of ordinary shoes but not winkle-pickers, which are not ideal for ballroom dancing. I found I actually enjoyed myself: I looked forward to going and sitting around the edge of the studio waiting for my class to begin. I had bought myself a pair of the very latest fashion accessory – a pair of Hush Puppies. These were a suede shoe that every night before going dancing I carefully brushed with the little wire brush that came free with them. You had to be careful to brush them with the grain, rather than against it, so they looked pristine – I'd stopped being a Mod but being well turned out was still important for me.

At the beginning of April, in the midst of the build-up to our taking the bronze medal, Linda and I had to miss a week of classes.

'I'm sorry, Pauline, but we can't be here next week because we're going to Spain on holiday.' I think I may have said it a little more loudly than I needed to because I was proud of the fact that I was going abroad. Apart from visiting the coast on a few short breaks with Mum, and later with my mates, I had never done anything so exciting. Naturally it wasn't just Linda and I going on holiday. It was Linda's parents that had asked me if I'd like to join them on a package holiday – although I'm sure that Mr Baker didn't use the word package. Nowadays it seems almost impossible to believe that going abroad was considered so unusual; in the mid-sixties it was mostly the rich and famous that travelled, but relatively small numbers of people were beginning to sample foreign food, foreign money, while naturally avoiding the water. My mum never did go abroad, on holiday or for anything else. People took these 'inclusive holidays' and spent the rest of the year talking about it.

We were off to Sitges, about 25 miles south-west of Barcelona on the Costa Brava. In the mid-sixties it was a small place with very few hotels, but it was developing a reputation for being a little different, although I knew nothing of this. All I knew was that we were going to Spain, a country from where the great Real Madrid came from. Today Sitges is a large resort that boasts of being 'one of the hippest gay holiday spots in Europe'; in 1966 we still thought being gay was just being happy.

Harry Baker, Linda's father, worked in Hatton Garden making jewellery and could be described as being upwardly mobile, although none of us knew what that meant. He was a dapper little man – he looked a bit flash to me, but not in a bad way – he had a grey moustache that matched his hair and he lived in a very nice bungalow in Bexley with his wife Joy. Our flight was from Gatwick airport on a Saturday afternoon, which left plenty of time for Mrs B to go to the hairdressers for her regular shampoo and set. Unlike today when everyone travels casually, we were all dressed to the nines. Harry, in particular. He was wearing an open-necked shirt, a paisley cravat, all topped off by a blazer with gold buttons. Just before I'd left home to go round to the Bakers' from where we were leaving for the airport, Mum got in a bit of a panic in case I didn't have enough spending money.

'Len, you be sure to pay your way, don't miss your round. I'd be so ashamed if you let us down.'

With that, she slipped me an extra 20 quid. I already had a tenner, so if you think of average wages then it was like having £900 to spend. I was only going for a week! There was no chance of me not paying my way.

Despite never having been on a plane before I don't remember much about the flight itself. Although it was April it was beautiful and warm when we stepped off the aircraft and walked across the tarmac to the terminal building. If that impressed me, then the hotel was even better. I had my own room with a balcony. Linda, naturally, shared a room with her parents. I'd only stayed in English bed and breakfasts before, so this was just like being in a movie. One thing that didn't impress me was the food. There was no way I was even trying paella. Harry Baker took everything in his stride and acted as if it was an everyday occurrence eating strange and exotic foods. I spent the whole week living on chips, partly because my mum had told me that they ate horsemeat, so I assumed everything was either horse or pony. Harry was equally blasé about the bathroom.

'What's this, Mr B?' I said, pointing to the bidet.

'That, son, is for washing the sand off your feet after going to the beach,' said the worldly Harry Baker.

'Blimey! They think of everything in Spain.'

On our first morning on the Costa Brava we naturally went to the beach. We'd noticed from the hotel that there was a large bay and a smaller bay; the larger one was fairly busy, while the small one was completely deserted.

'Let's go and enjoy some peace and quiet at the small one. Far more exclusive,' announced Harry.

After breakfast Mr Baker led the way, followed by Mrs Baker, her blonde hair piled high like Zsa Zsa Gabor. Trailing a little way behind were Linda and I. Once we got to the beach we spread out our towels on the beautiful, golden sand while congratulating ourselves on how clever we were to be smart enough to spot the opportunity. After half an hour or so of sunbathing I decided it was time for a swim to cool off. I'd been in for a little while, swimming and sometimes floating on my back, all the while marvelling at how much warmer the water was than in Brighton. Just then I noticed what looked like a small log come floating towards me. My first thought was it must have drifted all the way across the Mediterranean, probably from Tangiers or somewhere equally exotic – I'd remembered seeing Tangiers on a map during a geography lesson. Just as that thought finished another entered my head.

'Oh shit!' I shouted. I couldn't help myself. And that's exactly what it was. Next I noticed dozens more small logs floating towards me; I was out the water like a shot. No wonder the beach was deserted – this was where Sitges' sewers emptied into the warm, beguiling Mediterranean waters.

We decided being part of the throng was definitely preferable to the exclusivity of our deserted beach. We picked up all of our stuff to trudge back the way we came to the larger, more crowded, beach. Spreading our towels amongst the deckchairs and other towels, Linda and I once again set about getting a golden tan. Mr and Mrs Baker sat underneath one of those colourful beach brollies, about a dozen feet away. A few yards in the opposite direction was an English couple stretched out on their blanket. At least we assumed they were English because they were as white as we were; 20 minutes later it was confirmed.

'We're just going in for a swim. Will you keep your eye on our stuff?' said the man in a broad Brummie accent.

'No problem,' I called back. 'We're not going anywhere.'

Not long after they had gone in the water two Spanish

teenagers came wandering along the beach and sat down right next to the couple's stuff. I kept an eye on them to see they weren't out to nick anything, while the two lads surveyed the beach.

After a couple of minutes I nudged Linda. 'Here, take a look at those two.'

One of them had picked up the English couple's camera. I assumed they were pinching it and was just about to shout out when one of the boys got up, pulled down his trunks and turned his knob towards his mate who quickly took a picture. It was all over in seconds. The two of them calmly got up and put the camera back where it was, before sauntering off down the beach. Linda and I were the only ones to have seen what had happened; we decided not to say anything. I've often wondered if the chemist said anything after the film was developed.

In some respects it was surprising that I was on holiday with the Baker family at all; my first meeting with Linda's parents had been less than auspicious. We had been going out for a few weeks when I was invited to her parents' house one Saturday night for dinner. As I pulled up in my Jaguar, Mr Baker opened the front door, giving me a casual half-salute, half-wave, as if he was acknowledging my car. I parked in their drive behind Harry's Ford Anglia. Inside their Bexley bungalow it was the very height of modern sixties fashion.

Once we had sat down Linda's dad said, 'Can I offer you a glass of Mateus rosé, Len?'

I'd never had one before and wasn't quite sure what it was, but I said yes. It was not quite as nice as I had anticipated, possibly because it was served at room temperature.

'We've ordered an Indian takeaway, they'll be delivering it shortly. Have you had Indian food, Len?'

'No, Mr Baker, I haven't.' I didn't even know you could have a meal delivered. Then I thought to myself, well they do live in a particularly posh part of Bexley and maybe that's what you do on a Saturday night. I remembered seeing a restaurant in Bexley called the Taj Mahal and wondered what the food was going to be like; I was about to find out.

After chatting for a while about nothing in particular, the doorbell rang.

'That'll be the takeaway, let's go through into the dining room,' said Mrs Baker.

The dining room was mostly G-Plan furniture but they also had spiky funny little chairs, with spindly little legs, placed around a circular dining table. Over it hung a lamp, one of those that could be lowered from the ceiling by pulling it down to whatever height was best suited to create the perfect ambience. We sat down at the table while Mrs Baker laid out the little tin foil dishes full of the Indian food in a neat formation in the centre of the table. I stared at the various dishes having no clue what this was going to taste like, other than a vague recollection that someone had told me that Indian food was hot and spicy. I also had no clue as to what was in each dish, although they all seemed quite brightly coloured. I may have had a Jaguar but I was way out of my comfort zone. Added to which, generally speaking, in our house the rule was, if your granny cooked it then you ate it and if she didn't, you didn't.

Just before we are about to start helping ourselves to food Mr Baker stood up. He was dressed in a yellow cardigan, shirt and tie; he gave a small cough to indicate he had something important to say.

'Len, it's so lovely to have you and to have had a little chat before dinner. It's a pleasure to welcome you here and I do hope you enjoy the hospitality of our modest home.' What's coming next? I thought. 'Len, why don't you propose a toast?'

I'd never been called upon to do anything like this before and didn't know that's what people did when someone came around for dinner on a Saturday evening. I reminded myself once again that this was Bexley. I pushed back my chair and went to stand up, and as I did I headbutted the lamp, which had been lowered to about three feet over the table. Unfortunately, rather than just swaying backwards and forwards, the glass lampshade shattered into thousands of tiny pieces, most of which landed in the tin foil dishes that were laid out before us. I found myself repeatedly apologising for my clumsiness.

'Len, don't worry, we'll call the takeaway and order some more.'

'No, no, Mr Baker, it's all my fault. Let's go out to dinner, the least I can do is pay.'

I was so embarrassed by what had happened that later I even went and bought them a new lamp. Still, it held me in good stead with the Baker family from then on.

Back to the holiday, and after our first disastrous day things settled down. Cocktails followed days on the beach – further evidence of the Bakers' sophistication – then dinner and a few drinks to round off the evening. After about four days I noticed that a young Spanish guy who worked in the bar was paying Linda far too much attention. What was worse, she didn't seem to mind. He wore tight black trousers, a crisp white shirt and a black waistcoat; with his sleek black hair, he was quite a looker in a Spanish waiter kind of a way. I actually got jealous, something that hadn't happened to me before.

The following night I said I was going to go up to my room as soon as we finished dinner, to which Linda said, 'I'll sit with my mum and dad for a bit.'

I didn't like the whole scenario; I felt she was too familiar with this waiter. The next morning I had a blazing row with Linda before trying to get a flight home, but of course I was on a package holiday and flights couldn't be changed. The final two days were not much fun, and so when we got back home I finished with Linda. I knew that I was being daft, but she had wounded my pride and I wasn't having any of it. However, there was one problem, a big one. I was due to take my bronze medal in ballroom dancing in a couple of weeks and Linda was my partner.

The Tuesday after getting back from Spain I decided to go up the Erith Dance Studio to tell them of what had occurred, or at least that Linda and I were no longer a couple. I was really fed up because I really enjoyed the dancing. All the way there I worried about whether or not Linda would be there and about exactly what I was going to tell them at the school. I got to the studio 15 minutes early so I could get in and get out before anyone else showed up.

'I'm sorry, Miss Tolhurst, but I'm afraid my partner and I have split up and so I won't be coming any more, because it's all couples and everyone is paired off. It means that I couldn't possibly get it together in time to take my medal exam.'

'That's a real shame, Len, because I think you have talent.' At this, I felt myself go a little red in the face. 'You are doing so well that I think you would get a highly commended at your Bronze medal.' I reddened a little more.

'That's all very well, but I can't just dance around by myself can I? It's best that I just nip off now.'

I turned tail and headed back down the stairs. As I reached the bottom, Pauline, Miss Tolhurst's assistant, came out of the studio and called after me. 'Len, Len, Miss Tolhurst wants to have a word with you, can you come back upstairs?'

Back up the stairs I trooped.

'Len, I've got an idea. I've spoken to my daughter Cherry and she's said she'd be happy to dance with you for the three weeks until you take your medal. That's right, isn't it Cherry?'

'Yes, Mum,' said the petite 16-year-old that I was used to seeing behind the tea bar. I'm not sure, before that fateful moment, that I even knew she was their daughter and I certainly had no idea she could dance; was I in for a shock.

'Well, that's all sorted isn't it, Len?'

'Err, yes, Miss Tolhurst. I guess it is.'

I looked at Cherry who was pretty but couldn't help thinking – she's just a kid.

I had to admit dancing with Cherry was way easier than with Linda, not because Linda wasn't okay – it was just that Cherry had been dancing since she could walk and lived in a household that was 100 per cent dance. Cherry had done all her medals, she was a really accomplished and lovely dancer, and so it certainly made me look so much better because I had a fantastic partner.

In the run-up to the medal examination Henry Kingston would pop in as he had done before and I began to notice that he took a keen interest in what we were doing. On the day of the medal test Henry Kingston stood and watched, and afterwards he said to me, 'I've watched you dancing with my daughter and I think you have the potential to become quite a good dancer – if you work at it. Would you like to continue dancing with Cherry, and I will give you private tuition? You can see how you get on; needless to say there will be no charge. She has never had any interest in dancing competitively, but you've changed all that, Len.'

'That would be great, Mr Kingston.'

Cherry must have told her dad that she enjoyed dancing with me, but I wasn't at all sure what 'dancing competitively' really meant. He would have been thrilled that at last she was entering fully into the family business, rather than just serving the teas. It was just like my old dad had said. 'Len, you're just a leaf in a stream.' The luck of that Spanish waiter making me jealous had given me an opportunity that would change my life for ever.

Chapter Six

A White Tie ... and Tales

Achieving bronze-medal standard with Cherry's assistance was none too difficult, especially when you factor in the advantage of being taught by one of the world's top coaches. It's fair to say that dancing began to take over my life. I was no longer in a class alongside Mr and Mrs Rose, the rotund couple, or Tommy the plasterer; I had been let into Henry Kingston's inner sanctum. Having just had my twenty-second birthday I was still a little unsure about dancing with Cherry, who was so much younger than me, but her talent overcame all my apprehensions. What had happened to me was a bit like travelling economy and suddenly being upgraded to first class on a flight – not that I knew anything about all that at that point in my life.

It was an incredible experience to be coached by Cherry's father, although initially we were still only doing the waltz and the quickstep. His teaching methods were rigorous and centred upon the fact that it was vital to perfect each and every dance, to have it so ingrained upon your brain that you never, ever lose the technique. Even today I can look at dancers and instinctively know something is wrong. I can look at a couple's heads and I know there's something not right with their feet, because I know the rise and fall is all wrong. Initially I learnt this from Henry Kingston's coaching: he taught me a lot about the technique and the kinetics of movement. It's probably the same for an orchestral conductor who knows which violinist, among a whole symphony orchestra, has just played a bum note.

Cherry and I would practise week after week and I kept thinking perhaps this week we'll move on to the slow foxtrot or the tango, but no, it was the waltz and quickstep over and over – or more like round and round. Henry would show me some slight variations or extra steps that I could put in to move us across the floor more freely, the slight changes that help to give you (what appears to be) effortless progress around the dance floor. I came to appreciate the tremendous subtleties of dance and how this makes the difference between the good, the really good and the brilliant.

During the summer, having learned some additional dances, I was beginning to feel a lot more confident. One day Henry made a suggestion. 'There's a big competition run by Pontin's that has its final at the Royal Albert Hall and I think you two should go in for it.' I was a bit shocked, but before I could say anything he continued, 'As you may well know, Len, the first dance grade is novice, and this is an event for novices. If you win three novice events you become a pre-amateur and then if you win three events at that level you become an amateur. So if you really want to progress in this business it's time to start along the road.'

It's somewhat different nowadays but that was the form back then; novice was the lowest echelon of competitive dancing and I was very much a novice.

Pontin's holiday camps had been started by Fred Pontin in the late 1940s to give people an affordable place to go on holiday at the seaside in Britain. They not only offered accommodation but there was also an extensive programme of nightly entertainment of all different kinds, although the emphasis was very much on family fun – it was all very *Hi-De-Hi.* During the season, at every one of their 30 camps, Pontin's ran competitions; including darts, Miss Lovely Legs, the Most Eligible Escort, Miss Pontin, singing contests and not surprisingly dancing. If you won through the various rounds you eventually ended up at the final at the Royal Albert Hall. It meant that we would have to spend a week at a Pontin's holiday camp. At the end of the season one of their camps was designated as the 'host camp' for the dancers and so the winners from all 30 camps throughout the summer would go there for the first phase of the dance-off. It was the same process for all the other competitions, although each one took place at a different camp.

If we wanted to qualify for the later stages, Henry explained that we would initially have to go to Camber Sands, which is near Rye in East Sussex.

'Before you go there's one thing you're going to have to do, Len,' Henry told me. 'You'll have to get yourself a tail suit.'

When I told my mum she was over the moon. 'Oh, Len, you'll look lovely, you'll be my very own Fred Astaire.'

Having loved dancing so much when she was younger, Mum was delighted that I had taken it up; if anything she was even more pleased than Dad and my stepmum were. She also really liked Cherry, who really was a sweet, lovely girl. This meant that, for her spoilt little Lenny, nothing was too much trouble.

'Len, you'll have to go to Savile Row to have your tail suit made,' Henry announced, as if this was the most normal thing in the world. 'Everyone does.'

'Oh right.'

'Yes, and there's only one tailor to use – Hawes and Curtis.'

When I told Mum all she could say was, 'That's where all the toffs go, Len.'

'I know. Henry said that they've been tailors to the Duke of Windsor and Lord Mountbatten. They make all of the Duke of Edinburgh's riding clothes as well.'

And now Len Goodman's tail suit, I thought, but didn't dare say anything sarcastic to Henry as I sensed this was very important to him, nor did I say anything to Mum, who was equally impressed, although for different reasons. Henry explained to me exactly what I had to order and so on the following Saturday morning I caught the train up to London.

'May we be of service, sir?' the Hawes and Curtis assistant asked.

'Yes, mate, I'm a ballroom dancer and I would like to have a tail suit made.'

He was probably shocked when he heard my East End accent, but of course he didn't bat an eyelid. 'Ah, perfect, sir.' He was like an even posher version of the man in *Are You Being Served?*

Henry had told me the suit needed to be made from barathea. I knew it was a fabric of some kind, but I'd never heard of it.

'It's got a lightly ribbed or pebbled weave in it, Len, it looks brilliant when you dance.'

I told the tailor that it was barathea or nothing and added, as instructed, that the trouser leg had to be no wider than 16½ inches at the bottom.

'It must just break over the shoe and the jacket must be cut very tight in the body.'

'Naturally, sir,' said the tailor.

While I was there I ordered two wing collar shirts to be made; I also ordered ten detachable wing-collars to go with them. In total it came to £100, a huge amount of money, especially when you think you could get a suit at Burton's, underneath the Erith Dance Studio, for 15 quid. Before the rather common business of money was discussed I had to be measured; this turned into a real pantomime.

The man who had originally greeted me turned out to be the under-tailor, the man who did all the writing down of measurements and recorded the finer points of the suit that was to be made. The man who did the measuring was the master tailor.

'Yes, sir, we have 14½ inches from shoulder to spine, got that Mr Lucas?'

'Fourteen and a half inches, Mr Jenkins.'

This process went on for ages, with every conceivable measurement being called out by Mr Jenkins and repeated by Mr Lucas, the latter getting more camp as the whole thing went along. No chance of this going wrong, I thought to myself, no wonder it costs a lot.

'Where would we like the tails to reach down to, sir?' asked the master tailor.

'Oh, I'm not sure.' Bugger, Henry had not mentioned that. 'Can I use your phone?'

'Hello? Mr Kingston? They're having a steward's enquiry here about how far the tails should reach down. Oh, right, to the bend at the back of my knees. Yes, Mr Kingston, it's all going swimmingly.'

Having got all that sorted all that was left was to be measured for my white waistcoat.

'Right, we're all done, sir. We'll be in touch in due course so that you can come back for your first fitting.'

'First fitting? How many are there?'

'There's three, sir, we always do three fittings.'

He said it in such a way as to make me feel more than a touch daft for not knowing something so obvious. With that all sorted off I went; three weeks later I was back in Savile Row for my first fitting.

The camp writer-downer was in charge of the first fitting. After I'd put on the suit, which was all covered in white stitching, he got down to work on ensuring everything was as it should be. He spent what seemed like an overly long time dealing with my trousers. This was the first time in my life that I'd had a man push his arm up between my legs and around my bum.

'How's the fork, sir? Are we all right with that?'

Bloody hell, I thought, a bit personal having a bloke shove his arm up around your Jacksy. Fork was their polite way of referring to my crutch.

'I think we should let it out a little, don't you, sir? It does feel a little tight there, doesn't it?' As he said this he was kneeling at my feet gazing up at me. With all this close contact sport I was quite relieved when all three fittings were finished. Apart from having to hand over £100 for the privilege I was really excited about getting back down to Kent to show everyone my new tail suit.

When I got home Mum was waiting for me. 'Put your suit on, Lenny boy, I want to see it before you go down the studio.'

I dressed in my wing collars, which were as stiff as a board, my white bow tie, the white waistcoat and finally the suit itself. I felt brilliant.

'Oh Lenny, oh Lenny. Oh, oh, my lovely boy.'

To Mum it was worth every penny – and more.

Then it was off down the Erith Dance Studio where I went through the whole routine again. As I came out of the toilet Cherry and Henry Kingston were waiting for me. With just two weeks before the Camber Sands competition I'd left it tight to get the suit, so everyone felt a sense of relief. Henry was also insistent that we should practise with me wearing my tail suit as he felt it made a difference.

Cherry looked at me and smiled, so I knew she liked me in it.

'What do you think, Mr Kingston?' I asked, thinking to myself that I did look pretty dashing.

'Oh yes, Len, oh yes. It's fabulous.' As he walked around me, he ran his hand across my back and shoulders. 'There's not a crease, Len, it's just perfect. I told you they were the best. Okay, take hold of Cherry and let's see you do your first dance in your new suit. We'll do a quickstep.' Cherry came towards me but as I raised my arms from the horizontal it caused my tailcoat to ride up my back by about four inches; my head sank into the jacket as I metamorphosed from Fred Astaire into Quasimodo meets the Incredible Hulk.

'Len, Len, what's happening?' You can see what's bloody happening, I thought. 'Didn't you tell them you were a ballroom dancer?'

'Yes, it was just about the first thing I said.'

'Didn't they get you to stand in the dancer's hold position?'

'No!'

'Well, you should have made them do that.'

You were the one who sent me there saying they were the best, is what I thought, but I decided that he was so upset at this point that anything I might say would only make matters worse. With just two weeks to go before the competition I had no chance of getting a new tailcoat made.

At that moment Joy Tolhurst came in; she'd probably heard her husband's raised voice. 'Oh dear, Len, what have you done?'

What I wanted to say was I've been up to London four times, had three fittings, a man stick his hand up my crutch and, more to the point, my mum's done 100 quid and everyone is blaming me. At the same time I was resigning myself to the fact that I was not going to be dancing in tails, possibly not dancing at all. My big moment had been ruined.

Just then Henry shared his master plan. 'Look, it's too late to get them to do anything, we'll fix it.'

'How?' I very nearly swore, I was so frustrated.

A few minutes later Joy reappeared carrying what looked like two nappy pins.

'Stand still, Len.' I did as I was told before feeling the two former world champions behind my back fiddling around under my tailcoat.

'We're going to pin the jacket to your trousers, just where the fork in the tail is,' Joy told me.

'Won't it look odd having a jacket with a safety pin in the back?'

'Don't be silly, Len, we'll pin it underneath the jacket so no one will see.'

Having done it, Henry and Joy stood back to admire their work.

'Looks great, Len. You can't see the pins. Now take a hold of Cherry.'

They were right, my jacket no longer rode up and I was once again doing a passable impersonation of Fred Astaire. At least I was until they looked at my feet.

'Oh dear.'

I don't think Astaire ever had two inches between the bottom of his trousers and the tops of his shoes!

'It's not going to work,' I said.

'Oh yes it will,' said Henry as both he and Joy spent the next three quarters of an hour trying to get it sorted. I kept alternating between a man with no neck and a kid who'd outgrown his trousers. Finally they gave up on the nappy pins. Time for plan B...

They called in reinforcements. 'Pauline, can you pop round the haberdashery shop and buy some very thick knicker elastic?'

On her return she joined Joy and Henry as they set to work on my jacket. They pinned the bits of elastic to the back of the tails of the jacket and then took the elastic up inside the jacket, under my arms, across my back and pinned it to the inside of the jacket. It was so tight it virtually cut off the blood supply to my arms. Finally we had achieved a solution, but my brand-new tailcoat was not as God, nature or Hawes and Curtis had intended it to be.

Having sorted everything out sartorially-wise, it was time to begin practising in my new tails. I'd begun to get used to Henry's training methods, which were, to say the least, a little unorthodox. A few weeks earlier he said to me as we finished our session,'Len, do you have a small rucksack?'

'No, I don't but I think my stepdad has.'

'Well, ask if you can borrow it and bring it in with you next time,' said Henry.

I did and to my amazement he loaded weights into it and made me dance all evening while carrying it on my back. He said it helped to keep my back straight and my shoulders back. I can't argue with him, because it worked.

Another time he said to me, 'Len we need to work on keeping your arms straight.' He pointed towards the studio wall. Leaning against it was a contraption that looked part cross, part drainpipe and part medieval torture device. He took hold of it and strapped me to it with my arms resting in the bits that looked like guttering. By adjusting the straps it altered my arm position but it ensured that once I was in it there was no way I could drop my arms from the correct position. To begin with, it really made my arms ache, but in time I got used to it; it certainly helped to ensure I always had the correct posture.

'Remember, Len, your arm should be straight and your hand shouldn't look like it's revving a motorbike! It should be straight to.'

I'd spend hours just concentrating on that one aspect of my dancing: I did it over and over again until it became a habit, and was totally ingrained in my brain. Lessons once learned, never forgotten.

Quite rightly, from his point of view, Henry was not about to have me bugger off for a week alone with his lovely daughter. 'I'll be sending Iris with you to help out.'

Iris was another part-time teacher at the school and what he meant was for her to keep an eye on us. We had to book and pay for a week, but we went down the day before the competition and came home the day after. On the morning we were to leave for Camber Sands, Henry Kingston gave me a pair of cufflinks. They were gold with a little pearl in the middle – they were absolutely beautiful.

'Len, I'd like you to have these. I wore them when I won my first championship and I hope they bring you luck.'

It was such a kind and lovely thing to do. I still have them; those cufflinks are one of my most treasured possessions.

Henry also shared a vital piece of information with us. 'You'll be all right because a very good friend of mine, Frank Mayne, is the director of dance for Pontin's. I've told him you're coming, so you will win.'

Now if this sounds like it was fixed, it was, kind of, but we would have won anyway – trust me! Everyone else was just regular holidaymakers shuffling around and by this time we were getting very good. But it's also true to say there was some phoning around done back in those days. I'm sure Henry phoned Frank and said, 'Look, it's my daughter and her partner, they'll be okay, won't they, Frank?'

Not only were we very good, but also I was dressed in my tailcoat and the whole works, added to which Cherry wore a stunning dress and looked gorgeous. We looked like we'd just stepped off the set of a Busby Berkeley movie, while the regular holidaymakers wore whatever they had taken with them to the camp. I imagined the campers deciding to go in for the competition with a 'Come on, Flo, let's give it a go.'

When we finished our waltz and quickstep all the holidaymakers stood up and clapped. It was the first time I'd ever been applauded for my dancing and I was really chuffed. It was also the first time I danced to a real live band; previously it had always been records so that added another dimension to the whole experience. It's one of the things I love about *Strictly Come Dancing* and *Dancing with the Stars* – the live orchestra. I'm forever chatting with the musicians, all of whom really enjoy doing the shows. Back in the fifties and sixties there were thousands of musicians playing live all over the country, but the opportunities to do so now are far less. Every holiday camp had its own band and there's nothing like dancing to a full-size dance band.

Having won at Camber Sands we were told that the next round of the dancing competition was to be held over a weekend at Osmington Bay, which is near Weymouth in Dorset. We had practised really hard for the Camber Sands event and while I had looked forward to it, I hadn't, if I'm honest, been that bothered whether we got through to the next level; but having experienced the live band and everything else I was now completely hooked.

The Osmington Bay event was a whole different affair. It was obvious that there would be other novices, probably in a similar position to us: some of them may have been dancing longer and some may even have won some competitions. We on the other hand had the advantage of Cherry's dad coaching us. To get to the final we had to finish in the top 12, so the pressure was on – just a little bit.

Iris didn't come with us to Dorset in late October; this time Henry Kingston himself came along. This was serious. This was a bit like Arsene Wenger turning up to watch two Sunday pub teams on Hackney Marshes. I'm sure Henry knew all the judges and they couldn't have failed to know who Henry's daughter was – they had the same name! However, we were getting better and better from his coaching and, I have to say, through our commitment to practising. We also were developing a really good understanding as a dancing couple. Anyway, we finished in the top 12 and so it was next stop the finals.

We decided that appearing at the Royal Albert Hall in a tail suit with ladies' knicker elastic as an integral part of its design was perhaps not the best idea. It also took ages to adjust the elastic so the correct pressure was maintained. What would happen if it snapped during a dance?

'We'll go and see Hawes and Curtis together, Len. We'll get them to sort out their mistake,' Henry suggested, and so we went up to London together. When we walked into their shop in Dover Street we were met by the man who did the writing down.

'Oh no, sir, I don't think I can agree with you on that. It's certainly not our fault,' said the man.

If you'd spent a little less time fiddling with my fork then perhaps it wouldn't have happened, was all I could think. Despite his insistence that it wasn't their fault he was still mortified by what had happened and began to get a little more helpful. They started hacking the jacket about and a week later I got a perfect tailcoat. All for just £25 more.

Years later a mate of mine asked to borrow the suit because he was going to a fancy dress do. Afterwards he called me to say that he'd been sick over it and so he was getting it dry cleaned before returning it. I never saw it again and lost touch with the guy that borrowed it, all of which makes me sad, as it is one of those things I would love to have kept. So Norman Barrel, if you're out there and still have it, I'd like to try it on to see if it still fits.

There was no question: my remodelled tail suit perfectly complemented the Victorian splendour of the Royal Albert Hall. Having never been inside such a place before I was shocked and a little amazed by everything that day. The event was quite a feat of organisation, as all the various different finals were to take place over the course of one day; one minute it was the Miss Lovely Legs, next it was the ping-pong final. The dancing competition was scheduled for the end of the evening and so there was quite a bit of waiting around. The 12 couples took it in turn to dance to Joe Loss and his Orchestra, who were fabulous; a big step up from the holiday camp bands. We got down to the last six and in the final round the 11 judges decided we were the winners. Henry and Joy were there to see it; it was the proudest day of my life to that point.

Fred Pontin himself presented us with our prize and we had our picture taken with him and Henry Kingston. The fact is that Henry was held in awe by many of the professional judges, so it was no wonder they took notice of us. I learned a lot from my first competition. Ballroom dancing is much like a sport; dedication, training, fitness and a strong work ethic all come into play. Dancing is no different from serious sports. If you really want to progress to a high level it'll never happen without a huge amount of effort.

So, there it was: my first win in a novice competition. I was so elated I felt more like a world champion than the winner of a holiday camp competition. At the risk of sounding big-headed I felt like we were unbeatable, the confidence of youth, I suppose, but I knew how good Cherry was as a dancer and in Henry Kingston we had a brilliant coach. I remember lying in bed thinking this is my destiny, I could be a champion ballroom dancer, winning competition after competition and with luck some day I'd be a world champion. Naturally, it didn't quite work out like that.

The next week it was back to training. Before we started Henry had something to tell us. He was confirming my idle fantasies – kind of.

'As you know I'm very proud of you and what you did, but it's just the start. You've won one holiday camp competition and now you have a chance to enter another; this one's organised by Butlins in association with the *News of the World*.' He went on to explain it was called Dancing Stars of Tomorrow and it was another rung for novice dancers on the ladder of competition dancing, but he stressed that it was a step up from Pontin's.

'It'll be a lot stiffer competition than last time and you won't necessarily even make the final. There are some regional heats all over the country and the first three from each of these will go through to the grand final. It's at the Albert Hall again. There'll be 36 couples that will be whittled down to 24, and then the 24 will become 12, and then a final dance-off of six couples will decide the winner.'

There was one other problem, as Henry went on to explain.

'It's three dances: a waltz, a quickstep and a cha-cha-cha.'

I'd never ever danced any Latin American, a problem compounded by the fact that Henry Kingston only coached ballroom, never Latin – it was a case of never the twain could meet, in the world of professional dance coaches. Before I could object or offer a comment, which I'm sure Henry was expecting, because even then I was not slow in speaking up, he said:

'You will have to go to a Latin teacher. I have someone in mind so I will phone her tomorrow and book a lesson.'

The someone was a lady called Nina Hunt whose dance studio was in Balham. It's a strange thing but in the late sixties and seventies most of the top ballroom and Latin teachers were based in South London. There were Bill and Bobbie Irvine, Walter Laird, Len Scrivener, Sonny Binick, and Wally Fryer, a near-endless list of former champions. There are two different types of dance teacher: there's your bread-and-butter teacher who would just teach the general public social dancing, and then there are the coaches that only work with competitors. If you reach a certain level you went to one of the coaches. We, or rather I, was a long way from the standard that would normally get sent to a coach.

'Okay. Len, it's all arranged – you and Cherry will have a lesson with Nina Hunt on Friday.'

This was the equivalent of sending someone that had never played golf, other than pitch and putt, to have a private lesson with Tiger Woods.

Cherry and I went over to Nina's basement studio, which was just off Balham High Road; simply finding the place was a challenge. As we walked in, through what we took to be the door of her studio, we bumped into a lady.

'Oh, excuse me, are you Miss Hunt?' I asked.

'No, I'm bloody well not, she's next door.'

I later discovered that this was Nellie Duggan, the wife of

Len Scrivener, who I would later learn a great deal from. I also learned that Nellie was a lady known for speaking her mind. We hurried out and headed down an alleyway to a door that led to Nina Hunt's studio. I remember thinking, I hope she's not from the same mould as the woman we'd just met. As we walked in my jaw dropped. Having a lesson were John and Betty Wesley, the reigning British amateur champions; by this time I was beginning to keep up with who was who in the dance world. As Cherry and I sat in the small changing room, which was just a partitioned-off bit of the studio, I could hear them talking about fans and hockey sticks, and a whole load more technical jargon.

'Cherry, I'm really not sure about all this.'

'Don't worry, Len. You'll be fine,' said Cherry, trying to put me at ease.

'It's fine for you! You've been dancing since you were two, while I've been dancing for less than a year,' I reminded her.

At that point Johnny Wesley walked into the changing room and we walked out to the studio, which was about the size of a large living room; it also had a pillar slap bang in the centre.

'Hello, Cherry. How's your father? How's your mother?' asked the slim woman of around 40, who I assumed was Nina Hunt. It was as if I was invisible. Eventually, after chatting away to Cherry for a few minutes, she finally noticed me.

'And who are you?'

'I'm Len.'

'What would you like to dance, Len?'

'We'd like to learn the cha-cha-cha, please.'

'Okay then, show me your routine and we'll work from there.'

Luckily for me the Wesleys chose that moment to leave the studio, so sparing me the embarrassment of hearing me explain that we hadn't got a routine.

'What do you mean you haven't got a routine?' asked Miss Hunt, who clearly couldn't believe what she'd just been told. 'Well, just show me the basic steps, then.'

'I don't know the basic steps, I've never done the cha-cha-cha.'

As I heard the words coming out of my mouth I was thinking, why me? Can somebody get me out of here? I was just like most of the contestants on *Strictly Come Dancing* at their very first session. I felt humiliated, which is not something any of us enjoy. Then to my amazement Nina Hunt laughed. 'You know what? I haven't taught anyone basic cha-cha-cha for almost 20 years.'

With that she took hold of my elbows. And so it was that Nina Hunt, one of the leading coaches of Latin American dancing in the world, started me on the road to loving Latin American dancing. That first lesson made me appreciate the wonderful rhythms of Latin, the freedom that not being in contact with your partner brings. While I loved my ballroom I found, as the weeks progressed, that I actually loved Latin more. Not that we had long to think too much about it. We only had six weeks to master the cha-cha-cha before the first round of the Butlins competition.

Although I was still working at the docks for Harland and Wolff dancing was taking over my life. I spent every waking moment thinking about dancing and trying to be better at it. Even at work I was forever dancing around, and naturally all the blokes took the mickey: 'Show as your rise and fall, Len.'

One day we were sitting around chatting in our crib; it was the place our gang sat to have our tea breaks. I was telling them about our progress through the first round of the competition.

'We know, Len, we've arranged a coach to come up the Albert Hall when you do your dancing.'

'Leave it out, Jimmy.' I thought it was just the lads having another good laugh at my expense.

'No, really Len, we have. We've got a 53-seater charabanc organised. None of us have ever been anywhere like that and we thought it might be our one opportunity.'

'You're serious, aren't you?' I asked, knowing the answer.

'Oh yes! There's platers, welders and a couple of people out the office. We're not going to miss out on your big night.'

Come the day of the competition Cherry and I went up early to the Albert Hall so as to ensure we were not rushed; we wanted to be perfectly prepared. We were confident, because Nina Hunt had done a terrific job teaching me the cha-cha-cha from scratch. But while we had won the Pontin's competition with me in my tailcoat, this competition, because it included Latin, meant that the man danced in a dinner jacket – and obviously trousers. For my money the tailcoat hides a multitude of sins and so my technique, or lack of it, was going to be fully exposed. I was also very well aware that the standard of the competitors, from all over the UK, was going to be much higher this time.

As Cherry and I walked out on to the floor of the Albert Hall there was some nice applause, punctuated by shouts of, 'Go on, Lenny Boy!', 'Come on, my son!'

It was more like being at West Ham for a football match than it was a ballroom-dancing competition. At any moment I expected to hear, 'Come on the 'ammers.' The 50-odd dockers had enjoyed themselves all the way up to Kensington on the coach, crates of beer having lubricated their journey. I'm not sure whether it was the shouting of my workmates or the lack of a tailcoat or just my nerves, but it was not my, and consequently our, finest four minutes. When we came off the floor Cherry's dad was there to meet us.

'Len, I'm afraid to say you were terrible,' said Henry. 'I think you'll be lucky if you make it through to the next round.'

My first thought was, I'd blown it, which was quickly followed by, what would the lads say when I got back to work on Monday? I quickly put that out of my mind because they were probably too far-gone to actually remember much of what was happening. The compère read out the numbers of the couples who were to progress to round two and, much to my surprise, and even more to Henry's, our number was called; although 36 was the next to last, so we were on tenterhooks.

For the second round my nerves had subsided somewhat, but my confidence had taken a bit of a battering from Henry's criticism. This round was made up of 24 dancers and we danced much better and got through to round three – the last 12. From there we made it into the final along with five other couples. There were two from Scotland, one from Northern Ireland, and three from England, including Cherry and myself.

Come the final I was feeling very nervous, but I surprised myself with our dancing and thought we'd done far better than in any of the previous rounds; we were especially pleased with the cha-cha-cha. We may have been helped by the fact that the boys from Harland and Wolff were rather more subdued in their support; the booze-filled euphoria had become somewhat more soporific. Although they did give us a standing ovation as we came out, out of the corner of my eye I could see a couple of them sound asleep in their seats.

Waiting for the results was more nerve-racking than actually performing. The standard pattern is to do the top six places from first to last. As I stood there I thought, please let it be number 36. I was squeezing Cherry's hand so tightly I just about crushed it.

'In first place: number four.' It was one of the Scottish couples. Next up it was 24, then 31 – we hadn't made the top three. At that point another feeling kicked in. Please don't let us be last!

'In fourth place, couple number 36, Mr Len Goodman and Miss Cherry Kingston.'

In that one moment my feeling of invincibility was shattered forever, which was no bad thing. I realised then, and it's a feeling that's never left me, that it's hard work that makes winners. It has, of course, got something to do with talent, and there's also a little bit of luck that comes into play, but as the old saying goes – the harder I work, the luckier I become. Not that we had totally lost out, as the prize for coming fourth was a silver medal, which I still have. It is mounted in a little Perspex display stand, made for me by my dad's dad in his little garden shed.

Cherry and I were also picked to represent Great Britain in a novice competition against Holland. This called for another step up the ladder, but more for me, in that we had to dance a tango as well as a jive. It was back to Balham and Nina Hunt for more coaching. This time she didn't bother asking to see our routine.

'So, I'm teaching you from scratch, am I, Len?' said Nina with a smile on her face. You're probably thinking I'm referring to the tango, because coming from Argentina, which is obviously a Latin American country, then you might suppose it's a Latin dance, but that's not the case. The tango is a ballroom dance and it was Henry who taught us, and Nina taught us the jive. Originally the category we now call Latin American was Latin *and* American, so the jive being an American dance came under that classification.

On a Friday, a month later, we were on the coach for Holland along with the other couples who were competing from Great Britain, which included the two Scottish couples that had beaten us at the Albert Hall. The competition, which we won, was on Saturday and then we travelled back home on Sunday; the camaraderie was fantastic and we had a brilliant time. We got back to Cherry's house late on the Sunday evening to find that Henry Kingston had been rushed to hospital. The following day Cherry's dad died.

Chapter Seven

Standing On the Shoulders of Giants

When my mum's parents died in the 1950s it made me sad. I loved my Granddad Albert in his flat cap and his funny sayings. I loved my Nan, too, who made me laugh with her made-up rhymes, but when you're younger and an old person close to you dies it affects you in a different way from when someone who is closer to your age passes away. It's very different when it's a person you have come to know and like as a friend. And while Henry Kingston was much older than me, he had become my friend, but more importantly he was my mentor. I had already sensed that the opportunity he'd given me could be my one chance in a lifetime. It was not one I'd gone in search of, but because of him it had come my way. Initially Henry had been excited that Cherry was showing some interest in competing, and soon he began to see that we really did have potential, all of which makes it all the more tragic that he wasn't there to see us fully realise our dancing talent. So with Henry's passing I was left feeling both sad and, from a selfish point of view, frustrated and a little lost. I'd known that he had suffered from a bad back that he put down to dancing, but I later heard he'd been involved in a car accident that the doctors thought may have triggered the cancer that killed him. I was 22 years old; I'd been dancing for about a year. I felt that my world had been turned on its head. His death was so sudden and the shock so dreadful for both Joy and Cherry that, to begin with, no one thought about the Erith Dance Studio, but very quickly the realisation kicked in.

About ten days after Henry died, Joy sat me down.

'Len, I've got a proposition. Will you give up your job at the docks, turn professional and help me teach in the dance studio? Help us run it?'

'How can I do that? I only know the routines I've been taught.'

It was a bit like asking one of the celebrities on *Strictly Come Dancing* to start teaching. People who watch the TV show imagine they can really dance, but all they've done is to learn short routines and that's the limit of what they know. They have no understanding of the finer points of dance, the intricacies or whatever, and why should they? They're like someone that's learned one tune on the piano, albeit perfectly, but don't ask them to play another tune because they won't know where to start. It's not a criticism, it's fact, and that was precisely how I was. I was so inexperienced it was frightening. There was another problem: just like a male celebrity on the television I only knew my own steps – I had no clue what the woman should be doing.

What is it they say about necessity being the mother of invention? Well, Joy was about to invent Britain's first ex-dock worker-cum-welder dance teacher. She said, 'You can do it, Len,

I know you can. Here's how we'll manage. Cherry and I will show you what to teach before each class begins.'

Put like that it sounded really simple, and to some extent it was. I jacked it in at Harland and Wolf and before each class began we'd sit in the little office behind the tea bar where we'd go over the dances – again and again. Cherry and her mum would explain and sometimes show me. 'This is how the girl does it and this is how the boy does it. Have you got it, Len?'

'Sort of,' was my usual response. 'Sorry to keep asking this, but which one of you was the bloke?'

Naturally, Mum, Dad and my stepmum were thrilled. Their little Lenny had become a dance teacher; no more sweating it out at the docks. Obviously I was no overnight Henry Kingston, far from it. Joy took over the coaching in the upstairs studio; I was down in the lower room with Pauline and Cherry – all of which was fine, but I would have failed if I hadn't had one thing that has stood me in good stead throughout my life, and, as I said right at the start of the book, that one thing is my personality. It was also a lesson into why people go to a particular dance studio. As often as not they are attracted by the personality of the teacher, or not as the case may be. In a matter of weeks the Erith Dance Studio's classes had gone from quiet Joy to brash Len; it wasn't long before many of the pupils found my stumbling efforts too much to bear. Inevitably some people decided to hang up their dancing shoes.

In fact, I had exactly the same thing happen at my own studio about ten years ago. There was a girl who worked for me, who was very quiet and her personality was not very outgoing at all. She was very good at doing private lessons for couples, but she wanted to extend her repertoire and so she was always on at me to run her own classes and kept pestering me to give her the chance; I kept fobbing her off with excuses. I finally relented, in part because I was starting a new class of my own on a Thursday and needed to put an advert in the local paper. I suggested that she ran a class on a Sunday evening, a day when we were normally closed and so whatever happened with the class didn't really matter – it was better than nothing.

From the first week there were about 30 people there and to my surprise it seemed to go pretty well. Unfortunately, after three weeks of classes, the girl's mother called to say her daughter had appendicitis and was in hospital. I stepped into the breach and ran her next Sunday class – it was my dance school and naturally I thought I was a great teacher. Well, by the time she came back, three weeks later, there were just four couples left. The people who went to her class really liked the girl, who was more like a Sunday school teacher, and couldn't get on with me at all.

'Come on, shake your hips, girl, move your arse!' was not what they were used to hearing.

Not that I was quite so brash when I first started teaching, but the people who were used to Joy Tolhurst, world champion ballroom dancer, must have found it more than a little bit shocking to be confronted with me. At first I did some really stupid things. One evening Cherry and her mum were showing me some steps for the jive that I was to teach in class a little later. They demonstrated the change of hands behind the back; first they showed me the boy's steps and then the girl's steps. 'Have you got that, Len?'

'Sort of, but you'd better show me one more time.'

Once everyone arrived for their class we began by working on things that we'd done in a previous lesson. Following our tea break in the middle of the evening, I decided to leave the women chatting to get started with the men on the change of hands behind the back step in the jive. Having taught all the men how to do it they sat down and then I got the women up to teach them the step. Having taught them I said:

'Okay. Get back with your partner and do it together.'

All would have been fine, but for one small detail: I'd taught both the men and the women the men's part and the whole thing ended in a disaster. A minor catastrophe compared to what happened to me during a quickstep class a few weeks later.

On this evening there were about 14 couples and we were working on what's called the spin turn. While most people sort of got it, one couple just couldn't seem to manage it at all. As I watched them I could see that it was the woman who was having the most trouble and so I went over and said, 'Here, let me dance with you, it will be easier for me to show you where you and your partner are going wrong.'

At that point everyone else stopped dancing so that they could look at us. I'd already identified one of their problems; she was none too light on her feet. In the spin turn it was like trying to shift a Sherman tank; even getting her moving around the floor was really hard. I was literally pulling her around the turns with virtually no help from her. Very quietly, so that no one else could hear, I said to her, 'Could you just try and be a little bit lighter on your feet?'

With that the woman exploded. 'You pig! You dirty filthy pig!' She went crimson in the face and started shouting even louder. 'I've got a bad back. You pig!' She went on like a woman possessed, began crying and then went over to stand by her man so she could continue her tirade with his full support. 'I've never been so insulted in my entire life. We're leaving! Come on, George.'

With that she grabbed her man, who was close to half her size and weight, and marched out the studio door. She never came back.

It was a salutary lesson and one that actually prompted me to get better qualified. I read once that surgeons can only pass on 10 per cent of their knowledge, and the other 90 per cent is derived from experience; dancing is no different. As hard as Joy tried to teach me, and she did a good job, I always felt a fraud. I vowed to master the art of teaching. I'd been told that Latin technique was simpler than ballroom so I decided to get qualified first in Latin American. I bought a book on the subject, written by Doris Lavell; it was the official *Latin Technique for the Imperial Society of Teachers of Dancing*, no less. Not long after having ploughed my way through it, I thought that if she had written the book then who better to go to for some lessons?

I was already aware, having read Miss Lavell's book and talked with Joy about her, of just what an important figure in the dance world she was. She and her partner, Pierre, had been the most famous couple in Latin American dancing. I say 'had been' because Monsieur Pierre, a Frenchman, had died before I got into dancing. He, apparently, was a large man whereas Doris was petite, so they were something of an incongruous dancing couple. Immediately after World War Two, Pierre and Doris decided to go travelling in order to develop their Latin skills, as well as to learn new dances and techniques. They visited Brazil, the USA and Cuba. Havana in the late 1940s was a glamorous city full of glittering nightlife, casinos and holidaying Mafia bosses. In the immediate post-war years Latin American was considered a bit of a joke by the ballroom dance world, but thanks to the Lavells this reputation was changed for ever. They spent months learning from the great teachers and upon their return to the UK they set about formulating their own techniques to be submitted to the Imperial Society for approval. After months of deliberation the Society had still not decided whether their techniques were either good or acceptable.

The difficulty for the Society was that the Lavells' ideas were not just different, they were revolutionary – that's what going to Cuba does for you. For example, there were originally two types of rumba – the square rumba that was danced on the first beat, but the Cubans danced it on the second beat. When you tried dancing the Cuban way it felt as if you were dancing off time and out of rhythm, so it was no small change that they were trying to get the Society to accept. Unable to gain acceptance of their ideas they decided to return to Cuba for more lessons and research. Finally they came home with what they thought was the definitive technique; thankfully the Imperial Society agreed and their book became the bible for Latin American dancing for close to 20 years. Shortly after I went to Miss Lavell a man named Walter Laird brought out what has become the definitive book on Latin American, but his work could not have happened without the pioneering efforts of the Lavells.

In the dance world of the sixties and seventies there were certain ladies that had to be treated with the upmost respect; on no account were these women ever to be referred to by their Christian name. There was a Miss Josephine Bradley, she was always Miss Bradley, Phyllis Hayler who was likewise Miss Hayler and, of course, Miss Lavell. This was despite the fact that Doris Lavell had long since ceased to be a Lavell, having married a dancer named James Arnell who we all called Jimmy. About three years after first going to Miss Lavell, out of the blue, she said, 'Len, you may call me Doris.' That was it, I was in the club.

Doris was not only a great teacher; she was a great character too. She and Jimmy had a Rolls-Royce, but they hardly ever used it. Instead they used their other car, one of those French Citroëns that looked like they were made out of corrugated tin. They also had a yacht that was moored down in Monte Carlo harbour – it was a catamaran called *Soho Cat*. It wasn't dancing that bought these luxuries but Jimmy's family money. His father owned a string of garages called Blue Star; they were all over the South East of England in the sixties. When his father died he left Jimmy a sizeable sum that he and Doris enjoyed spending, but they never gave up teaching and dancing.

One day Cherry and I turned up at the Greek Street studio to be met by a distraught Doris – not that this was unusual as there was always some tragedy or crisis happening in her and Jimmy's life together.

'Oh Cherry, Len, we've had a terrible time. You know we have the two Alsatians, well it's Alphonso – he's been so bad.' They lived in Primrose Hill and had apparently popped over to Hammersmith to get something. 'We took Alphonso with us and instead of taking the Citroën we took the Rolls. We left the dog in the back of the car while we went into the shop. I swear we were only gone about 25 minutes, but Alphonso must have got frustrated or something. We had left the window on one side of the car open so he had some air. We told him to stay on that side so he could breathe it more easily. To encourage him to stay that side we put the armrest down. Do you know what he did? He ate the armrest!'

On another occasion she was talking to Cherry after our lesson had finished and said, 'This morning I went over to Bond Street and bought this dress in Fenwick's, how does it look?'

'It looks absolutely lovely, Miss Lavell,' Cherry said, because it did.

'Well, that's good because unfortunately they only had it in a 14, but I wanted to wear it for dinner tonight. Do you think anyone will notice?'

With that, she turned around to reveal that the back of the dress was stapled together to make it smaller. The bloke downstairs from the dance studio had a furniture business and Doris had got him to do it with his staple gun.

Still, we worked hard when we went to the Soho studio, because to become a recognised teacher with the Imperial Society takes a long time. First you have to become an Associate, which is quite an arduous exam. Then once you have passed that, you have to wait two years before you can take your second exam, which was then called the Membership but it's now known as the Licentiate. It's not just that there's a two-year wait to take it, it's because it takes you two years to learn all you need to pass the exam. You have to wait a further five years to take your Fellowship; so it takes eight or nine years to complete the process. During all this time I trained with Doris and we became very close friends. She was a wonderful teacher to whom I owe a great deal and a very good lady to have counted as a friend.

While teaching was now my day job, so to speak, competing was also very important to Cherry and myself – we were really ambitious. If you wanted to succeed in the competitive dance world it required not just skill and dedication: there was also a certain amount of politics involved in getting to the top. There were far less teachers then than there are now, which is what made the whole thing so political. When I began my professional career there were only four top coaches: Nina Hunt, Walter Laird, Doris Lavell and a chap called Sidney Francis. All of them had strong and differing opinions about dance. As a dancer, if you went to Doris you had to dance her way; if you went to Nina Hunt her methods were different, as were Walter Laird's, and Sidney Francis just had a mixture of them all.

As a competitive dancer you had to go to all these teachers because they also judged a lot of competitions. The truth was that unless you were in with them all, at least a little bit, and they knew you, you had a cat in hell's chance of doing well. Not that by going to all four guaranteed success because very nearly every serious competitive couple was doing exactly the same thing. It was an open secret that dancers went to all of the coaches but it was not the done thing to mention to a particular teacher that you had been having lessons with one of their so-called competitors. Being a bit more of a 'cor blimey, come on, Nina, let's sort this out' kind of a guy may have helped me: on the other hand she may well have been irritated with me being a bit over-familiar, but I got away with it. If others who went to Wally Laird dared to even mention Nina Hunt's name they were history. For whatever reason Doris liked Wally Laird and he didn't mind her too much, but mention Nina's name to Doris and that would start her off something rotten – they were the worst of enemies. I'm sure too that my dancing with Cherry, and their affection for the late Henry Kingston, also helped me get along, where others might have struggled.

Nina Hunt, as far as I know, never competed but she was a great coach, Walter Laird both danced and competed, Sydney Francis never competed, nor did Doris Lavell. Whereas technically Doris was very, very good, Nina Hunt was great at choreography. Walter Laird was great for taking Nina Hunt's choreography and teaching you how to do it much better; but for God's sake don't tell him it was her choreography! Nina Hunt had good ideas for steps and was good at showing you them, not teaching them, but showing you. It was just the same in ballroom dancing: there were certain ballroom teachers you would go to who would be good at teaching the quickstep while others would be good at other dances.

We also began being coached by Len Scrivener, the husband of Nellie Duggan, who I mistook for Nina Hunt when we went over to Balham for our very first lesson. Len was an absolute character as well as a lovely man.

'So what dance would you like to show me to start with?' enquired Len at our first lesson.

I said we'd try the waltz, so he selected a 78 record, put it on and we started to dance. Well, I was bloody amazed, and a little cross, because Len stared out of the window. What I didn't realise at the time was that he was watching our reflections. When we finished he asked, 'What were you trying to portray to me in that waltz?'

'Well,' I said, 'first of all I wanted to show you the beauty of the dance, a beautiful rise and fall, a lovely sway of the shoulders, a swing of the body as we moved through each bar of the music. We wanted to characterise some of the basic steps as well as some of the intricate moves that you can achieve during the waltz.'

'Well, you failed on every section,' Len replied.

So began the first lesson with Len Scrivener, a man who won the British championships two or three times – a legend and a maverick.

Len was an eccentric and over the few years having lessons with him we became very friendly. I was always trying to encourage him to go to Blackpool – the Mecca of ballroom dancing where they hold the championships every year.

'Come on, Len, you'll love it, what is the matter with you?'

'I'll never step foot in that ballroom ever again,' was all Len would say. It was daft because he was a legend as a dancer and an extremely good teacher whom the organisers would have loved to have been there as a judge. Finally, I think it was in 1974, he relented and said he would grace Blackpool with his presence. That was only half the battle, because Nellie was adamant that she wasn't going.

'We're never going up that bleedin' hole, you'll never see us in bloody Blackpool.'

After some more cajoling she relented and I said I would go and pick them up and drive them to Blackpool along with Cherry. I booked us at the Clifton Hotel in Talbot Square, and come the day of our departure I picked them up 8.30 a.m. At around 11 o'clock we decided to stop for breakfast at the services on the M1, and having parked up the four of us trooped into the place that had waitress service. I ordered a toasted teacake and some tea, Cherry and Len said they'd have the same and Nellie said, 'You know what? I'd like that early starter.' This was a cooked breakfast special.

'Ah, I'm awfully sorry,' the waitress said, 'but you can only have the early starter until 11.'

'Listen here,' said Len. 'It's three minutes after 11 and my dear lady wife would like the early starter so surely you can rustle that up for her, please?'

'No, I'm very sorry, it's only on until 11 o'clock,' insisted the waitress.

That was it. Without another word Len stood up and started shouting. '*Get me the manager!* Bring him to me this instant.'

It gave me an inkling into why he might have fallen out with the Blackpool people.

Nevertheless, word had gone out that Len was going to the championships. It became the buzz of the dance world: the Messiah Scrivener is coming to Blackpool. Whatever his faults he was a genius at teaching. One day when we were learning the tango, for which there was no better teacher, he said to me, 'Len, the whole dance is lacking any atmosphere, you're just going through the motions and there's no atmosphere.'

'Well, what is atmosphere?' I asked Scrivener.

'Atmosphere is the outward expression of an inner emotion.'

Brilliant!

On another occasion Len Scrivener taught me what I thought was a particularly difficult bit and after practising it with Cherry I couldn't seem to get it. The following week I went back and said, 'What you taught me really didn't feel right when I did it.'

He offered me some brilliant advice. 'Let me tell you a story about my dog Bubbles. I take him for a walk every morning and I meet a man named Mr Jackson who has a dog called Fluff. I've been seeing him and his dog now for years. Mr Jackson walked in a very strange way, he was buckled over and his right shoulder was very low and he was bent forward at a very strange angle. About six months ago I stopped seeing Mr Jackson and for several months he just disappeared. One morning, however, who should I see coming towards me but Fluff followed by a man walking perfectly normally, it took me several moments to recognise Mr Jackson. He was straight, straight as a ramrod, walking proudly. I was completely amazed at his transformation.

'"Mr Jackson where have you been?"

'He told me that during the war a piece of shrapnel had lodged at the base of his spine, which is what made him walk in that bizarre way. He went on to tell me that the doctors thought it would be impossible to operate. Then a new surgeon saw him who said he could do it, so he had had the operation and everything had worked out fine. Then Mr Jackson said something amazing, "So now here I am walking upright, but I must say it feels funny."'

This was Len Scrivener's way of telling me that how you feel when you dance is nothing to do with how you look.

One of my favourite dance teacher stories was one told to me by Walter Laird. One day he complained about the way I was dancing.

'Len, you're dancing too soft, you've got to get toned, you've got to get some toning in you.'

'Well, I understand what toning is but not how it applies to dancing.'

'Well, not like that, Len, because that's too stiff, I don't want stiff. Imagine a businessman who has taken his secretary on a dirty weekend to Brighton. She's 35 years younger than him and she's lying on the bed – naked. He's in the bathroom cleaning his teeth when he realises he's left his dressing gown on the other side of the room and he has to walk out of the bathroom, across the room, to his side of the bed. The way he walked? That's toning.'

It's the brilliance of the best teachers: they tell you things that lodge in your brain for ever. They helped me become a better dancer and helped me become a better teacher as well – not to mention the fact that I now know exactly how to walk naked around a bedroom.

There's a brilliant saying, 'If I have seen further, it is by standing on the shoulders of giants.' That's what I've always tried to do. These old teachers had great ways and that's how I learnt to explain things better. It's from them that I learned some of the funny expressions like 'all sizzle and no sausage'. Mind you, I also got some good things from my dad. He'd watch my competitive dances and say things like, 'I don't know what's right, but I know that's wrong.'

It's only fair to point out that I was never a world-class dancer: I'm not where I am today for being a dancing great! Much like in many walks of life, whether it's sports, the arts or something else where people are judged, you get the good and the great. I was a good dancer, whereas Cherry was a *great* dancer, which was a huge advantage for me and to us as a dancing couple. We also got where we did through hard work and perseverance, by working that extra bit harder than many couples. I capitalised on our advantage of having Cherry's huge talent to move us up through the ranks of competitive dancing.

However, much like in football, golf, horse racing or whatever else, from among the greats there comes, maybe every ten years or so, a true great – a legend. In the dance world it's these very few dancers or teachers that take Latin or ballroom to another level. They revolutionise the way that things are done. Well, that was never me. As a dancer I got as far as I did because I was blessed with having a great partner and was prepared to work harder than most.

Cherry and I were not only dance partners but we also became boyfriend and girlfriend. I cannot say we became a partnership in the living-together sense, because that was something that was much less common in those days. We became romantically involved, like many dancing couples, because we lived in each other's pockets. I don't want to make it sound mercenary and calculating, because it wasn't, and there is no denying that Cherry was a pretty girl. But we just slipped into our relationship from what started out as a kiss on the cheek, to a kiss on the lips and then, well, I'll just leave that to your imagination.

In the months and years after Henry died I worked tirelessly to become a better teacher, while at the same time working on being a better dancer. I learned from every teacher that has ever given me a lesson. Sometimes what I learned was a new or brilliant way to teach; other times a teacher perhaps showed me through their teaching method how not to teach. In dancing you never stop learning, which is why I've always said that dancing is just like life. All this learning, teaching and training was hard work even for a fit 25-year-old, but there was another more tricky problem that had been waiting in the wings for some time, and it was now time for it to take centre stage.

There had been talk for quite a while about Erith being given a bit of a makeover, a rejuvenation I think they called it. Things like that were all the rage in the late sixties. Finally in 1970 it happened, and the dance studio on Pier Road was, along with a number of other properties, cited for compulsory purchase by the local council. Their plan was to pull our building down and redevelop the area into a car park. Joy, Cherry and I wanted to keep the school going, and so while we looked for new premises we decided to move the school to temporary accommodation. Our theory was that we would soon find a new permanent home, but in practice we spent three long and difficult years running a dance school in the pub. It was the George in the High Street in Erith, and when I say it was in the pub it was actually behind the bar area in a hall-like annexe. While it was not the most salubrious of places it was a lovely big space, which in many respects was actually better than the old studio. We had our own entrance so our pupils could come into the hall without having to go through the pub itself. However, we soon found there was a downside. The pub toilets were at the back of our hall, which meant there was continuous traffic all through our evening sessions with men going to and from the john. At the start of the evening the men, on their way to the toilet, would quietly walk past the class with their heads averted towards the wall, repeating their routine on the way back. Unfortunately, after they'd had a few pints they would be foxtrotting up the side of the hall with their mates, looking not unlike Peggy Spencer's formation dance team who regularly appeared on TV's *Come Dancing*.

Before moving to the pub, and by way of a farewell to the

old Erith Dance Studio, we held a dance on the night before we were to vacate the premises. We booked Richard Gleave and Janet Wade, who had recently turned professional but were also the reigning British and World Amateur Champions, to give a demonstration. Richard and Janet later married and went on to become one of the greatest ever British professional dance couples, winning the World Championships eight times in all.

This was the first time I had organised anything like this; actually it was the first time I'd ever really organised anything. I was anxious to make a good impression on Joy and Cherry, but also I wanted to impress the pupils, who we hoped would continue with us at our new premises. The day before the event I checked over the equipment. We had one of those really large record players for the 78-rpm heavy-duty shellac discs; it was the kind of player on which you had to change the needle regularly to avoid damaging the records. It was connected to a large valve amplifier, which used to get very hot after it had been in use for a while. As well as checking the equipment I checked over our collection of Victor Silvester records, assuring myself that nothing could go wrong. My next task was to have a dry run of the full evening's programme: first of all I wrote it all down so that I had a detailed running order. I noted the times of the recordings, when Richard and Janet would enter, which track I was using from which record and so on; it filled several sheets of paper because I left nothing to chance.

When Richard and Janet arrived at the studio they gave me the music that they were going to dance to. This was a period when there was crossover between 45-rpm singles, 33⅓ LPs and 78s, so it was a complex business trying to organise different speeds, as well as different tracks. While Richard and Janet were changing in the upstairs studio I was busy playing records so our pupils could dance. And while our regulars were going through their paces I was going over things one last time to avoid any slip-ups. The Gleaves' first song was a waltz, track five on a Tony Bennett LP that they had given me when they arrived. Next up was a tango, track nine on an Edmundo Ros LP. Come time for their first dance and I put the needle exactly on to the start of the Tony Bennett track, and stood back to not only admire Richard and Janet's dancing but also to congratulate myself on my skill as a DJ; was there no end to my talents? There didn't seem to be, as the evening went off without a hitch, helped by the fact that every time Richard and Janet came to do another demonstration dance, my needle-dropping skills proved unfailing. When they finished I went to thank them. They both said how much they had enjoyed the evening, before Richard added: 'Len, could you let me have our records back, as knowing me I'll forget them when we leave.'

'Of course, Richard.'

I went back downstairs and picked their records off the amplifier cabinet where I had carefully laid them after putting them back inside their sleeves. To my horror I found they had melted and buckled. Not just the one next to the amplifier but the whole lot. Luckily I was able to buy them new ones. Richard and I are still great mates although he still occasionally reminds me of that night in Erith.

Many years later I had Stephen and Lindsey Hillier do a demonstration; it was before they were married. They had been British

Amateur Champions and had turned professional. By this time cassette players had replaced records, for the most part, so there was less to go wrong, or so I thought. Stephen gave me their cassette, which contained all the dances that they were to perform, briefing me as to when I needed to pause it between some of their dances so that they could change outfits.

'Len, all you need to do is press play when it's time for us to come on,' Stephen explained. 'We have this fanfare that we've recorded to announce our arrival.'

Times really have changed, I thought. When it was time for their entry I pressed play on the cassette player, fully expecting to hear the Hillier's fanfare. There was nothing, just silence. I had already given them the big build-up, announced their names, so I got back on the microphone. 'One, two...Stephen, sorry, nothing's happening.' Stephen then popped his head round the door looking less than impressed – he was probably thinking I'd messed up their big entrance.

'Are you sure you've pressed the play button, Len?'

'Yes, I'm sure I have.'

'Is it on side one?' asked the frustrated-sounding Stephen Hillier.

'Of course it is, but naturally I'll check.'

I couldn't help being a bit sarcastic. What does he think I am? Stupid? was what I was thinking as I walked across to the cassette deck. At the same time Stephen, dressed in his tailcoat, looking very suave, started walking across the room – we both arrived at the cassette player at the same time to see what I had done. I'd not only pressed the play button, I'd also pressed record, which meant I'd erased their precious fanfare as well as several minutes of their opening number. All I could do was apologise, while also going very red in the face with embarrassment.

Not long after we moved to the pub we decided to start a new beginners' class. This was going to be my very own class, not one that I had inherited from Joy after Henry's passing. We put an advert in the local paper. 'New beginners' classes teaching all dances for social success. Still the Erith Dance Studio, now relocated to the George public house. Commences Tuesday 10 September, 8 p.m. till 10 p.m.' We had high hopes of filling the class, which would be some worthwhile extra money for the business. We had some additional costs associated with the move; a casualty of our relocation was the tea bar, which couldn't be re-established in the pub's hall. Prior to our first class I went to buy a new tea urn along with some reject cups and saucers. Pauline, Cherry and I set all this up on a table at one end of the hall, although not too close to the toilet, and by 7.45 we made sure it was full of hot water, there was milk and sugar, and a plate of digestive biscuits, and so we were ready for the onslaught of new dancers.

By ten to eight no one had turned up. At five to eight, two couples walked in, but that was it, no one else showed up. I was hoping for at least 40 people, and here I was with just four. It was all a bit of a disaster, not least because to teach 20 couples takes a lot longer than just two; with more pupils there's a lot more banter, lots more stops and starts, and teaching the class expands to fill the available time. But not with two it doesn't. What I had planned to take two hours took just 20 minutes. I had to improvise and so, even with a lengthy tea break – 'Do have a second cuppa, we have plenty' – they had learned the basics in four ballroom dances and a smattering of Latin American as well. After it was all over the three of us sat down to talk it over. We were devastated. There was also the expense of the advert, which only added to the sense of failure. We were crushed. What we couldn't know at that moment was just how valuable these four people would be to the business; valuable because both couples came to me for lessons for over 20 years. They paid for that advert a thousand times over.

In 1973 we finally found a place for our new school. It was in Dartford: number 27 The High Street – it was a search that had taken close to three years. The studio was not ideal: it was over some shops, on the top floor above two floors of offices; there was a climb of 54 stairs to get to our new dance school. Once there, the pupils were confronted by four pillars around which they had to navigate. It was a case of beggars can't be choosers, especially as we were all fed up with teaching in the pub; it wasn't just the problems of pub-goers and their antics, it was the lack of security of tenure for the business, which was by now going from strength to strength. In Dartford we got a 21-year lease, with rent for the first seven years of £20 per week, which doesn't sound like very much, but it was a fair rent for the property.

We planned to open in a month on a budget of £1,000 to complete all the renovations and remodelling. It was every penny of our savings. We needed to lay a dance floor, build a tea bar, there were lights, a hi-fi system and there was the painting and decorating on top of all that. Luckily, when you run a dance school you meet people from every walk of life, from every background and from many different professions. There was a ready-made work force of electricians and carpenters but there was only thing I didn't have: someone to lay the floor.

Before our pupils could start to climb the 54 steps, everything involved in the renovation had to be taken up the same way. For most things it was a challenge, but when it came to the material for laying the floor it proved to be a nightmare. There was no choice but to bring in a specialist floor-laying company. On the first day the two men from the company turned up at 7 a.m. To me, not yet 30, they looked to be close to retirement age; they were not just past their sell-by, they looked past their use-by date. The plan was to unload their vehicle before the traffic got bad. It proved to be every bit 'a plan' as neither bloke would carry any of the heavy stuff: they were only prepared to hump the light stuff. After they had shifted a few mops and tins of polish we reached an impasse.

'Don't worry, I'll carry the heavy stuff up for you.' I must have been mad, but I was also desperate. On the back of their truck were eight foot by four foot by one inch sheets of chip-board that were to be laid across the whole of the studio floor to provide a firm base for the actual dance surface. In all there were 40 pieces of these seriously heavy sheets; after five sheets I knew I had bitten off more than I could chew. As I walked out to contemplate my sixth sheet I bumped into Polecat Smith, an odd-job man I knew from around the town; his main trade, if you could call it that, was taking lead out of car batteries.

'Whacha, Len, you look like you're sweating a bit.' Polecat wore a railway man's cap that had once had a shiny peak to it but after years of straightening his cap with hands covered in battery acid it had eventually rotted clean away. His cap now looked more like something that a nineteenth-century US cavalryman might have worn.

I had first got to know him through my old mate Pete Dawson. We had gone to Polecat's home because Pete needed a reconditioned car battery.

Polecat lived on Dartford Marsh in three railway carriages, none of which had wheels; these were all linked together as a bizarre substitute for a normal home. As we drove up the dirt track leading to Polecat's place he eyed us suspiciously, while at the same time he continued examining one of his horse's front legs.

'And what can we do for you?' he said, as if he and the horse were in partnership. We had heard he was suspicious of strangers. We'd also heard that he sometimes ran errands for a notorious gypsy family. Apparently, if the gypsies were having problems with anyone they sent Polecat along to hit them over the head with a hammer; not exactly a scene out of *The Godfather*, but I'd heard it said that he got three quid a time for his efforts.

Pete said he wanted a car battery so Polecat became somewhat less suspicious and invited us inside. We entered the first railway carriage, which was obviously his 'living quarters'. Instead of normal seats there were a couple of bench seats out of a Ford Zephyr: sitting on one of the seats was a donkey.

'Go on, get out, you stupid bloody donkey.' As Polecat started waving his arms around, four chickens appeared from beneath the seat, fluttering and squawking about the place. By now our eyes had adjusted to the gloom inside the carriage, a gloom that was barely lifted by three naked 40-watt light bulbs that were strung along its length. In the corner was a sink, which had no taps on it; next to it was a bizarre-looking kitchen cabinet with two opening cupboards at the top and a centre one that pulled down to make a work surface, and this was all resting on two piles of breeze blocks. In the corner was a 14-inch Bush black and white television set with a convex-like magnifying glass in front of it to make the picture watchable.

'You boys wanna a cuppa?'

'Err, no thanks, we've just had one.' I imagined it would result in a case of acid poisoning at the very minimum. We ended up paying for a battery for Pete's Cortina and left as quickly as we could.

All of this explains how I came to be on passing acquaintance terms with Polecat Smith. 'Want to earn yourself a fiver, Polecat?' I asked, thinking it was probably going to be a lot harder earned than hitting someone over the head with a hammer – although not potentially as costly.

'Sounds good, what is it?'

'Well, I've got to get all these chipboard sheets up to the third floor.' I'd hardly finished speaking and Polecat had grabbed two sheets and was off up the stairs. At that moment Alan came along: we only knew him as Alan, although we never called him that, except to his face. Everyone called him Neanderthal Man, because he truly was the missing link. He was barely five foot tall but his arms reached down past his knees.

'Hello, Alan, want to earn yourself a fiver?'

Very soon the two of them were carting the chipboard flats, the floor sander and every other piece of equipment and materials from the back of the floor-layer's lorry to the top floor of the building. I haven't seen Polecat around for years so I assume he's dead now. It's strange because there are not those kinds of characters around any more; then again maybe I'm now moving in different circles.

Two weeks before the renovations were scheduled to finish I put an advert in the paper to announce the grand opening of the Len Goodman Dance Centre. Following the failure of just the two couples turning up for the new class at the pub years earlier I had learned a valuable lesson. Rule number one – never place the advert on anything but the front page of the local paper if you want a decent result. My front-page banner announcement invited new and old pupils to come along, admission was free, there were free refreshments and the evening would run from 7 p.m. until 10 p.m. One hundred and fifty-four people – new faces, old faces, some of whom I hadn't seen for years – made it to the top of the stairs. We were on our way. I had achieved my destiny: I was a dance teacher in Dartford.

Chapter Eight

Success Comes in Cans

The three years between the Erith Dance School closing in 1970 and our new school opening in 1973 were a mixture of good and bad times – although they were much more the former than the latter. Most of all they were very busy times. We were on a roller-coaster ride of teaching, competing and demonstrating, not only in the UK, but also all over Europe, and especially in Germany. We never seemed to slow down, but I must admit, they were also very exciting years. Whenever you start something new, especially when you're young and full of energy, you get carried along on a wave of adrenalin. Mum and Dad were pleased that things were working out so well for me. With the benefit of hindsight I have no doubt that they had their doubts that their Len would amount to anything very much. I was still living at home with Mum, but was also seeing plenty of Dad and Rene; all in all family life was fine.

The first competition Cherry and I entered after our two at the Albert Hall was the Kent Championship at the Royston Ballroom in Penge. This was back to the reality of dancing competitively when you're just starting out. I soon found that different judges liked different things and there wasn't necessarily a pattern to what they liked and didn't like. It's just like when I'm on the television judging now: sometimes I feel very differently from one or all of my fellow judges. While certain things are 'by the book' other things come down to personal taste. In the Kent Championships it had been a split vote. Some of the judges liked what we did, although not enough and we ended up coming third; we won a fiver. I also came third in the raffle, winning a six-foot length of hosepipe. I never did find out exactly what it was for because it never seemed to reach far enough when I wanted to use it. A year later we won our local championships.

It was a struggle to try to make it as professional dancers as well as running the dance school in the pub. Without a lot of help from Mum, I would have to have gone back to a proper job. For a while I even sold insurance for an American company to tide us over because there was not a lot of money to go around; Joy and Cherry were quite rightly taking the lion's share. But then Cherry and I had an enormous bit of luck around the time the Erith Dance School was closing. The first was through Henry Kingston's friend, Frank Mayne, the Dance Director of Pontin's who telephoned us right out of the blue.

'Len, I was wondering if you and Cherry would like to do some demonstrating for us?'

The gods had spoken, or at least one had.

Holiday camps had a pecking order as far as popularity was concerned. Top of the tree was Butlins, with Sir Billy Butlin and his Redcoats; next came Pontin's and the Bluecoats; later on came Warner with their Yellowcoats. Later still Fred Pontin started his Pontinental camps, which started to spring up in Spain – very posh if you could afford it. The Bluecoats at Pontin's were the entertainment staff and they became mega-stars, a bit like Britney Spears or Paris Hilton are today. Everybody wanted to have a photograph with them and were proud when they sat down for a cup of tea at your table. From what I understand the Bluecoats had no shortage of girls to take back to their chalets. I asked once where Jack, one of the good-looking boys, was. 'He's got chalet rash.' I didn't like to ask what that was.

The chalets were little more than wooden sheds in rows. They had a bed and a wardrobe with bunk beds for kids – but no television, unlike today where each camp has its own TV station broadcasting what's on. The main building was a much more substantial affair; it was also where the ballroom dancing took place. If the camps had a restaurant this was where it would be. Camber Sands was self-catering, so each chalet had a small kitchen with a gas stove and a fridge. At the end of the night's entertainment everyone would sing 'Goodnight Campers'. I'm sure it sounds corny but remember, after six years of war and the end of rationing in the fifties, it all seemed so sophisticated.

Frank Mayne from Pontin's said he would like us to do, not just one show a week, but also a whole series of them. We were to demonstrate on a Monday night at Camber Sands, Tuesday we were to go to Lowestoft to a camp called Pakefield, from there we would drive up to Great Yarmouth. Here there were two camps, right opposite one another – Seacroft was one and the other Hemsby. It meant that we could drive home on a Monday, while on Tuesday we stayed at Pakefield and drove up to Great Yarmouth on Wednesday night. The only downside to this whole plan was the fact that we needed to drive home immediately after we'd finished our second show at either Hemsby or Seacroft because we couldn't afford to be away from the school for any longer than necessary, but there was a huge upside – we got £25 per show, £100 per week which was a fabulous amount of money in 1970.

Not only was it good money, but also it helped me to develop as a bit of a showman, a role that I naturally played up in my classes. My gift of the gab came in handy yet again. All the entertainment at the camps was free, which meant people showed up for things whether or not they were interested; if people pay for something they go out of their way to enjoy it more. It was difficult to make a show out of just demonstrating a bit of Latin American dancing so I would get on the microphone and start the banter – it became my trademark. I learned a lot about working a crowd, and in some cases a lot less than a crowd. By the end of the last week in September, the end of the season, there might be 15 people in a camp ballroom designed to hold hundreds. They'd often all be old-age pensioners and half of them would be asleep. My technique was simple: I would step out and imagine I was on the biggest stage in the country, with the place full to overflowing. Having said that, during the height of the season it was really buzzing, the ballrooms were full and the Bluecoats organised dance competitions; everyone had a ball.

The other great piece of luck came about because we would go practising twice a week at one of the ballrooms in and around London to mix with other dancers. I really believe that you should practise alone to become good, but you also need to go into an environment where there are better dancers so as to learn from them and to improve your floorcraft – the ability to get around people on the dance floor. Outside of the holiday camp season we would go to Sydney Francis' studio in Balham on a Monday night, Tuesdays we would go to the Hammersmith Palais, because that was always ballroom dancing night, on Wednesday we went to a bloke called Bob Burgess in Dulwich and on Thursdays to Benny Tolmeyer's studio.

One weekend Cherry's mum had made her a new practice dress, so all day Monday, while we practised at the pub, Cherry kept saying, 'Let's go over to Balham this evening.' I wasn't so keen. Having spent four hours working solidly on our routines I wanted a night in. However, I finally relented despite feeling knackered. My heart definitely wasn't in it but I knew that she wanted to show off her new dress to all her dancing friends. Not that Cherry was overly bothered about dancing that evening: it was all about the dress and so we mostly sat around watching others. I knew that she wanted to see how the skirt flared up when she danced, and so when a jive came on she said, 'Oh come on, Len, don't be a spoilsport.'

We jived and as soon as we'd finished we sat back down; Cherry was happy, her skirt flared perfectly. A minute or two later a couple came over and said in heavily accented English, 'We think your jiving is brilliant.'

'Where are you from?' I asked.

'Ve're from Germany and ve're here for another three days. That gentleman,' said the man, pointing to Sydney Francis, 'said you give lessons and ve vere vondering if you could teach us?'

He told us his name was Charlie Coster and introduced his wife, Marlena. The following day they came over to the pub and

I gave them a lesson: in fact I gave them a two-hour lesson for the next three days. It was the best accidental investment I've ever made. They explained to me that in Germany things were done very differently. Over there they have dance clubs, which are all run by amateurs, with a head person that is a professional dancer.

'Ve'd love you both to come over to our club to teach us some more.'

'That would be very nice, wouldn't it, Cherry?'

With that, I thought no more of it until a couple of weeks later we got a call from Charlie.

'Vould you come to Germany for us and teach in our club? Ve can get you eight hours of teaching, for you and for Cherry, that's 16 hours of teaching each day. Ve vould like you to come for three days to Dusseldorf.'

It was all delivered with Germanic precision. When it came to the fees that was the really amazing part. He was offering four times what we got per hour in Britain, plus they paid our accommodation. All we had to do was get there.

It was not just the money that made the trip to Germany worthwhile; the people at the club all turned out to be lovely as well. The professional in charge of their club was Gunter Dresen who also had a formation dance team. He asked if we would be prepared to go back to Germany two weeks later to help train them.

'Sure,' I said.

The only drawback, as Cherry pointed out as soon as we were out of earshot, was the fact that we'd never done any formation team dancing, let alone training. I had never even watched it. If the formation came on, I went to the bar.

'Yes, I know, but for 50 quid an hour we can learn,' I reasoned.

I taught the team for three days and changed some bits around. It was actually quite straightforward. I found different pattern changes, easy steps, and quickly realised that I saw it all in my head as I talked about it. To explain more easily where the dancers needed to be in order to make patterns on the dance floor I used eight penny coins – the big ones, pre-decimalisation. As I moved the coins around the table I'd say. 'Right, you two are going to go up there and you two are going there.' But even I was surprised a month later when we got a telegram saying they'd won the German championships, when previously they had never come better than third.

For years and years Cherry and I went to Germany for three days every two weeks to train their formation team, take classes and give private lessons. They bought our house and made us a small fortune, all because Cherry had a new practice dress and wanted to show it off. When I was working for the American insurance company they sent me on a course and one of the things a trainer said very definitely applied to this situation. 'Success comes in cans, not in can'ts.'

Whenever we taught in Germany, Gunther always paid us in cash and after one longer than usual trip involving extra classes, we were heading home with a lot of money, all in 20-mark notes. Cherry didn't like flying so we most often drove. We would go to Dover and take the ferry to Ostend from where it wasn't a bad drive – mostly motorway and autobahn. In the early seventies exchange control was in force, which restricted the amount of money we could take out of Britain. The limit of 50 quid presented us with no problems, as we knew we'd come back with a bundle of cash. On the way back the Customs and Excise stopped us at Dover.

'Where have you been?' asked the officer.

'We've been teaching people to ballroom dance.'

'Oh yeah, really?' He was really sarcastic. 'Would you open the boot?' I got out of the car and opened the boot. 'Have you got any money?'

'Yeah.' I had nothing to hide; there were no limits on what you could bring into Britain.

'How much?'

'I don't know, I haven't counted it. Where is it, Cherry?'

Cherry reached over to the back seat and produced a carrier bag. Inside were the bundles of cash held together by elastic bands.

'Miss, I think you better get out of the car too,' said the officer.

That was their cue to start dismantling the car. The back seat was removed, the tyres were deflated and the inside door panels unscrewed. I don't know what they expected to find. I kept saying, 'But we've shown you the money, why would we be hiding any? I've been teaching people to dance. Look, we'll show you a bit of cha-cha-cha if you want.'

They weren't having any of it; they were convinced they'd stumbled on Bonnie and Clyde. Having turned the car upside down they naturally found nothing. They just put it all back together and let us go. I'm not sure they even said sorry.

In addition to our regular trips to Germany we were incredibly busy in the UK demonstrating all over the place. Our first demonstration as professionals was for Doris Lavell in her Soho studio; it was a lot less lucrative than Germany – she paid us three quid. It was another one of those lucky breaks because Phyllis Hayler saw us at Doris Lavell's and asked us if we would do a demonstration for her Mardi club she ran in Hammersmith every Tuesday night. Phyllis (though we were still calling her Miss Hayler) was a brilliant ballroom teacher. However, while her club was impeccable it did have one drawback – the floor was very slippery. To counter this I used one of the oldest tricks in a dancer's repertoire – three-in-one oil on the soles of both Cherry's and my dance shoes. I did it right before we went on, but on one occasion I must have overdone it somewhat because as we came out on to her immaculate maple floor all you could see were our footprints: you could practically trace all the steps of our routine. While Phyllis must have noticed she was very nice and didn't say a word about it. When it came time to go she gave me an envelope in which I assumed was the fee. 'Thank you, Len, very much, a very lovely demonstration. Cherry, you're beautiful and so was your dancing.'

The first thing I noticed was how fat the envelope was and I thought, blimey, she must have really loved it and given us a bit extra. When we got in the car I opened it up and it was full of foreign stamps. I nearly chucked them out of the window, but luckily I didn't. The next day she telephoned.

'Len, I think I gave you the wrong envelope – that was for my nephew who lives in Hong Kong and collects stamps.' She sent us our three quid by post.

We were asked by Bob Burgess, another former world champion and a leading coach to demonstrate at his studio in Dulwich on the first Saturday in each month. The format was slightly different to some of the others, as he liked us to do our dem after which Cherry and I had to judge his pupils in a fun competition. It was no easy task as the couples were far from good and there was little to choose between them. One particular week the competition was a waltz; both Cherry and I were pretty stumped as to who to choose as the winner from among the dozen or so couples. Once they finished I quietly said to Cherry, 'I'll just pick one at random.' I stood up and gave a little speech, while looking around the room thinking, who am I going pick?

'Well, I must say how very impressed Cherry and I were with the standard of your dancing. We thought you all danced very nicely. We all know that one of the key elements that we look for in the waltz is rise and fall. I thought it was epitomised tonight by you, sir, and your partner.' I pointed to a gentleman; up he stood, followed by his partner. As they walked towards me to collect their prize I was horrified to see that he had a gammy leg and limped, so it was impossible for there to be any rise and fall when he danced.

Another chap I did a show for was a lovely man called Derek Brown who has a dance studio in Peterborough. As usual I was giving it all my usual patter; by this time it had become a right little routine. I had a little joke about each dance; I would say how the rumba is a dance of love, so you have to think of Romeo and Juliet or Anthony and Cleopatra, or in our case it was George and Mildred, who were very popular on the TV at the time.

'It's a very exciting night tonight because it is 15 years since Cherry won her first championship.' Everyone clapped and Cherry smiled.

'Yes, it was at Crufts.'

Derek was paying us the unheard-of sum of £30 and while it had to cover our petrol it was still a great earner. I learnt a lot about running classes from Derek, in particular how to advertise correctly. He also got me a plum job with the IDTA, the International Dance Teachers Association. This organisation's head office is in Brighton and at the time a vast number of their members were in the North of England. Derek was on their committee so Cherry and I were asked to demonstrate at their congress in Blackpool. It was a dinner, dance and cabaret; this one dance set Cherry and myself up for years to come. Work came flooding in from all over the North and the Midlands; the phone wouldn't stop ringing, as we were booked sometimes for a double header. We'd go to Dewsbury at eight and then be up the road in Leeds for 10 p.m; we must have got 50 jobs through 1971 and '72.

A man named Ken Rainer who had a studio in Blackpool booked us for four shows over a single weekend: one on a Friday, two on Saturday, one in the afternoon for the kids, one in the evening for the adults, and another show on the Sunday. However, after the Saturday evening show my confidence took a real knock. I had changed out of my dance clothes and popped into the toilet. I was standing at the urinal when a punter came in and stood next to me. 'I didn't think much of that show, did you?' said he without taking his eyes off the wall in front of him.

'Nay lad, me neither.' I'm not sure if my imitation northern accent fooled him.

Shortly before we opened the Dartford school I went and spent a couple of days with Derek learning all the little things that help make a dance school successful. Like most things in life it's attention to detail that makes things work; invariably success follows along behind.

In the early seventies we were doing over two hundred shows a year. We might not have been the best demonstrators but we must have been the busiest. We drove thousands of miles and this was way before there was a half-decent motorway network. We were lucky in that Pauline took care of things back at the dance school, which allowed us to do what we did. Sometimes we did a double demonstration – a ballroom and a Latin. It would be Cherry and I doing the Latin show with another couple doing a ballroom show. One time we did a show at a car manufacturer's social club with the great Bill and Bobbie Irvine, the couple I'd first watched as a reluctant teenager when they gave a demonstration. At the time Cherry had a chihuahua called Cha Cha; I'm none too keen on dogs, and to make matters worse, Cherry took hers to demos. Bobbie loved dogs as well and she had two pugs, although they were not with her on this occasion. Bobbie came into our dressing room and made a real fuss of Cha Cha, when it was time for us both to go off and do our dances she insisted that the chihuahua was placed on her mink stole so it wouldn't get cold or lonely. When we got back there was an awful smell in the dressing room because the dog had done a poo on Bobbie's stole. I started calling her Miss Irvine again for a while after that.

The day I told Dad that Cherry and I were getting married he told me another of his little homilies.

'Len, imagine that inside of you are maybe ten metronomes that tick. You've got a hobby metronome that takes care of your interests outside of work; there might be gardening one, a country walks metronome or maybe even a poetry metronome.' As my dad is telling me this I'm thinking, bloody hell, where's this going.

'Of course, Len, you've also got a sex metronome. Now, the ideal partner is one whose metronome ticks in time with yours. You love going out to dinner, she loves going out to dinner. When you make love it's beautiful, she loves it, you love it. You love going down to the seaside spending time together just strolling along the beach, and so does she. It's simple: your ideal partner is one where all ten metronomes tick in time. Now imagine you're with someone who is virtually perfect, except that you love poetry and she doesn't; so your little poetry metronome is still there, but it's unfulfilled – in fact it's hardly ticking. Everyday you go to work on the train and most days you're reading a poetry book. One day it just so happens that a woman gets on the train and sits opposite you and takes out a book of Robert Browning's poems. You tell her how much you love poetry and especially Browning and suddenly you're in conversation with the woman. You start seeing her on the train regularly and the talk is all poetry and that one metronome, the one that's been starved for so long, is ticking off the scale. Next thing you leave your wife because this metronome has been starved for so long. You end up leaving a wife who is perfect in every other way. The fact is Len, it's just one metronome out of the ten. Be careful not to get things out of kilter.'

Cherry and I got married on 27 April 1972, two days after my twenty-eighth birthday. With the clarity of hindsight I realise that life sometimes fires warning shots across your bow. I'm probably no different to most people in that I've resisted all the tell-tale signs designed to make you stop and think. It was now a case of carry on regardless. Two weeks to the day before our wedding my father was feeling unwell. He had pains in his chest. Luckily, and probably stupidly in some ways, he drove to his doctor's surgery as soon as he felt them. As he sat in the waiting room hoping to see the doctor, he had a massive heart attack. It saved his life. The doctor later said that if he hadn't been there he would definitely have died. The doctor came straight out of his room and attended to Dad, and within no time he was rushed to hospital. Ten days before the wedding Dad had a quadruple bypass, and two days later he was on the road to recovery, but still in hospital. I should have taken this as warning number one: postpone the wedding.

But things were too far gone with all the preparations and I felt pressure from Cherry and her mum, and who can blame them? On Monday 24 April we all went to the church for a dress rehearsal, and everything seemed to go off without a hitch until the vicar dropped his bombshell, not that he intended to.

'Have the banns been seen to?'

Always the joker I was back as quick as a flash. 'We don't want a band thank you very much, an organ will do nicely.'

The vicar had a look on his face that said, 'very funny, but not very original'. 'Yes, so I assume the banns have been read for the past six weeks. The reading of the banns is a legal requirement for a church wedding, they must be read out for three successive Sundays before the wedding.'

'Well, no, err, I guess not.'

'Well, I'm afraid the ceremony cannot go ahead,' said the vicar.

At this point everyone – Cherry, her mum, Pete Dawson my best man and the bridesmaids – all turned to look at me as if to say, why didn't you get the bloody banns read?

'I've never heard about banns, it's not my fault I've never been married before!' With that I turned to the vicar. 'Surely I can do something, who can I pay?'

'It's not that simple. There's only one thing you can do. You need to go to Canterbury and get a special licence from the Archbishop.'

With three days to go before the big day it was a pressure I didn't need. I spent most of my twenty-eighth birthday on the phone talking to what seemed like everyone in the Church of England at Canterbury trying to get this special licence. They said I could go to Canterbury the following day to collect it. As I put down the phone to the Church of England man it rang again. It was the Black Prince Hotel in Bexley where we were holding the reception.

'I'm sorry, Mr Goodman, but I'm afraid our kitchen has caught fire and we're going to have to move your reception. But don't worry, we've arranged for it to be held at Bigley Manor in Bromley.'

Now apart from the fact that this was ten miles away I'd heard that it was a nice place so that was no big deal. But, it was another one of those warning shots.

Finally the big day arrived and after all the upset, rushing around and generally hectic time I guess it was inevitable that I had a hangover. My stag party was not one of those affairs that seem more common today where we jet off to some Eastern European city or another; I had to content myself with Costa Alota – a Greek taverna in Welling High Street. There were just the four of us: myself, Pete Dawson, Muzzletoff Mike, a Jewish friend who was always saying mazel tov, and 'Dollar' Dixon. Dollar's dad had a chain of furniture shops and was pretty well off. His dad was always giving him money so when we were in our teens and were skint we'd ask Dollar to lend us two bob, and he'd always say the same thing. 'There you go, have a dollar.' This dates from the time when there used to be four American dollars to the pound and so a dollar was five shillings.

Before heading for Costa Alota we went to the pub for a couple of pints of Watney's Red Barrel. The restaurant had recently changed from an Italian to Greek, but had retained its name. The first thing on the table, even before the menus, was a jug of Ouzo.

'That's not enough, we need one of those each.' We drank directly from the jugs so things quickly got out of hand. It was another of those skirmishes with foreign food – the kind my nan would never have cooked. My problem was I was so hungry by now that I could have chased a horse and eaten the jockey as well. Various plates of starter type dishes began to arrive. Muzzletoff had been going on about the fact that it was customary to smash the plates in a Greek taverna. Dollar got so fed up with this that he picked one up off the table and smashed it over Muzzle's head. The owner was over in a flash standing next to Muzzletoff who had minced beef and olives in his hair.

'No smashing the plates, please, not until later.' Come the end of the meal the 'special' plates for smashing arrived and we found we were all pretty good at it.

Pete came around at ten o'clock on my wedding day and we drove down to Plumstead and spent the morning in the Turkish baths. We had a massage and a shave, you get a lovely close shave in the heat, and by 12.30 we left the baths feeling a lot better than when we went in. On the way to the church we went via Joyce Green Hospital to visit Dad.

'Are you sure you're making the right decision getting married, Len?'

Another warning.

'Yes,' I said, but really I was thinking I don't know. The trouble with dancing marriages is that you don't get an opportunity to meet other people of the opposite sex. Cherry and I had lived in each other's pockets. She was fed up with living at home and was pushing for months about setting up together. It was definitely too late to turn back now.

Pete and I arrived at Christ Church in Bexley Heath at 2.45 p.m. and waited for the bride. When she came in she looked absolutely lovely. The ceremony went off without a hitch and after the usual photographs we all went to Bigley Manor. After a glass of champagne everyone sat down to enjoy the meal. The starter had just been put in front of everyone when the Maître d' came over and whispered in my ear. 'Can you please come and take a telephone call from the hospital.'

My father had had a relapse and was not expected to make it through the night. Rene had not known if they should call or not but the doctor had convinced her she should. Back at the top table I tapped my glass.

'I'm sorry but I have to go to the hospital.' I explained what I'd been told and said for everyone to enjoy themselves, but it put the mockers on everything. I spent the night at the hospital and when I got back Cherry somehow blamed me for leaving – her mum was none too pleased either. To be honest I don't think she ever forgave me for messing up the wedding. But what could I do?

Within a couple of days Dad improved and was out of danger so Cherry and I went off to Paris. After two lovely days we drove to Dusseldorf for the second half of our honeymoon. Our friend Gunter Dressen had a beautiful log cabin in the White Forest in northern Germany. It was a wonderful place, extremely luxurious and even had a sauna, which was a bit of a novelty if you came from Kent. There was a hide you could go up into, and if you were there before dawn you could watch the deer feeding. It was the perfect place to spend a honeymoon.

After a week at Gunter's cabin we went to do a little bit of teaching with the Dusseldorf formation team. Cherry and I also spent time working on our own competition dances, as the British Championships were due to start in the third week of May. Our German formation team were flying over to England to compete at Blackpool, which was going to make it interesting for us. Back from our honeymoon we went straight to our new house. We had bought it several months before we were married; it was a really nice detached house in York Crescent in Bexley. I'd got the details from the estate agent who made an appointment for us to go and look it over. When we got there who should be the owner but my old headmaster, the one who reckoned I'd amount to nothing.

Not that we had long to enjoy our home: no sooner were we back than we went into some last-minute serious training. Cherry and I were entered into a new competition to be held at Blackpool. It was The British Professional Rising Star Championship, which was open to all but the top six finalists from previous years' British Championships. It meant that anyone in the world could enter, so competition would be stiff. We went for a lesson with Nina Hunt two days before the competition, confident we had a chance of making the final. Nina soon put the kibosh on that. She seemed to find fault in almost everything we did and was always mentioning how well several other competitors were doing. In particular she picked out Harry Koerner from Germany, Sam Sodano from America and Robert Ritchey from Australia. It was not going to be easy.

But there was one thing that I hadn't quite twigged about all the people that Nina mentioned: all of them went exclusively to her for lessons – we did not, so we were not on her list of favourites. Having said that it was great kudos if a pupil who was exclusive to you won a competition; then again perhaps it was just mind games. Nevertheless Cherry and I went back and practised until midnight, determined to do well in Blackpool.

On the Thursday morning we popped over to the hospital to see Dad before heading off on the long drive to Blackpool. To say it rained fails to do it justice; it poured for the whole journey, not helped by the fact that just as we were passing Birmingham on the M1, with the wipers at full bore, the one on the driver's side just flew off. I spent the rest of the journey leaning over, looking out of the passenger side trying to get us there in one piece. We arrived at around eight o'clock that night; I was totally knackered. We stayed at the Claremont Hotel, one of hundreds of hotels and guesthouses along the front; after checking in and unpacking we went down to the lounge for a sandwich and a cup of coffee. Paddy Shanahan was holding court with a group of dancers. Paddy had been dancing for years and was coming to the end of his dancing career; his results had got worse and worse, a mix of age and the tremendous influx of Japanese couples who were, by then, coming to Blackpool. Paddy was what you would definitely call a character – the older he got the harder he found it, but the funnier he became. If he was flagging when it came time for a quickstep he would stoop down to tie his shoelaces. It was amazing how many times Paddy's laces came undone, but it used up 20 seconds and he would miss the first 16 bars of music. Paddy was busy telling anyone who'd listen stories about his dancing years. He had just begun one about his wartime exploits, a time when he was a very popular demonstrator, but having no car he and his wife June, who was also his dance partner, would arrive by bus; he'd be in his tail suit and she in her ball gown. One time they were doing a show at the Locarno in Streatham. Unfortunately it was pouring with rain and they had to walk from the bus stop. June had on a new dress, which she made during the few days running up to their performance; sadly time was against her and instead of finishing it properly by sewing on the feathers she glued them on. As they danced, the feathers, having warmed up in the room and having previously got soaking wet, came unglued. Paddy said it looked like a chicken pluckers' convention; feathers were flying in all directions and the whole floor was covered.

Cherry and I didn't hang around too long as we needed to be early to bed for our big day. I went to sleep going over my routines in my head. Friday morning it was up to the Winter Gardens to practise, which we certainly needed. There were 53 couples entered into our event, with entries from 24 different countries. We were split into four heats, and we had to dance five different dances: the rumba, the samba, the cha-cha-cha, the jive and the paso doble.

Cherry had a new dress, white with red spots with shoes to match; I had traced all over the shoes with a penny then filled in the circles with red paint. The dress, made by a woman called Doris Brace, was a brave decision; Cherry was nervous that it might be too different so she had packed another just in case she lost her nerve – there was no doubt in my mind: I loved it. We were number 12 and I felt great when Alex Warren, the chairman of the judges and the compère, called our number for heat one – I was totally up for it. Nina Hunt was sitting in the front row, but she never even gave us a second glance.

Running concurrently with our competition was the senior, over 35, ballroom championship. It meant that once we had done a round of dances they then did a round, which gave us time to rest and recover. This went on all through the evening. In the third heat there was an American couple, Vernon Brock and Betty Donohue. I didn't see them dance on the night but saw them on the following Wednesday night and he was truly brilliant; his dancing was totally different. Every now and then a couple will come along who revolutionise the standard of performance, taking dance to a new level. The problem with being different is that sometimes people take a while to work out if your different is good or bad; that's exactly what happened to these brilliant Americans. Vernon and Betty baffled the judges, who are not allowed to discuss things amongst themselves during a competition. Should we mark them high or not? It was a bit like the King's new clothes: they were all thinking they were brilliant, but all were frightened in case they were the only one who marked them into the finals.

We were chosen as one of the 24 in the quarter-final; this was to be run in two heats. When we had finished Cherry and I sat down behind the stage, not wanting to be too near. I've always thought it terrible to stand right by the front waiting for your number in case it's not called; if it isn't, you have to walk away in full view. Good old Alex Warren, he called out our number – we were in the last 12. Cherry's spotted dress and shoes were a hit with everyone: they helped us to stand out. While we sat exhausted but exhilarated after dancing in the last 12, Cherry and I talked about our chances. She was convinced we'd make the last six, but I was not so sure. I started going through the list, sure we had no chance. When the names were read out we had made it, but so had Harry and Doris Koerner, Robert and Helen Ritchey along with Sam Sodano and Pat Hogan, the three couples that Nina Hunt had mentioned when we trained with her. I looked round at the other finalists and I realised we had beaten so many couples that we had never beaten before, but neither had we beaten any of the ones in the final. Whether it was adrenalin or a will to win I don't know, but I danced with an energy that I never knew I possessed, added to which Cherry was at her brilliant best. After the final we sat exhausted. Walter Laird stopped by where we were slumped to say, 'I have never seen you dance so well.'

They announced the winners of the seniors' competition first before Alex Warren stood up to announce the results of the Professional Rising Star Latin Championship. 'In first place from Bexley...'

I never heard anything else because I was the only bugger from Bexley! I was up and running on to the floor, with Cherry somewhere miles behind me. I suddenly stopped so she could catch me up and we went over together to the person presenting the prizes. I was absolutely ecstatic when we received our trophy and a cheque; I couldn't help looking across at Nina Hunt and winking.

To be honest we shouldn't have won; Vernon Brock and Betty Donohue were actually way better than us. It was just that the judges didn't know what to make of them. Dancing is no different from anything else. Sometimes you get the breaks, and that's certainly what happened to us that night. Not that it was the end of our week of competing. The next morning I called Mum to tell her what had happened – she was so excited – and Cherry and I spent the whole day in a state of euphoria; we bumped into all sorts of people, all of whom told us how well we'd done. Much of the credit for us competing at all should go to Cherry, because of her great enthusiasm. Of course, I loved doing well and can only try to convey the excitement I felt when we won. I was clear from the outset that doing well in competition got us more work, whether it be demonstrating or teaching.

On the Monday it was the Ballroom Rising Star Professional competition and from an entry of 63 we made it through to the last 24, which was not bad considering we only practised our ballroom dancing when the Latin practice was not going well – we were far from disappointed with the result. In any event our focus was on the professional Latin championships which were to take place on Wednesday. Cherry and I were confident, perhaps too confident, and we fully expected to make the semi-final and maybe the final, bearing in mind that we had come first, with only the top six in the world missing from our earlier competition. In simple terms that put us seventh best in the world, but in actual fact it was a bit like the Olympics where someone tries to compete in both the 10,000 and the 5,000 metres. All the couples that we had beaten a few days earlier beat us, including the fantastic Vernon Brock who made it through to the final having not been able to make it into the last 12 four days earlier; it was a dance too far and a salutary lesson.

Thursday was the day the formation team from Germany was to compete. The day before the competition the teams were allowed rehearsal time, following which several of the other formation teams' coaches tried to get my team banned.

'On what grounds?' asked Madame Ilet, who was in charge of the festival. Her first line of defence was simple: 'This is just a rehearsal and so how do you know that the routine won't change?' That evening Madame Ilet spoke to all the other coaches and told them they were all being ludicrous. Several said we were breaking the rules on steps, on hold, and we included too much solo work; none of it stood up.

We also had a secret weapon, Klaus Hallen, a young guy in the team who was crazy on music, who would later become a very successful record producer; he made albums of strict tempo dance music, with orchestras featuring impersonators singing the songs. He created music for our routines that was totally unique, featuring a little bit of cha-cha, followed by a snatch of samba, a rippling of rumba, a pinch of pasa doble and some jive. This constantly shifting sound-bed enabled the dancers to create a unique style of formation dancing. Probably to everyone's surprise – except us – we came first; it completed a memorable week. I was really pleased because what we did helped to revolutionise formation dancing, mainly because I knew absolutely nothing about it before I started. Previously it had all been very basic and teams would stay in patterns for a long while, whereas I introduced constantly shifting patterns based more on professional routines. With everyone else plodding around, suddenly along came the Germans, not previously recognised for their talent, and blew everyone away.

It was the culmination of a fabulous Blackpool festival, although I didn't realise it was the last proper Ballroom or Latin competition I would ever enter. Why did I stop? I actually got fed up with the politics of the business, the fact that you had to placate and schmooze people that you really didn't like, because you dare not upset them, as they were judges. It cost a lot to compete and the politics of trying to keep yourself in the running by saying the right thing to the right people was not really my thing. One day I said to Cherry, 'Why are we putting ourselves through all this? Do we want to keep slogging our arses over to Balham or up to Connie Grant in Sheffield for lessons, or Eric Hancock in Liverpool? Let's kick it into touch, the school's working well and we'll get no more demonstration work by competing.'

Cherry wanted to carry on, but I talked her round.

We did, however, kind of compete, but just in one-off events over the next couple of years. Probably the biggest one-day event in the dance world was, and still is, the International Championships that are held each October at the Royal Albert Hall. There are only four competitions: the professional ballroom and Latin American championship and an amateur ballroom and Latin American Championship. One of the highlights of the event was a form of cabaret, just before the finals – it was dubbed, 'The Duel of the Giants', in which two couples compete against each other. You had to be invited to participate, an honour in itself, by Elsa Wells who ran this charity event with her husband, Joseph Petenski, a mega-rich businessman.

Elsa Wells called us after Blackpool to see if Cherry and I would like to do it, not in 1972, as she already had her duel lined up, but in 1973. I was a bit reluctant at first, thinking of all the work it would create; particularly as for an exhibition dance there needed to be lifts and that was something we hadn't done before. There were two stipulated dances – a rumba and a jive – along with the exhibition number. Elsa eventually talked us into it. The first thing we did was to call John Delroy to ask if he would help us put together a routine for the exhibition number; John had danced seven times in the duel and was a legend.

I've rarely thought of anyone in my business as a genius, but John was a true one, both musically and as a choreographer, yet in the pecking order of famous people he wouldn't be halfway up the list. He told me on the phone that he only did two-hour lessons, before giving me his address in Lewisham, south-east London. Cherry and I drove over there and parked in his street but we couldn't see anything that resembled a dance studio. There was a man up a ladder so I asked him if he knew where John Delroy's dance studio was.

'That's me,' he said and down he came.

He was in his late forties or early fifties, with long curly hair and a bandanna around his head – not your typical dance coach. He took us down into the cellar of his house where he had a very small studio. John was a New Zealander and half Maori; his ability to bring out the best in his pupils was truly amazing. We sat and discussed which exhibition number we should do and I said, 'With my personality I would like to do a comedy number or at least something with comedy in it.'

John agreed, suggesting an Apache – it's a French dance that features a sailor and a prostitute who fight, a very passionate number. After a little more chat we started the lesson with a 30-minute warm-up which was all ballet – it was the start of me loving ballet. According to John, 'All forms of dance comes from ballet, ballet's the mother.' From then on every lesson started with this warm-up, which I really enjoyed. He showed us some basic lifts, although his ceiling was so low that we often had to go out into the garden to do them properly.

Before our next lesson my mission was to find the sheet music for the Apache; John suggested Chappell's, the music shop. A couple of days later up I went to Bond Street where their shop had been for about 150 years; a nice old gentleman said they might have what I was after. 'He took me down into their basement where tens of thousands of folders of sheet music were stored. They had it and I handed over my £2, taking the music, with all the band parts, to John the following week. John had arranged for a keyboard player to be there to play it. It was very clinky clonky, fine for rehearsal but it actually made learning the dance quite hard. I wasn't overjoyed by the tune, but John told me not to worry, it would be fine. John's partner, Christine, helped us with the lifts and for the next 18 months we tried to master every aspect of this dance.

After the 1973 Blackpool Championships in May we learned that we were to compete against Gerd Weissenberg and Helga Steuwe, who'd just won the British Rising Star Championships. It was like the world cup of 1966 all over again – England versus the Germans. In between teaching and demonstrating in Europe and the UK my passion became this Apache. For the Albert Hall event there were always two bands – Victor Silvester did the ballroom and from the other side of the stage Edmundo Ros and his band played the Latin American. It was Edmundo's band that played for the Duel of the Giants, so we needed to get the band parts rearranged for his particular orchestra. I telephoned him to ask if I should get the music arranged.

'What would be simplest, to use your arranger or shall we get it done?' He said his guy would do it, so I went to Edmundo's flat in Swiss Cottage, in North London, to meet the famous bandleader and his arranger. It had the most enormous lounge, like something out of a Hollywood movie. You could have got 12 settees in it; in the corner was a baby grand piano. I sat down with the arranger and he went through the music. To me it still sounded weird beyond belief.

Having sorted it out we chatted about what Edmundo was going to play for the other two dances. I thought it would be a shame to waste the chance and asked if there was any chance that he could play 'Maria Elena', a song made famous by Jimmy Dorsey in the 1940s, as the rumba and a Herb Albert & The Tijuana Brass tune, 'So What's New', as the Jive. I also asked if when he counted the band in for the rumba rather than just do it while facing his band could he say it into the microphone. Cherry and I planned to start on the first beat of music whereas normally you would wait a couple of bars to start. This would give us immediate impact.

When I told my mum what we were planning she called the Albert Hall and booked a box for her, Alex and several of their friends. On the day of the competition, to help us get even more in the limelight, I went up to the top of the Albert Hall and paid the six spotlight operators a fiver each to follow us more closely. Everything is fair in love and dance. There were three foreign judges from the dance world but their duty was only to assess the level of public applause, so it was imperative to get the crowd on your side. I'm one of the lucky people who don't suffer with nerves when it comes to dancing or talking; I am what I am. The compère was Albert Rudge, a charming man and a good golfer, who had a marvellous speaking voice.

'Ladies and gentlemen, we come to the highlight of the evening – the Duel of the Giants. The contestants will dance a rumba and a jive together, then separately an exhibition number. First the rumba.'

As Edmundo said, 'One…,' Cherry walked forward towards me and I lifted her off the ground. The whole audience started clapping. As the music began we were off and Gerd and Helga were still standing there. They were in total shock because in the rehearsal Cherry and I just marked it; we didn't actually do the lift. We were brilliant, even if I do say it myself. In golfing terms poor old Gerd never got out of the clubhouse and we birdied the first two holes. We then tossed a coin to see who would dance their exhibition dance first; we won the toss and elected to go second. I never saw Gerd and Helga's show dance but could hear only mild applause. For us the crowd went mad, there was laughter and applause, and when we finished there was a standing ovation: our win was overwhelming. Afterwards Gerd said he didn't realise you could do lifts but looking at Helga, a big blonde Bavarian baby, she was very definitely built for comfort and not speed.

In dancing terms it was my most exciting and fulfilling night, but a total one-off, as we never did it again. Unfortunately it wasn't filmed, but I do have a recording on an audiotape. The man who was in charge of the band volumes for some reason taped everything and afterwards he mentioned to me that he had it. I nearly bit his hand off for it. I wish I could teach the routine to someone else because it was so fantastic, what John Delroy did in this one routine. Unless I pass it on to someone it will be gone for ever and it needs to be seen again.

The next day Elsa Wells phoned to say how marvellous our performance had been and invited me out to dinner at her home in Knightsbridge. She asked if we would do the duel the following year.

'Elsa, as much as I'd love to I've got to stop, it's consumed us for a whole year.'

With some persuasion we agreed to do it again in 1975, two years later. We didn't mess about; we went straight round to John Delroy to discuss our next duel. In between, Gill McKenzie, the organiser of the Blackpool Festival, asked us if we would appear in something similar in 1974. We agreed and danced a more classic number to 'Exodus'. We won, which enhanced our reputation as the leading exhibition dancers.

The 1975 Duel of the Giants was a very different kettle of fish. Our challengers this time were Peter Maxwell and Lynn Harman – legends in the world of ballroom and Latin American. They are one of the few couples to be British Champions and World Champions in both ballroom and Latin, not only that but British Juvenile under-12 Champions, Junior under-16 Champions and Amateur World Champions. They had just won the British Professional Latin American Championship and they were going to dance against poor old Len and Cherry Goodman. We needed a very special idea to even stand a chance and I had something I thought could work – but it very definitely needed John Delroy to turn it into something special.

I was going to be a dirty old man and Cherry was going to be a stripper. Once again a huge amount of practice was required. When the big night arrived I felt the tightening in my stomach just prior to going on to dance the rumba and jive. We were neck and neck judging by the applause; while we had lifts and were spectacular, Peter and Lynn are just great Latin dancers and are known for a wide range of speciality spins. We again won the toss and danced second on the exhibition number. Theirs was a classic semi-balletic number and from the applause it went down very well. We had worked out another very special entry, which instead of having me come on via the stage, as most people did, I entered from the opposite end of the hall, walking through the audience, to the signature tune of *Steptoe and Son*. I was dressed as Harold Steptoe, a chair was placed in the middle of the floor and down I came and sat on it. Cherry then came on via the stage, helped down the stairs by Bill Irvine. She danced to the classic David Rose number, 'The Stripper'. Cherry's dress was white with long chiffon-type handkerchiefs attached by Velcro, and each one had a huge rhinestone attached to it. As Cherry danced she peeled them off and threw them towards the crowd; because of the weighty rhinestones they flew like little chiffon arrows.

The crowd loved it and as she stripped I moved my chair ever closer until she took off her feather boa and hooked it around me to drag me to her. From there it was a somewhat more traditional dance, but with lots of lifts. At the end the applause was great and the compère Albert Rudge asked the three judges to assess the applause that the audience had given for us and Peter and Lynn. It was too close to call and Albert asked people to applaud again. When they finished, the head judge walked over to Albert and whispered in his ear. 'The winners, Len and Cherry…' We'd beaten the world professional Latin champions.

From Kent professional champion in 1969 to second in the International Professional Latin in 1970, to the British Professional Rising Star in 1972 and the Duel of the Giants in 1973 and now in 1975. Twenty years later I won a Carl Allan award, which is like the Oscars of dance teachers. But I'm sure you know that awards are like piles: eventually every arsehole gets one.

This was the culmination of Cherry's and my dancing career. With all that was going on with the school it might seem that competing was in some way secondary to us but that was never the case. We loved the adrenalin buzz of competing, and naturally the thrill of winning was brilliant. If you are thinking, it sounds like all the Goodmans did was dance you wouldn't be far wrong. Cherry and my relationship was entirely based on dancing: it was more of a partnership than a relationship. Whether it was competing, demonstrating, talking about the school, teaching at the school or over in Germany, it was dance 24/7. As husband and wife we didn't have a lot of time for anything that normal couples do. We were no different from lots of dancing couples that marry because they dance together. Some dancing relationships last a lifetime and do so very happily. However, lots split after the dancing finishes, because once you've stopped you look across at the person next to you and think I've got nothing else in common with you. The likelihood is she's looking across at you thinking – what am I doing with you? It's a recipe to split and that's exactly what happened to Cherry and me.

Chapter Nine

Monte Carlo or Bust

The break-up of my marriage can be traced back to way before we even got married; it was as a result of going to Monte Carlo the year after Cherry's dad died. It was also the fault of Benny Tolmeyer, one of my best friends in the dance world. I say fault, but Benny was totally innocent of any wrong-doing: it was just that he introduced me to casinos and the south of France. And before you all start thinking I gambled away our fortunes and Cherry was too upset to be able to stay with me, then you couldn't be more wrong. For the most part our trips to Monte Carlo and the Sporting Club were very happy times. It was a chance to get away from dancing, demonstrating, competing and teaching.

Benny was a Dutchman and one of the first Europeans to make a breakthrough to the top flight of ballroom dance; he was also a bit of a character. We had first met at Benny's studio in Tooting in 1970. Cherry and I used to practise there from time to time. Benny would pop into his studio from his home, which was right next door. He knew Cherry's dad, which is probably why we got talking in the first place, and thereafter we often had a quick chat after we had finished our session. One evening as we were gassing away a problem developed in the social club that adjoined his studio. It was owned by Charrington's, the brewery company, and it was from them that Benny had use of the studio dance space in exchange for managing the social club; Benny did it under sufferance.

Suddenly, just as Cherry and I were about to leave, a terrific racket started up from inside the social club. It turned out to be two blokes that were a bit worse off for drink playing on a slot machine. They had got fed up putting two bob bits into the machine with no payouts, so in frustration they had tipped it on its side and were kicking the life out of it. Poor Ron, the dapper little barman, had come around from behind the bar to try to calm things down and got a smack round the ear for his trouble. The rule of the club was they didn't come into the ballroom and the dancers didn't go into the club; as far as the dancers were concerned they were a rough lot, and the club people just thought we were a bunch of nancy boys. Benny ran towards the door into the club and instinctively I followed him. One of the two slot machine bullies was a biggish bloke – obviously the leader of the dynamic duo. The other was a smaller bloke who was sat on a bar stool watching his bigger mate kicking the crap out of the slot machine – he was applauding. Ironically the dancer Paddy Shannahan, which I only found out later, owned the fruit machines in the club.

The bigger bloke, on seeing Benny come in, stopped kicking the machine and took a swing at him instead. As he did I grabbed him and bundled him to the ground. Having worked in the docks I knew how to handle myself and dancing does make you pretty fit. I pinned him down and tried reasoning with him.

'Calm down, you big girl's blouse, you're going to hurt someone.'

Witnessing this the little one perched on a bar stool decided to launch a pint glass in my direction. It hit me on the forehead and cut me, which strangely didn't hurt: it was probably the adrenalin. Seconds later blood started gushing over me and my trapped – and shouting – adversary. It must have looked worse than it was because the little one made a dash for the door where he was met by the police. Having collared him they took the big bugger off my hands. He was all covered in my blood, and I was taken down the hospital. The upshot of all this was I had six stitches in my head and a life-long friend in Benny.

Benny had first come to London in the early fifties in an effort to further his dancing career. His partner was Sylvie Silve, an English girl, and together they got to the professional finals in Blackpool in 1955. I'm pretty sure he was the first European ever to do so. He went on to become one of the leading coaches, teaching many of the top couples. He had a lovely way of talking, in a kind of broken English. When you had a lesson with him and he was about to put a record on, instead of saying, 'Well, let's try it to the music' he would say, 'Let's do it to the orchestra.' I'm not saying Benny's English wasn't good: it was turns of phrase with him – he also swore like a trooper.

Nina Hunt's husband was Demetri Petridis, a Greek who was also in the dance business. When Benny first met him, years before, he was introduced to Benny as Demetri, pronounced Dem-e-tree. For some reason Benny got it in his head that his name was Jimmy Tree. From then on he called him Jimmy to his face. If he was telling others about him he'd say things like, 'Yes, I was judging with Jimmy Tree.'

The week after the fruit machine incident Benny and Sylvie took Cherry and I out for dinner by way of a thank you for helping over the aggro. We went to the Palm Beach Casino in Berkeley Street, just off Berkeley Square in the West End; it was my first visit to a casino – unfortunately for my bank account it wasn't my last. Over dinner we chatted away, getting along great; for Cherry and Sylvie it was the start of a very close friendship. During dinner Benny related a story about another well-known Dutch dancer named Eric Van Dyke. I'd never heard of him but evidently he was an amateur dancer who used to come across to the UK from Holland every couple of weeks. Somehow or another he got in with a bad crowd of blokes; Eric and his partner began smuggling. Among all the diamantes on his partner's dress they would sew a few real diamonds; gradually over time they increased the number of gems until they attempted the big one and covered the whole dress with real diamonds. They thought they would never be caught, but somebody must have tipped off the police and Customs. They were waiting for them and nabbed them when they came off the boat. A pretty dress covered in gems that just failed in becoming a great scam.

After dinner Benny and I went to the gaming floor, while the girls stayed at the table for a coffee and a chat. Benny loved to play roulette and after watching him for a bit I had a little walk round and decided to try my hand at Blackjack. I knew all about pontoon, or 21 as we often called it, so I thought I'd probably manage it fine. I changed up a fiver and half an hour later when Cherry came looking for me I had £21 – a £16 profit. How I wish now that I'd lost because if I had a done I'd probably never have played again. The fact that I tripled my money encouraged me to join the Palm Beach Club as I was leaving.

Cherry and I had picked Benny and Sylvie up from their house so we drove them back home after a great evening. On our way to Tooting, Benny and Sylvie told us that for the past two years they had gone on holiday to Monaco; they said how great it was, how much they loved it and why didn't we join them this summer? On the spur of the moment we agreed, and so in the middle of August off we went by train. We had to change in Paris and had some time to kill so we went for dinner, which proved to be Benny's undoing. On the sleeper train from Paris to Nice we had a couchette with bunk beds that pulled out from the wall; Benny and I slept on the top ones with Cherry and Sylvie below, like four kids on a sleep-over. After we put the lights out I lay there listening to the rhythmic clickety-clack of our train thinking how glamorous it was to be going to Monaco when my thoughts were interrupted by the roar of a huge fart coming from Benny's bunk. I suppose it was the rich Parisian food that caused a chemical reaction in his stomach. Whatever it was I just roared with laughter, Sylvie was most indignant and Cherry acted as though nothing had happened. Benny acted all innocent, pretending to be asleep. Within seconds the smell reached me, probably because I was on the same level as Benny. It was so bad that in an instant I was up off my bunk and into the corridor, followed immediately by Sylvie. 'Do you think it was a squeaky rail?' asked Sylvie.

Having arrived at our apartment at Monaco, which was a few roads back from the promenade, we unpacked and settled in. Around about 5 p.m., we went out for a bite to eat and a look

Winning 'The Duel of the Giants' at the Royal Albert Hall in 1971.

I was always being told I needed a kick up the bum.

Steptoe and Cherry in 1973 – see what happens when you eat your spinach.

Me with the German formation team winning the world championship.

Cherry and I at dinner with some of the icons of the ballroom dancing world. On the left of me are Nancy Duggan and Len Scrivener, and behind Cherry you can see Billy and Bobbie Irvine.

Lesley and me during my Peter Sellers phase.

A wonderful life – a fag and a game of crib. My dad and I played and kept score the whole year.

Christmas 1986 with my boy James.

The answer to my prayers – two women who say nothing.

With Craig, Arlene and Bruno – a picture speaks a thousand words.

The very first publicity shot for *Strictly Come Dancing*, May 2004.

Fiona Phillips with Brendan Cole – who said she couldn't dance?

The 2007 champions, the very talented Alesha Dixon with Matthew Cutler.

Carrie Ann Inaba with Bruno and me on *Dancing with The Stars.*

'Hello Dolly' – Bruno and me with the legendary Dolly Parton, and (left) with Barry Manilow.

Fame at last, I appear in the *Beano* in December 2007.

My film star's trailer at ABC television in Los Angeles.

Me with a poster of my younger self on my 60th birthday.

Spot the Tiger – two golfing legends.

I am never happier than with my old golfing buddies. Brian, Mike, Richard and me at Carnoustie 2002.

round Monte Carlo. We walked into the square with the old casino and the Hotel de Paris; outside was a fantastic array of expensive motorcars – this was the life all right. Benny knew of a small restaurant just off the square, one where you could sit outside to eat; we all thought it sounded perfect. When we got there who should be sitting just a few feet away from us but Sacha Distel, the French singer whom Sylvie idolised. Much to our embarrassment, over she went and chatted away. We were out of earshot so could hear nothing, but after just a few minutes she was sitting at his table acting like they were long-lost friends. Pretty soon she beckoned to us to come and join them. Over we went and we all sat chatting and drinking with Sacha; I thought this must be a normal everyday occurrence in Monte Carlo: you just sit down and start having a chat and a laugh with a superstar. A few years later the same thing happened, thanks again to Sylvie. This time it was Demis Roussos, the huge singer who wore shirts that he must have got from rent-a-tent – he was another of her favourites.

After an hour or so Sacha made his excuses, probably thanking God he'd got rid of us, and we had dinner. All too soon it was time for bed. I wasn't so keen, wanting to soak up the atmosphere, and after a bit of arm-twisting I managed to get Benny to take me to the casino; Cherry and Sylvie said they were off back to the apartment. Benny was insistent that he wasn't going to play, but was happy to take me in to show me what was what. It was like walking into a museum; and there was a gorgeous restaurant along the side called the Blue Train. In the casino the minimum stake was too high for me, but I knew once Benny got in he would have to have a 'spiel' as he always called it. He changed up 1,000 francs, about 100 quid back then, and headed for the roulette table. Within ten minutes of sitting down Benny had won a packet. Next he was giving me a 10,000-franc chip with strict instructions. 'Len, whatever happens don't give it to me back.'

Off I went to change it and by the time I was back at the table Benny gave me another 10,000-franc chip; the instructions were the same. By the time we walked out of the casino, about an hour later, Benny had turned £100 pounds into £5,400. Remember this was in 1970, which makes it worth somewhere close to £100,000 today. When we got back to the apartment Sylvie asked how much Benny had lost.

'I won a bit,' said Benny.

Then the guessing game started. They got nowhere near and even with some prompting still only got to £5,000.

'That's close enough,' he said.

It was the biggest win he ever had. He explained that he put a chip on 22, which came in, and what all proper roulette players do is to then put more back on the same number in case there's a repetition. He also put money all around the 22 and, bugger me, it came in again. He increased his stakes and the same thing happened: 22 was where the roulette ball landed for a third time, the odds against this happening must be millions to one. After he finished explaining all this to the girls he reached into his pocket and got out the most enormous wad of notes. The casino wanted to give him a cheque, but he said no, I want the cash. Benny went to the kitchen and when he came back he gave me 10,000 francs, £1,000.

'What's that for Benny?'

'Listen, Len. I wouldn't have even gone in there and had a bet if it hadn't been for you. That will pay for your holiday, it will pay for your travel and hopefully it will give you all your spending money as well.'

I resisted but Benny was insistent and he was right. It paid for everything and we had money left over when we got back home.

From then on we went to Monaco every year. Sometimes we went by train, sometimes we flew and just once we went by car, but we always met up with Benny and Sylvie and had a brilliant holiday. In 1976 I was banned from driving for six months for getting three speeding tickets, which in those days was an automatic ban. I really needed to be able to drive with all the demonstrations we were doing all over the country, so I decided to go to court to try and contest it. My case came up at Greenwich Crown Court and I felt sure my gift of the gab would get me off; I was, I pleaded, only doing 38 in a 30-mile-an-hour limit. The court was full of policemen, all there to deal with their respective cases; I was scheduled to be the second person to come up before the magistrate. My confidence quickly ebbed away when the man before me, who was also there for speeding, was asked if losing his licence would affect his employment.

'Yes,' he said. 'I'm a milkman.'

He got a six-month ban. I went into the dock and the clerk read out my speeding charge.

'Your name?' said the clerk.

'Leonard Goodman.'

'Your occupation?'

'Ballroom dancer.'

From around the court and amongst the gathered group of policemen there was tittering; from others there was out and out laughter. It really bugged me.

'What's so funny?' I asked.

'Be quiet,' said the magistrate.

'Well… I don't see what's funny, do you?'

'Quiet,' said the judge a second time.

For me there was no letting up. 'You tell me what's funny.'

In addition to getting a £25 fine for contempt of court I got a six-month ban and a further £20 fine.

Losing my licence proved to be something of a nightmare because I always drove to wherever we were demonstrating, which I never minded. I had a Daimler Sovereign that helped ease the pain of miles and miles of motoring. Cherry could drive but she refused to drive the Daimler saying the bonnet was too long for her; we spent the next six months in her Ford Cortina. Luckily my six-month ban ended two weeks before our annual trip to Monaco, so I suggested that this year we drive there instead of flying. In the middle of August we set off from Dover for Monte Carlo. We were in no hurry and so we took three days, enjoying a night in Paris and another in Lyon on the way south. We would often meet other dancers in Monaco who were also there on holiday and this year was no exception. Robert and Linda Bellinger were there, as was Peter Maxwell, who had just won the Blackpool Professional Latin American Championships; Peter has now probably become one of my closest friends in the dance business.

After our two weeks we were asked by Peter if he could have a lift back to England as British Airways was on strike and he had to get back for some work. The plan was to try and get back in just one day, so we left about five in the morning; a case of foot down and go on the autoroute. We hadn't been on the road long and were just outside of Avignon when smoke suddenly started appearing from under the bonnet; I knew it was most probably the head gasket. We ground to a halt on the hard shoulder and pretty soon a police car came along. They arranged for a truck to come and we were loaded on the back to be driven to Avignon. None of us could speak French and to almost everything I asked there was a shrug and those two little words from the French mechanic, 'C'est impossible.'

It all boiled down to the fact that they had no Daimler parts and so we were stuck. The 'we' was Cherry and me, because as soon as we got back to Avignon, Peter nipped off to the train station and legged it home. Eventually we managed to get a place on the car train from Avignon, which meant me bribing people to push the car on to the train; after we arrived in Calais it was a repeat procedure, and then in England too. The AA took us home from Dover docks. We were four days late, several thousand francs poorer and it cost another £1,000 to get the engine sorted at the garage in Bexley.

Our last Monaco holiday was in 1977 for which we returned to our normal method of getting there – we took the plane. We spent our days on the beach. One thing I used to really enjoy was watching films at the lovely outside cinema right on the promenade down at one end of Monaco. They screened English films; as we sat back to enjoy the movie a waitress came round with drinks. They started at about eight o'clock and afterwards we would go into the Sporting Club. One evening while we were in the casino having a drink we struck up a conversation with a Parisian named Michel. He was olive skinned, handsome, about my age, and may have been of Moroccan descent I think. He obviously had a bit of dough as we saw him at the casino most nights playing roulette on one of the tables with a minimum bet of 1,000 francs. A couple of evenings later I was playing blackjack and when I finished I wandered back to where Cherry and Michel were sitting having a chat.

'Michel has got us two tickets so we can go and see Manhattan Transfer tomorrow night,' said Cherry.

'That's brilliant, Michel, thank you so very much. They're one of my favourite groups.'

Cherry and I had a wonderful night at their concert and so I couldn't wait to thank him the next day. Michel was once more very gracious and offered to take Cherry and me, along with Benny and Sylvie, to dinner at the Café de Paris in the square. We had champagne, beautiful food, brandies afterwards; it was a fabulous night. What a generous man, I thought. The next day I paid the price, but not from a hangover; something I had eaten hadn't agreed with me. I felt in no mood to move far away from the nearest bathroom so while the rest of them went off to the beach I stayed in the apartment sitting on the balcony reading a book. It really wasn't much of a tragedy but when they came back in the evening and suggested dinner I decided my stomach still needed to rest. Off the three of them went for dinner.

When Cherry arrived home it was about 2 a.m. I'd been asleep for a while. She told me that she, Sylvie and Benny had been to Jimmy's, the disco attached to the Sporting Club; we had been there often. It was at the end of a pier and when it was warm they slid the glass walls back so it felt like you were dancing out in the middle of the ocean. I went quickly back off to sleep and the next day I felt as good as new, so it was back to our routine and a trip to the beach. Around lunchtime Michel came sauntering up the beach and sat down with us and chatted away in his broken English; we arranged to all go to the open-air cinema that evening. For the last few days of the holiday I spent most of the day at the beach on my own. Cherry regularly went off into town to go shopping, which was most unlike her as we usually spent our days all together, sitting around, chatting and soaking up the sun.

All too soon it was time to leave for home. It wasn't quite a case of see you next year to Benny and Sylvie because we saw them regularly in London but we always talked about our next trip to Monaco.

Not long after we got back from holiday I was due to leave for Johannesburg to judge the South African Championships and do some teaching. Having been a successful competitor it was a short step to becoming a judge. When I say a short step it was not that I immediately jetted off around the world judging in glamorous places. First of all I did some judging in dance schools, then in regional competitions, then the Kent County Championships and then I got on what was called the Sunday circuit, which was the step before doing some of the larger regional competitions. I'd served my apprenticeship and so it was nice to reap the rewards.

One day, between arriving home and my leaving again, Cherry said we'd had a call from a guy named René Roulin. He had a dance studio in Vincennes, just outside Paris; we had been there many times to teach and demonstrate. While the standard there was not as good as in the UK we both enjoyed the place. René was a dapper little chap with a pencil moustache. We would only have to suggest going somewhere or doing something and

René was on the case. On one occasion Cherry said she would love to go to the Lido. '*D'accord*,' said René, and he drove us in his car, parked right outside and in we went; we had the best table, there was champagne and no charge! He was one of those blokes who seemed to know everyone; even though we couldn't talk French, by the way he spoke you knew he knew his way around. René wanted us to do some teaching, but the dates coincided with my trip to Johannesburg.

'No problem, Cherry, why don't you go and I'll do the South African job as planned.'

When I got back from Jo'burg, Cherry said it had all gone very well and René had as usual looked after her extremely well.

'He asked me if I had any old dance dresses for sale as some of his pupils are about to do a competition and they need some. You remember we talked about me getting rid of a lot of those old dresses of mine, the ones I never use? All they do is sit in the wardrobe, collecting dust, so I said I'd sell them to him. René also said he would like me to do some more teaching for him.'

'That's a good idea, Cherry, it'll free up some space in the wardrobe and earn a few bob at the same time.'

So in a few days Cherry went off to Paris, but not alone. She had a car full of dresses and she took her mum with her. She said Joy needed a bit of a holiday.

The day after Cherry left, Benny called me; it must have been a very hard call for him to make. 'Len, Cherry has gone to Paris to meet Michel, the Frenchman from Monte Carlo. Her mother has gone too because Cherry is going to leave you and she wants her mum to meet her future husband or whatever they plan on doing.'

'You what?' was about all I could manage. I was practically speechless. I was so bloody mad at Cherry for what she was doing, but I was also mad at myself for being so naive. 'So that's why she learning all those little French phrases.'

Benny knew because Sylvie and Cherry were very close. Not that I felt any bad feelings towards either Sylvie or Benny. In these situations it's best to try not to take sides. When I put the phone down I just sat in the chair thinking about what a shitty thing it was. I wasn't so much mad with Cherry; she had found someone else that she'd fallen in love with. Sometimes it's impossible to fight those emotions, but I was hurt; hurt that she had done it, hurt by the way I found out and hurt that she had gone over to France behind my back. With hindsight I knew that ours was a dancing marriage, one that lacked that spark of real love. Cherry was not the one and only, but it was still a bugger at the time.

The more I sat there, the madder I got. As the old saying goes: don't get mad, get even. Well, whether I got even is a matter of opinion, but I certainly got mad and retaliated in the only way I could think of.

Our house was about a mile from Cherry's mum's house in Bexley Heath. Joy lived in a cul-de-sac; you had to climb up 10 or 12 stairs to her bungalow. There was a front lawn that was raised up above the pavement so that anyone walking by the house on the pavement couldn't see Joy's garden. Over the next two days I took everything of Cherry's that I could possibly think of, all of her clothes, her minks, her jewellery, records, a nest of tables her mother had given her, and laid everything out neatly on her mother's front lawn; thank God it didn't rain. The postman must have thought it was some kind of house sale! I then had the locks changed on our house. I knew she would take her mum home first, and so I put a note through Joy's front door. It just said: 'Don't come back, I know everything'. I also phoned everyone with whom we had shows booked, it was about 80 in all, to tell them that Cherry and I were no longer together and I wouldn't be able to fulfil my obligation to demonstrate. Then I packed a suitcase of my own and went to tell my mum and dad. After that I got in my car and went off to the Lake District for two weeks to a lovely hotel called Old England on Lake Windermere.

When I got back there was a letter from a solicitor saying Cherry was starting divorce proceedings. There was no surprise in that, but it surprised me that she knew exactly how much money we had in the bank. At the time it really upset me because she left me for a multi-millionaire, but all she asked for was our savings. Of course she was entitled to her share, but in these situations it's hard to be rational. All I could think at the time was how it would wipe me out for quite a while.

About three years later I was walking through Bexley Heath, where I had gone to buy a music system from a nice shop called Young's. They sold record players with variable speeds and pitch control, which was great if you wanted to slow down a cha-cha-cha a notch. After I'd ordered it I walked out of their front door and bumped straight into Cherry, who I hadn't seen since she buggered off to Paris.

'Let's go and have a coffee over in Hydes, shall we, Len?'

It was lovely to see her; the anger had long gone in me and she seemed very happy. She told me she had two kids, which was certainly a surprise. After we talked for a while I just blurted it out.

'You know what, Cherry, the one thing that really got to me was the fact that you cleaned me out when you went off with your multi-millionaire French bloke.'

After I calmed down, we talked a while longer and said our goodbyes; I thought nothing more of it, other than I was glad to have got it off my chest. Three days later a cheque arrived from Cherry and a note to say sorry. I'm so glad, not for the money, which was nice, but because it put a full stop on things for me.

Chapter Ten

It's a Family Affair

With Cherry gone it totally put the kibosh on me demonstrating: it's a bit difficult to do it on your Jack Jones. It made a big hole in my income. It was what bought us our lovely detached house in Old Bexley, which I was still living in, it got us a nice car, which I still had, so I wasn't complaining. It was the dance school that ticked over, bringing in steady money, so for me it was back to teaching four or five days a week – no hardship because I've always loved that aspect of my work. This was also when I discovered disco, along with just about everyone else in Britain, but it wasn't a discovery I made for myself. Outside of work I found I enjoyed being on my own, suiting myself as to what I did and when I did it. I started doing things I hadn't done much of while Cherry and I were together; one of the best things was going for fish and chips every Friday night.

Aldridges, the chippy, was in Bexley village and the only challenge I faced every Friday was getting there before they closed – at ten o'clock on the dot. My last class finished at 9.30, so time was tight as I had to lock up as well as drive there. As often as not, as I walked through the door at 9.57 p.m., Mr Aldridge would turn the sign around from open to closed. He would then stand by the door to let anyone who managed to get in before the curfew out and to stop anyone getting in – there was never any budging him, even if you were a regular.

One night I just got through the door with barely seconds to spare, but I was not the last: another guy followed me a second or two later. I vaguely recognised him but couldn't remember from where. After the two people in front of us had been served and ushered out, it was just me and this other bloke. Mrs Aldridge was serving and she assumed we were together.

'What can I get you boys?'

Simultaneously we said, 'Cod and chips please.'

'We've only got one piece of cod left, I'm afraid, so which of you is to have it?' asked Mrs A.

'You have it,' I said.

'No mate, you have it,' said the other customer.

'No really, you have it.'

The debate on who was to have the one remaining piece of cod went on for a bit, with neither of us wanting to take it. With Mr Aldridge anxious to close up I finally said:

'Look, I only live two minutes away – why not come back to my place and we can share it.'

'Okay, sounds good to me. I'm John Knight by the way.'

Back at my place it was a bit like a scene out of the Bible, with me dividing up the fish, luckily I had a new loaf of bread in the house. We sat and enjoyed cod and chips and a beer, chatting away like we'd known each other for years. We discovered that we were both members of Dartford Golf Club, which solved the mystery of where I'd seen him before. We arranged to play golf the following Saturday afternoon. It was the start of a friendship that has lasted 30 years. It was a friendship rooted in our mutual love of golf, but as time went along we found we shared a sense of mischief, we laughed at the same things and we were both single blokes in our early thirties. We were a whole bunch of trouble.

My working day began about 2 p.m. with private lessons, which lasted until about five, classes followed this for children and then there were adult classes until about 9.30 or 10 p.m., from Monday to Friday. John owned shops selling wallpaper and paint, called Mr Discount. He later sold out to a firm named Fads. All the shops had a manager, allowing John to play golf pretty much any morning; we'd each found a new golfing buddy. We would meet at the golf club around nine o'clock and have nine or 18 holes depending on what else either of us had on. John and I had more fun and laughs than in any other period of my life to that point. We have similar personalities, and we look alike – lots of people think we're brothers. With our love of fun and practical jokes we had plenty to occupy us on days when the weather put paid to golf. Some days we would sit and talk about going into business together. Wine bars were the big new thing at the end of the seventies. We sat for hours discussing every little detail of ours; we even had a great name for it – Chez When. Some ideas sound better when you're drunk. We spent a lot of time on detailed research – probably the best bit of it as a business venture.

John and I were great playmates and were always getting into mischief, like the time we tried selling a boa constrictor belonging to a pet-shop owner that had a shop next to one of

John's Mr Discount stores. Wilf, the guy who owned the pet shop, came in to say, 'I've got to pop opposite to the dentist. I'll be about 20 minutes. I'll put a sign in the door saying if anybody wants anything to come in and see you. Is that okay, John?'

Well, bugger me, but the first person that came in asked, 'How much is the snake?'

'Ah, the snake, that'll be £3 a foot.'

John also had some swag shops; they were like pound stores today. One day he bought a container load of some stuff called Gunk.

'It's green, slimy and treacly-like stuff that you can throw against a wall and it'll trickle down it. It looks revolting.'

We were on our way to play golf and John had a can in his car. Most mornings the course was very quiet and this morning was no exception. When we finished our round we filled the hole where the flag is with Gunk. We really had to force it in. We then hid behind a building so that we could watch the next golfers who came along. As it happened it was two ladies. One of them was about to putt and the other went over to the flag to take it out, and, of course, as she did out oozed the squelching Gunk; it was like a scene out of *Ghostbusters*. The green keeper turned up and the three of them stood studying the situation; they probably thought they had struck oil. Knighty and me were hiding behind the building; we must have looked like a couple of schoolboys.

John bought a shop in Dartford, which had been called Kerr's, and was originally a gentlemen's and ladies' outfitters. Some of the workings of this shop are now in Dartford museum. It had one of those pneumatic systems where the money went shooting upstairs somewhere to the accounts department who then sent back the receipt and any change. John had decided to turn Kerr's into another swag shop. One day, on our way back from golf, we nipped in to check on the progress of the builders. While Knighty was talking to the joiner I was poking about the place and came across a dismantled mannequin. As I was checking it out John came over.

'Oh, look at that poor lady, why don't we put her back together again?' Having done so John suggested it was rather unfair to leave her naked, so we took her along to Dorothy Perkins – four doors along from John's shop – to buy her a frock and a hat. We christened her 'my dear' and decided to take her with us to the pub for lunch. The two of us walked into the King's Head in Bexley and sat her at a table, John put a fag in her hand and we went up to the bar to order two pints and, 'A gin and tonic for madam.' We sat talking and then had a sandwich. We left without her and for all I know she may still be there.

Through John I met another one of my best mates, a travel agent named Mike Colley whose business was in Bexley Heath. Normally if we popped in to see Mike we parked in the car park of Hyde's, which was one of those old-fashioned department stores. Hyde's was just across the street from Mike's shop but when we got there we found their car park was closed, as they were laying tarmac.

'No problem, Len, we'll go and park at the back of Colley's shop.'

As it was raining we decided to go in through Mike's back door, but the only problem was that we were not sure which one was his as there was nothing to say which back door was which.

We took pot luck and rang the bell, and as the young lad opened the door John realised it was the jewellers next door to Mike's travel agency. John was wearing an old Harris Tweed jacket and had his hand in his pocket.

'It's a stick-up,' said John.

Instead of seeing the joke, the lad pressed the panic button and ran to the front of the shop and out the main door. He then ran into Mike's shop and they pressed their panic button. The two of us decided to make ourselves scarce and crossed over the street into Hyde's – to hide. It was just before Christmas and so we sauntered into Santa's grotto – Santa was rolling himself a fag. Afterwards we told Mike Colley it was us; looking back we were bloody lucky to have got away with it.

I was fortunate that I had great help in the dance school that supported me during this period, because I probably spent way too much time having a great time. It was as though I'd escaped from something. Don't take it as a criticism of Cherry: she and I had just fallen into our situation so I was just making up for what I perceived as a bit of lost time. We had really worked hard to build the Dartford school with Saturday morning children's classes, adult beginners' classes, classes for medal tests and lots of private lessons. Cherry had mainly done the beginners, while I mostly did the competitors. The funny thing with beginners is that some that come to a new class stay for just a week, don't like it, and you never see them again; others come for five or six weeks just to learn the basic steps. Then there's some who come for 20 years. I've even got people that came to my studio in the seventies that still come today. Some came as singles, met someone at the studio, married and they've got kids. Sometimes there was even great drama at the dance studio. One night a biggish man, who had been coming up to the school for about six or eight months, collapsed and stopped breathing. Fortunately two pupils who also happened to be nurses were there because he would have been brown bread if one of them hadn't given him the kiss of life and the other one pummelled his chest. He recovered, so it's easy to see the funny side of it, because as this was going on everyone sat around the edge of the dance floor looking on as though they were watching *Casualty*.

One of my regular hangouts during the late seventies was a pub called the Fox and Hounds, which was in Green Street Green, just outside of Dartford. I would often pop down after work about 9.30; my mates had been there for hours so they were all nicely loosened. In actual fact, I wasn't used to pubbing it: it wasn't my thing because I never really had the opportunity while I was with Cherry. The landlords were Howard and Christine Smith, a really lovely couple with whom I became very friendly. Christine originally came from the Isle of Wight and was always taking the mickey out of me because during this period in my life I tended to go out with their barmaids. The pub was a ready-made dating agency. One evening I went in and there was a very attractive girl behind the bar – my first thought was 'nice of them to get a new one in for me'. Her name turned out to be Lesley, but she was not a new barmaid at all: she was a friend of Christine's who was just up visiting from the Isle of Wight.

They say opposites attract; well, Lesley and I were like chalk and cheese. Me a scatterbrain, game for the lark, always up for the crack, whereas she was quiet, sensible and about to take up a nursing training course at St Bart's Hospital. John Knight,

Howard and Christine all encouraged me to take her out while she was visiting for the week, not that I needed much encouragement, as she really was a looker. Well, we hit it off from the first date, despite the fact that I wasn't used to sensible conversation. One date led to another and we landed up going out virtually every night until she went home to the Isle of Wight. Then the strangest thing happened to me, something that had never happened before. When she left I actually found I missed her. I decided to telephone her on some pretext or other to see if she had got home safe. After a little conversation she said, 'Why don't you come down to the Isle of Wight next weekend?'

There was no playing hard to get from me. 'I'll be down Saturday morning.'

The following Saturday I was on the eight o'clock ferry. I remember thinking as I paid for my crossing how expensive it was for just a couple of miles of water. I stayed with Lesley, at her mum and dad's bungalow in a room in the roof. Lesley's parents, Les and Maureen, were a nice couple and I really enjoyed myself. Lesley was five or six years younger than me and she had already told me that she had been married before, although over the weekend a little more came out about her ex-husband. He was a bloke called Wilf Pine who had managed Black Sabbath. Lesley and Wilf had got married in Connecticut, with a whole bunch of Mafia bosses as guests!

Lesley told me they had a house in Wimbledon and their friends the Osbornes – that's Sharon and Ozzy – used to stay there. This was a long time before they found fame on the television as a celebrity couple living the Hollywood dream. Sharon's father was an infamous music business manager named

Don Arden, who seems to have had a very colourful life, if what I've read is anything to go by – this was the world that Lesley had left behind.

Once I got back from the Isle of Wight and told John Knight a little about Lesley's background he went from encouraging me to go out with her to saying I should have nothing to do with her because of her ex.

'You never know what he might do, Len, or worse, have somebody else do! It could all turn very nasty. Top tip, mate, if anyone comes to your door wearing sunglasses, don't answer it.'

The problem was that I had fallen in love with Lesley, so anything he said I just ignored, or, more accurately, put to the back of my mind.

Over the next few weeks, before starting her nurse's training at St Bart's, Lesley came to Kent a couple of times to stay at my house. Once she started training she stayed in their halls of residence, which were more like a prison than a hall. Her room had a bed, a sink and there was a communal bathroom – it was a long way from luxurious and all a far cry from driving around in her ex-husband's white Rolls-Royce and mixing with the stars. I would nip up to London to see Lesley and I must admit to not being very supportive of her ambition. Having said that, she was also quick to point out to me how much better my dance-school business could be if I ran it a little more professionally.

I had no drive financially or for anything else really. I was happy with my dance school and having fun with my mates, but Lesley was much more ambitious and saw there was a good deal more potential from my business. According to Lesley her ex wasn't the most attentive of husbands, and while I might not have been the most attentive of husbands to Cherry I think all things are relative and I came out in front on that one. Lesley needed little encouragement to realise that nursing wasn't her forte and so after a very short time of us being in a relationship I convinced her to give it up and come and live with me and help me with the dance school. At first Lesley was a bit like me when I started to teach: she was just one step ahead of those she was teaching, which is all you need to be. I was the sort of front man for the whole thing and with Lesley and others who helped at the school we began to grow the business.

Things rolled along pretty nicely for a year until out of the blue Lesley dropped a bombshell. She was pregnant. My initial reaction was a mixture of disbelief and uncertainty. Was this what I wanted? I was 36 when we found out that we were to have a baby, which at the time was a little older than most people when they have their first child. At that age you've become used to a way of life that suits you and it's a mix of shock along with some trepidation as to how you'll cope. My overriding fear was one of having to face up to the responsibility. We weren't married but that didn't make me feel any different about the situation. However, we had never even talked about having a child together, which made the shock even greater.

A month or so before the baby was due we started work on the bedroom that was to be the nursery. I say 'we' because despite a life-long aversion to all things DIY I was determined to do something for myself for once. Lesley knew that this wasn't my strong suit but despite her counselling against it I went off down to Mr Discount to buy some brushes, a roller and emulsion. The future nursery had some fitted wardrobes in it in which Lesley kept many of her clothes; they had louvred doors, which was the very height of modernity back in 1980. In addition I bought four plastic dust covers so that I could cover literally everything. I was taking no chances. I covered everything not just once but twice. I placed the steps in the middle of the room and decided to emulsion the ceiling first. Not wanting to cover myself in paint I stripped to my underpants. I naturally left my socks on and found an old straw hat of Lesley's to avoid getting too much paint in my hair. I had barely taken two steps into the room when, on account of still wearing my socks, I slid on the plastic sheet and went arse over tit on to my back. All would have been well had I not been holding a full two and a half litre can of emulsion with the lid off. It flew up into the air and I watched as the paint came out of the tin, seemingly in slow motion, before it flew all over the louvred wardrobe doors. Despite her advanced state Lesley came running up the stairs on hearing the crash. Instead of seeing if I was mortally wounded she went straight over to the wardrobe; as she opened the doors she looked at me; we both knew what to expect. Just about every piece of clothing was covered in paint.

This incident followed close on the heels of another monumental cock-up a couple of weeks earlier. This time it was Len, the cleaning man. For some unknown reason I decided that the dining-room table was dusty and needed polishing and so I went down under the sink and got out the furniture polish. I gave the mahogany table a lovely spray all over and within a second it started to foam up. I thought, this is going to come up lovely and shiny. As I went to put the can down, I noticed that it was a can of oven cleaner. I stripped the whole bloody table. It was then I decided that do it yourself and domestic work was not for me.

On 26 January 1981, a Monday, I was woken up by Lesley. In my half-awake state all I could hear her saying was something about 'waters' and 'breaking'. I thought she meant a pipe had burst or we had a leak – up I jumped. 'Where, where?'

She explained the baby was on its way; off we went to West Hill Hospital where I was actually quite well known. In the previous year I had done a marathon dance with all the kids at the dance school. They had to dance for five hours, every hour having a ten-minute break, and the money we raised went to the children's wards at West Hill. We bought four special beds that tipped up and they put a plaque on each saying, 'Presented by the Goodman School of Dancing.' All the dance school kids were invited to go to the hospital to see what they had achieved.

After hanging about at the hospital for a while it was obvious that nothing was going to happen right away. One of the nurses suggested that I had time to go off and do anything I needed to do; she got no argument from me, as I'm no good with medical matters. Lesley was lying there and probably couldn't have cared less what I did.

'I'll pop down the school and get the microphone that's broken and then take it to Jimmy Dides.'

It had gone on the blink and whenever I had anything like that, Jimmy's was the place to get it fixed. His shop was in Hyde Street and had been in his family for over 100 years. Jimmy also came to the dance school, so on the previous Friday he had said to me to let him have it, and he would have it fixed by the Monday, as it was most likely just a loose wire. When I collected it he wouldn't even take any money, as it was just a soldering job. One of John Knight's Mr Discount wallpaper shops was just two doors from Jimmy's, so I popped along to see him to tell him that Lesley was up the hospital. Before I could say a word John looked at me and said, 'Are you from Radio Kent?'

'Yes I am, I've come about the complaint that your floor is slippery and people keep falling over.' With that I thrust my mended microphone under the lady's nose. 'How's it for you?'

She rubbed the floor with her foot and said, 'The floor's fine, it's not slippery at all.'

'I'm here in Mr Discount in Dartford High Street where I'm speaking to one of the customers and she has agreed that the floor is no problem at all.' Just then another customer came in. 'Madam, could I ask you? Is the floor slippery?' I out-whickered Alan Whicker.

'No, it isn't.'

'Well, this is Len Goodman for BBC Radio Kent.'

With that, I walked out and never even told John what was up at the hospital.

Back at West Hill things hadn't moved on at all. Lesley was still groaning with no sign of anything about to happen. By four o'clock in the afternoon there was still no action on the baby front and classes were due to start at five. Lesley said, 'Why don't you go down and start the classes?' I had got somebody covering it but I left the phone number with the nurses in case there were any developments. At eight o' clock the phone went to say things had started to hot up, so I left and was back up at the hospital in five minutes flat. Lesley was going into theatre; I had no intention of joining her.

'Are you coming in?' said the midwife.

'No, I'd better not, I'll faint.'

'Oh, come on, you'll be fine.'

Rather than keep on arguing, in I went and parked myself at the head end rather than the business end; I enthusiastically joined in the urging.

'Come on, girl, you can do it. Better out than in.'

Finally, at 9.25 p.m. on Monday 26 January, James William Goodman arrived in the world; two days later and he would have shared a birthday with my dad. Now James was not my first choice of a name; the debate as to what to call him, if he was a boy, had been going on for weeks. My first choice was Len, but everyone, despite my spirited defence, soon discarded this.

'Think about it! Len is such a good name. If he's an engineer then he can be Len, if he's a little bit gay and artistic, Lenny, if he becomes an author, Leonard. Its such a versatile name.'

There was no way I was winning the argument. My next choice was Harry, but this was quickly rejected. Of course, once Prince Harry came along every other bugger's called Harry. According to Lesley's mother, and we had a real row over it, it's an ugly name and lacks class. So James it was, after my grandfather and William after one of my uncles.

To say I was overjoyed is an understatement. Once Lesley was back in the ward I couldn't stop gazing at the funny little thing. I tried to slip the midwife a 20-quid tip but she was having none of it. After I left the hospital I couldn't stop smiling. I was so proud. The next day I bought a £20 Marks and Spencer's voucher for the midwife and two £10 vouchers for the other two nurses that had helped with the urging. After a bit of an argument they accepted them. It was money well spent. Having asked myself if this was what I wanted, I now had the answer. It was definitely the thing I wanted most in the world.

Before all this business with babies, something happened with teenagers and the young that was a huge and totally unexpected bonus for the school. It had started in 1978 and in a completely accidental way; to begin with it was something I was totally opposed to. I was a ballroom and Latin American teacher: that's what I loved and that's what I liked teaching. But this was the year that disco had taken off, thanks to *Saturday Night Fever*. Everyone wanted to learn to dance like John Travolta and Karen Lynn Gorney, and there was no one in Kent to teach the moves.

There was a young lad, Ken was his name, who was about 19 who used to come to the dance school to help out a bit. He went to see *Saturday Night Fever* over and over again and started to nag on at me about going to see it. He said we could teach people to dance like that. I went to see the film. I didn't like it much to be honest; so it wasn't a case of 'cor, what a film', but I took his point and we decided to try and capitalise on it. We worked out some little things that we could teach and then put an advert in the paper. 'You've seen the film, you've heard the music, now learn the dances. *Saturday Night Fever* class commencing next week.' Well, come the day and the hall was full: there were people down the 54 stairs and halfway up the High Street in Dartford. I ended up having to cancel loads of other classes just to fit in extra *Saturday Night Fever* fanatics – it was packed night after night. The fact was the school had not been bringing in a huge amount of money and, while I wasn't quite down on my uppers, it revived my flagging finances. Thirty years later we still have 300 kids that come to do disco dancing and street dance, all as a direct result of that film. Lesley had encouraged me to start disco classes and when *Grease* came out, followed by *Fame*, the floodgates opened; the seam of gold turned into a whole goldmine.

Lesley also had a very good idea, and suggested that we should get a freehold property as the Dartford school was leasehold and offered no security. Whereas my epitaph will be 'He couldn't be bothered', hers will be 'Let's get on with it'. She was absolutely right.

As usual Lady Luck smiled on me, this time in the form of Margaret Radcliffe. She was a dance examiner who regularly came to us so that kids could take their dance medals. There were actually very few schools that Margaret went to because she lived in Folkestone and didn't drive, which meant she only did places that she could reach by train. One Saturday after she had finished the examination, we sat having a cup of tea and chatted about dancing in general. Towards the end of the conversation I said, 'Margaret, if ever you are examining in a dance school and it's a nice property and you hear they might be selling, can you let me know?'

'Len, that's amazing you mentioning it, because just last week I examined in Gravesend for a man named Leslie Mineer who has got a lovely ballroom dance studio. About four months ago he had a heart attack and so he's looking to retire to Spain with his wife and he's about to put it on the market.'

Margaret had to give me his number because I'd never heard of either him or his studio. I didn't hang around and as soon as Margaret had left to catch her train home, I was on the phone.

'Well, yes, I am going to retire and I'm so glad you phoned me because I would hate it to become something other than a dance school because I've had lots of pupils who have been loyal and I really would love somebody to keep it going.' We arranged for me to go up to Gravesend and have a look at his place early the next week. It was an old Victorian semi-detached house; the whole of the back garden was a building, which housed the dance school. It was perfect and I bought it for £47,000. It became a very important feature in my life for all sorts of reasons and I still have it.

Lesley had a lot of drive, and while that was a good thing, there was also a downside to the get-up-and-go aspect of her personality. Lesley didn't feel very comfortable living in my house at Hill Crescent because it was the home that Cherry and I had once shared; I can understand that. And we had only three bedrooms, one of which was James's nursery and the spare was used as an office, which meant there was no room if anyone came to stay. That was the practical side of things, but I was happy with it because for one I didn't have a mortgage. But Lesley made her case and in the end I agreed that if she found somewhere nice then we would move.

I must admit I was bloody awkward about the whole idea of moving. Whenever Lesley found somewhere she thought might be suitable I found fault with it. I could see her point of view, but I liked my home and I didn't go out of my way to be accommodating. However, like most men I'm pretty keen on a quiet life, although I've done my best to avoid having one. One morning in the spring of 1981 Lesley announced she had found the perfect place to set up our new home. It was about six miles south-east of Dartford in very small hamlet called Culverstone. She read me out the details.

'It's called Rose Cottage, a lovely six-bedroom house set in two acres of garden with woods extending to 14 acres, and there was also a two-bedroom cottage in the garden. It's on the market for £108,000.'

I think I said something like, 'It can stay there too.'

But Lesley was undaunted. I didn't know it at the time, but she had already been to see it once or twice and had decided that if I was to be won over, then timing was everything. Lesley had been waiting for a glorious spring morning and this day was just that. I knew there would be no peace so we went over to have a look at it. She was right. It was beautiful, the bluebells had just come out in the woods, the gardens looked immaculate, the sun was shining, there were three beautiful greenhouses glistening in the sun and before I even entered the house I fell in love with the place. Once we got inside, a fire was glowing in the grate, you could smell the coffee brewing and I swear they were baking a loaf of bread. It was the perfect pitch. I shook hands there and then saying, 'If you can wait while I get my house on the market the deal is done.' Luckily my house sold very quickly to the first people that came to see it. They paid £67,000 for it, which was a great deal as Cherry and I had bought it for just £13,000.

In August 1981 the old occupants vacated Rose Cottage and we moved in – I had to admit the house seemed perfect. It was within easy striking distance of both dance schools, which made it easy for me. Lesley was left to sort out the house; I was having nothing more to do with decorating. I put myself in charge of the garden; from never having taken any interest in gardening I found I loved it. Being a bloke, the first thing I did was to go straight out to buy a sit-on mower; I used to drive up and down even when the grass didn't need cutting. A day or so after moving in, I was mowing, sipping my tea as I did so, when a rough-looking bloke came up the drive. He looked as though he'd had a hard life and I guessed he was past retirement age.

'Hello,' he said, 'I'm Bill. I live up the road. I saw you moving in the other day and wondered if you needed a gardener or handy man?'

I didn't know I did but looking around the garden I knew it was a bit of a handful so I just said, 'Yes.'

I'm so glad I did. In time I learned that he had been a bare-knuckle boxer and a circus trapeze artist, but he turned out to be not just a lovely bloke but also a hard-working one, and an invaluable help.

The first thing I needed help with was the cesspit, but this was out of Bill's league. 'You'll be needing ol' Tom.'

If Bill didn't know how to do something, or something was too big for him, he always knew a man who could. Tom came round and from then on he would turn up once a month to empty it. The funny thing he did after emptying the pit, never before, would be to ask if he could use the toilet. Afterwards he would always say the same thing as he climbed back into the cab of his wagon.

'I like to put a little bit back into the job.'

After a year or so I managed to get main drainage from an estate on the opposite side of the road and had the gas laid on rather than the oil-fired central heating. I must admit I missed Ol' Tom's visits.

To begin with I thought I would only need Bill in the summer to help mow and suchlike, but I had underestimated the size of the task. In the autumn there were so many leaves because of the wood that we were knee deep in them – they needed cleaning up. Come winter it was snow! The drive was 100 yards long and that needed clearing, then it would be a pane of glass out of the greenhouse, then it would be planting seeds for the vegetable garden. Bill and I spent hours discussing how to improve the garden. We had lovely rhododendrons everywhere but we decided we needed a new one to fill in a particularly bare spot. A couple of miles up the road, near Sevenoaks, was a specialist rhododendrons centre where people came from all over Britain to buy special plants – the owner exhibited at the Chelsea Flower Show so he was obviously top drawer. His place was not so much a garden centre, more like a huge wooded area, maybe five or six acres, with little clearings in which were the plants. I drove up there and parked the car but there appeared to be no one around so I started having a look for myself. I wandered through the woods and about ten yards into the first little clearing I was looking at this largish bush that I thought would be just right. I had just touched its leaves when suddenly a man shouted, well almost screamed.

'What are you up to?' I jumped as if I was a shoplifter getting caught in the act. I spun round and a huge scruffy-looking man was stomping towards me. 'Don't touch anything and don't talk directly at the plants, just whisper.'

Suddenly I felt uncomfortable; here I was in the middle of a woodland glade whispering to a man in case the plants heard. 'Step away from that Japonica neurosis' – I think that's what he called it – next he's going to tell me to keep my hands where he can see them.

'What do you want?' he snapped.

'Well, I've come about a rhody. I'd like to get a nice rhododendron. I want quite a big one about the size of an armchair.'

'What sort of soil do you have?'

'It's normal,' I said. 'Just normal soil.'

'Is it loamy?' It was beginning to feel more like the Spanish inquisition than buying a plant. I assumed he wanted me to say yes, so I said:

'Oh yes, it's very, very loamy.'

'Ah good.' I liked gardening but I was no Alan Titchmarsh. After a 30-minute interview it was agreed that I could have one of his plants if he could place it where he felt best in my garden. I agreed, thinking well once he's gone I can dig it up and put it where I want it.

'Could I have it next week?' He looked at me as if I'd asked if I could tie him to a tree and whip him with a holly bush!

'Next week? Next week? You can have it in October.'

'But that's four months' time.'

Apparently, as he explained at some length, there was no touching anything until October. There was no discussion. I would just have to wait.

When it arrived it was a bush as stipulated, about the size of an armchair, but the root ball was four times bigger than the plant. The lorry had a digger thing stuck on the back and the gardener dug a hole about six feet deep by six feet wide, then a crane attached to the lorry lowered the plant into the hole. The look on the gardener's face was that of a son burying his beloved mother. I fully expected him to say a prayer as it passed into the hole. Instead, his only words to me were, 'and I'll be back.' He said this in a threatening manner as though if anything happens to that shrub you'll be in the hole and the rhododendron will be out. I realised that gardening is a lot more complex than I had imagined.

Near to the where the rhody was planted was the large stump

of a tree that had been cut down before we bought the house. Bill and me had tried, unsuccessfully, to dig out this stump, although with hindsight it was a daft thing to attempt. Finally Bill suggested getting Arthur Chamberlain to do it.

'Arthur's got the right equipment, Len.'

I knew Arthur because he had done some fencing for us with his son and he was a good bloke.

'Oh, that won't be any trouble for me and the boy. We'll come and do it next week.'

Between them taking a look at the stump and coming round to remove it, I went up into the attic to put some stuff up there for storage. While I was rooting around I found a plastic skull: it said on it that it was the property of some hospital or another, so it was one of those that must have been used for training. Despite this it looked very real. I brought the skull down so that Bill and I could stuff some earth in it, put a twig poking out of the eye socket and then put it in an old sack before burying it at the base of the tree stump. All this was a few days before Arthur and his son were due to arrive. Come the day, and it was not Arthur, but just his son and another old boy. Old Bill and I chatted with them for a bit before retreating to the utility room where we had a good view of them dealing with the stump. Soon enough they dug up the sack and probably thought it was a crock of gold or something. Arthur's son picked up the sack, turned it upside down and out fell the skull. Well, the lad fell backwards and landed on his bum, so shocked was he. He shouted out and next thing the two of them are in their vehicle heading out the driveway. Before long the police turned up along with Arthur, his son and the old boy; the police began putting plastic tape around the 'crime scene'. I had to come clean and tell them. I got such a bollocking for wasting police time, despite the fact that it wasn't me that called them.

Not only was Bill great around the garden, he was also James's best pal. From the age of two James would spend all day, every day, in the garden with him, and the two of them became inseparable. I loved watching old Bill and James messing around in the garden. I also found I loved being a father much more than perhaps I would have thought if you had asked me before I knew Lesley was pregnant; although I sometimes found being a dad a bit of a challenge. I'm sure I was no different to many fathers in that I remembered what my own dad had done with me when I was a kid. He had a few rules that he used on me, which I tried using with James. The first rule was, no meant no, and yes always meant yes, whereas maybe also meant yes as well. When I was about five or six there was a cheap sixpenny toy that I wanted. My dad had told me, no you can't have it, and nothing would make him change his mind, despite my crying or begging. Years later he said the sixpence was of no consequence but you have to teach that no means no and if he gave in to me over this toy then the battle was lost. Interestingly my dad was the complete opposite with James. If he wanted a toy or something Dad never said no to him. One day I asked my dad why he was never like that with me.

'Len, your role as father is to bring him up properly, my job as grandfather is to spoil him rotten.'

The funny thing is, when I was 16, Dad talked absolute rubbish, but by the time I was 21 he spoke only pearls of wisdom. It was amazing how intelligent he became in five years. I'm sure that is a quote from somewhere but it's so true. I used to think, 'oh shut up, you silly old sod', when I was a teenager but several years later I found that what he said was right on the money.

At three years old James went to nursery in the village hall so I made sure I had the mornings off so that I could take him. Two ladies run it and two parents were asked to stay each day to help out; it was on a rota and so once every couple of weeks I was expected to stay. Unfortunately I lasted just one week. I was asked to read a story about a frog and a fairy to five or six kids: no problem with that I thought. I tried to make it a little more exciting by using a froggy voice and a squeaky one for the fairy. Things started off okay but I soon ran into trouble when the fairy and the frog met.

'Hello, Mr Frog,' I said with a squeaky voice. 'Hello, pretty fairy,' I said with a gruff froggy voice, that with hindsight sounded more like Darth Vader. Immediately a little girl started crying and this started a chain reaction amongst the whole nursery, and every kid started crying or whining. The two ladies came over to suggest it would be better if I didn't come back again.

As James was just coming up to five years old he went to a convent in Gravesend. I believe the only tangible thing you can give a child is education and the convent had a good reputation for discipline and schoolwork. It was a 20- to 30-minute drive to take him to school in the morning; in the evening it was a repeat performance. I used to take James to school whenever I could but I was spending a lot of time abroad, both judging and teaching. I had started working abroad much more in the year after James was born. I had been back in Germany working regularly as well as going to America and even Japan. Getting the job in Japan was the strangest thing. I had never been to the Far East, until, one morning at 3 a.m., the phone rang. It was a man called George Fujimura who was like the big dance boss of Japan, who I only knew by reputation.

'Hello, Len?'

'Yes.'

'We want you come to Japan to judge Japanese championship. Okay?'

'Yes, lovely.'

'I send you details.'

'Thank you very much, very kind of you, George, to think of me.' Despite him waking me up, I was ecstatic at the prospect of going to the Far East.

The next day, again at three in the morning, the phone went.

'Len Goodman?'

'Yes.'

'Very sorry, George Fujimura here, I thought I was speaking to Len Armstrong. We don't want you.'

Shortly afterwards they got in contact again, properly this time, and I went to Japan for the first of many visits.

As well as all the travelling, I was busier than ever at the dance school with classes and private lessons, which all added up to Lesley becoming thoroughly sick of our lifestyle. I was often not getting home until ten o'clock and the last thing I wanted was a conversation, as I'd spent the whole day talking. I kept telling myself, and Lesley, that I had to work while it was available, but looking back I perhaps should have eased up a bit. There was another problem in that Lesley was feeling increasingly isolated, living down a country lane with virtually no neighbours. She found the drive to and from James's school just allowed her so little time to do anything else. The rural dream turned into something of nightmare and there was only one logical alternative: we needed to sell up.

Chapter Eleven

Nearly a Very Grave End

The decision to sell Rose Cottage proved to be a watershed in my relationship with Lesley; it was one of those decisions that seem to have repercussions way beyond how it appears at the time. It would eventually lead to me spending most of the nineties in limbo, and I don't mean the dancing kind. Approaching 50 I couldn't really complain about my lot, but it wasn't what you'd call an exciting existence; it was like I was treading water, and this time turned out to be the unhappiest period of my life. Love had flown out the window. But for James's sake I didn't want to split up. We became like too many couples that simply stay together for their child's sake. Deciding to sell Rose Cottage was the easy bit: doing it turned into a nightmare situation of legal wrangling, lawyers, barristers and unpleasantness all round.

Before I bought the cottage I had a full structural survey completed, as I didn't want to be caught out in any way; luckily it came back saying that there were no serious problems with the house. However, just before we were about to exchange contracts Lesley and I were there looking at the curtains. While

Lesley was inside measuring up, I was walking around in the garden when I noticed that one of the walls of the original cottage had a slight bow in it. I'm not sure how come I even saw it, because I certainly wasn't looking for it. The next day I called the surveyor to talk it over with him.

'Look, you haven't mentioned this bow in the wall which even I can see. Should I be worried about this?'

'I did notice it, but I've checked it and it isn't a problem – it's perfectly sound, but I will go and have another look at it. If that's what you want, sir.' A couple of days later he called me back to confirm it was not a problem. I called the man selling the house who said that If I was worried about the wall he would write to my solicitor to the effect that – at least as I understood it – should anything happen in the future with the wall then he would pay to put it right. Worries over. The surveyor had said the wall was fine and my solicitor got a letter saying the seller would pay for it to be fixed if anything untoward should happen.

I didn't spend my days at Rose Cottage worrying about it, and we lived there happily, but I did every now and again check to see how the wall was looking. Over time it got steadily worse, to the point where after four years an inch and a half gap had appeared between the window frame and the wall. I decided to meet with my solicitor; he suggested we have another surveyor look at it.

'Mr Goodman, this is dangerous, you've got to get this shored up otherwise the whole side of your house could collapse.' This was just a local surveyor, so I decided to get a second opinion. I called in one of the biggest surveying firms in Britain, who've got offices in New York, Hong Kong and God knows where. They cost me a small fortune but I wanted to be certain before getting the surveyor who originally looked at it under the cosh. My main priority was the urgent need to get it put right; it cost me 18 grand!

Not that I thought it was costing me anything: I assumed that because I had the letter from the previous owner I was covered. I was just ensuring the bloody house didn't fall down. Unfortunately the man I bought the house from didn't see it quite the same way as I did and we inevitably ended up in court. One of the lawyers involved in the case said:

'Mr Goodman, this is an open-and-shut case. We cannot lose.' Of course it was anything but and although we had written evidence from the biggest company in the world, with offices God knows where, things went badly from the start.

To prove everything I had done, I got a professional photographer to record the before and after; I had enough pictures to publish a whole book of photographs on the rebuilding of the wall. The judge decreed that this was inadmissible evidence and wouldn't accept it. At that moment I thought all was lost, but thankfully the other side were not as confident of their case and offered to settle out of court for £12,000. I had asked for £18,000 but thought what the heck, better to get this whole charade over and done with so I was all for accepting the money. I was talked out of it, with people saying things like: 'They wouldn't have offered to settle otherwise, would they, Mr Goodman?' I allowed them to change my mind and the open-and-shut case in my favour ended up going against me. I had to pay my costs, their costs and the £18,000 it cost me to fix it. It wiped me out for years. In the first instance I had no option but to increase my mortgage on Rose Cottage.

There's no doubt that it affected my relationship with Lesley.

Any lingering doubts we had about staying there disappeared, but there was another more practical reason in that James had developed asthma and the doctor thought the damp air there, because of all the surrounding trees, was a factor. We put Rose Cottage on the market and it sold for £140,000, which would normally have been a pretty healthy profit. However, the court case cost that and more of the so-called profit.

We had not the money to buy somewhere else that we really liked, so as a stopgap we moved into the flat above the dance school in Gravesend. We went from six bedrooms and several acres of garden to a dance school in the back garden. James had the bedroom on the top floor, while we had the bedroom on the third floor. For a start I was overworked in the school: it's a place where you have to be upbeat, full of fun. It's like doing a performance. When I arrived home I was drained and I just wanted to relax. I didn't particularly want to talk; I just wanted to chill out and unwind. In retrospect I should have balanced work with play – all work and no play made Len a dull boy.

After enduring a couple of years in the cramped dance school flat, during which time our relationship went further downhill, we bought another house, which in its own way proved to be just as disastrous as the cottage. We had spotted a lovely development of 13 houses on a private estate in Gravesend called Brontë View. We went and viewed the show house and I fell in love with it. They were detached homes, advertised at £204,000, which they were building one at a time. Having been told they were all virtually the same as the show house we said we'd have the next one. I'd managed to accrue some money from having lived in the flat and so we had enough to put down a deposit but it still meant a pretty hefty mortgage. Not that we, or anyone else who was buying houses at the time, bothered as prices were moving upwards so quickly that we made a profit before we even moved in. The next house they built after ours went for £210,000 so that was six grand in the bank already. Even before we had moved in they sold another for £213,000, and then two more went for £220,000. Just as we finally moved into our house they sold one for £230,000 so we contented ourselves with having made £26,000. We couldn't quite believe it...sure enough we were right not to.

One of the best things about living in the flat in Gravesend was being able to walk James to school. Seeing him in the evenings was difficult because of my teaching commitments, so the morning was very much our time together. I began to pick up on James's dislike of the convent school: he would mention it all too often as we walked there, but I put it down to kid's talk. When is a kid ever that happy with school? Being smacked every day by a middle-aged woman was the norm for me when I was at school; I hear people pay good money for that kind of thing today.

One Wednesday morning I took James to school but unfortunately I forgot to pick up his gym stuff – his plimsolls and shorts and top. It was my fault, I should have remembered; how many kids at that age know what day of the week it is? Apparently when it came time for gym the teacher in charge made James stand on a chair in his underpants, because of forgetting his stuff, while all the other children had their PE lesson. James was a very sensitive little boy and so when I went to pick him up in the afternoon he was distraught. I was furious that they had humiliated him and so the next morning James stayed at home and I went straight up the convent to tell them I was pulling him out of the school. Decision made, and not a difficult one; the question was what to do next.

There were two things that came into play in deciding on a new school for James; one was the fact that he definitely followed in his old man's footsteps in that he wasn't the most academically gifted of kids. He tried harder, a lot harder, than I did, but his mother and I knew that singing and dancing was a more likely option than brain surgery especially after a girl he sat next to at school announced, 'I mustn't sit next to James Goodman 'cos he's a dumb-dumb.' Charming!

James loved coming to the dance school and although we never ever said, do you want to join in with the other kids, one day he suddenly did. From the outset it became clear he had a talent for it. Lesley and I decided we should enrol him into Italia Conti, the theatre arts school, near the Barbican. It's the oldest school of its type in Britain and so we thought it perfect for James. As luck would have it there was a coach service that went from Gravesend to London Bridge. From there it was a tube to the Barbican and then a short walk. Every weekday he and I caught the 7.30 a.m. coach to take him to school. I did the trip for six weeks, first me showing him the way, and then James showing me the way; after six weeks James started doing the journey alone. He was nine and a half, coming up ten, and this did a great deal to build his confidence. Best of all, though, James was suddenly in an environment that was perfect for him; he went from hating school to loving it.

Sadly it came to a point where being with Lesley was just impossible for me, and I think she couldn't stand being with me either. We were always arguing, which is no environment to bring up a child. It was just history repeating itself, because I'd grown up in similar circumstances 30-something years earlier, so I had some idea of how difficult it could be. I was the one that made the actual decision to split up. Lesley decided to move back to the Isle of Wight and 12-year-old James went with her. It put paid to Italia Conti but we were lucky that James got into a really good school, a normal one, not a stage or theatre school, although on the island there was a programme called Stage Coach, where we enrolled him, that encouraged his talent. I bought them a bungalow on the Isle of Wight; we discussed how much she would need, along with the house, and just settled it amicably. There was another small bonus for Lesley in that half the Gravesend dance studio we bought was in her name. It was to do with business and VAT, which at the time my accountant advised was the best way to do it. Today the school is rented and Lesley still gets half the money, a just reward in some ways, as it was her idea in the first place. But having said that it's my side of the story and Lesley probably has a very different take on things.

With Lesley and James gone I was living in the house in Gravesend, which by the day was reducing in value. My 'so called' £26,000 profit of a couple of years earlier when we first moved in had turned into a thumping great loss. As every week went by it was worth less and less. I eventually sold it for £148,000; I virtually gave it away just to be out of it and release myself from the mortgage payments. Not surprisingly they're now selling for £400,000. I went back to my bolthole, the flat above the studio in Gravesend. It was something of a low point in my life, because while I was happy to be free of the negative atmosphere that two people living together in unhappy circumstances create, I was stony broke. The cost of Lesley's place and paying the mortgage on the worthless Gravesend house meant that I had been working my nuts off. So there I was, 49, coming up 50, pretty much skint, living in a two-bedroom flat over the dance school in the aptly named Gravesend – things could only get better.

Better is always a matter of someone's opinion; for me it was better in that I was no longer living in a doomed relationship. I was not the only one in this situation: John Knight had got married in the eighties but his had also broken down. John and I went back to our old ways and spent too much time playing golf and having a laugh. I missed James a lot and so whenever possible he would come up to stay during the school holidays. We'd often go out for the day together, usually somewhere fairly local. One time I asked James where he'd like to go and he said Alton Towers. Well, this was a fair drive so we decided to turn it into a weeklong tour of British theme parks. We did Thorpe Park and Chessington World of Adventure before getting to Alton Towers; on the way back we did Longleat Safari Park.

The dance school required, and got, a good deal of my attention, as I was not going to let things slip. I needed the money to deal with my responsibilities and I had also worked too hard to let it all disappear; apart from anything else I kept telling myself that I was totally unsuited to any other kind of work. Somewhat unbelievably I was still riding on the back of the *Saturday Night Fever* and disco boom of years earlier. Throughout the eighties and on into the nineties large numbers of people were still wanting to do pop dancing; we had 400 or so kids that did it every week. I also saw this as an opportunity to try and encourage some of them to take up ballroom and Latin

American, although if I'm honest I think that Latin was a bigger draw for most of those that did take it up. Martin Cawston and Julie Tomkins, a professional dancing couple that came to me for lessons, helped me with this idea. They came from East Anglia and were only partners on the dance floor. They also did some teaching for a guy who had a studio in Orpington and after I'd been coaching them for a while I suggested that they come and teach Latin and Ballroom dancing for me, specifically with the kids. Having Julie and Martin at the school was brilliant because both of them were not only good dancers; they were also very good teachers.

Besides concentrating on making the school more successful I was also doing a lot of judging; Japan was by this time a regular trip, one that I really enjoyed. I also judged the United States Ballroom Championships, which are in Miami every September. Then in 1993 I was asked to judge the open section of the Blackpool Championships, which is the pinnacle of a judge's achievement. I'd previously judged the exhibition section, the one that Cherry and I won all those years ago, I judged Junior Blackpool, the closed National British Championships, but I had never actually judged the premier dancing competition in the world. It's strange, because judging Blackpool brings you far more kudos than judging the world Championships, which I'd already done. In those days there was a panel of 11 judges that adjudicated at each event and these were drawn from a pool of 25 judges. In the dance world it's a bit like becoming a Knight of the Garter; it's certainly a very select group. From a career point of view this was it, I was in with the most respected judges in the dance world – once you've judged Blackpool you've cracked it. I was even asked back several more times during the nineties, so I must have been doing something right. Although I'm making a joke of it I was very proud of this and still am – it's a great honour.

I embarked upon a relationship with Julie, the teacher from the dance school, she was responsible from bringing back my passion for ballroom and Latin dancing once again, having let it dwindle in favour of disco. As I turned 50, and as is so often the case when you get to these milestone years, it encouraged me to reflect a little more on what had been and what the future might have in store. I was getting on a bit now, there was no escaping the fact; I'd been teaching for 30-odd years. I ran a successful dance school and I did a bit of judging, which all suited me fine but I certainly had to work hard for my daily bread.

One day I was sitting in John Knight's office chatting when he did the most amazing deal. One of his many businesses was a tile firm; he bought and sold wall and floor tiles. As we were talking the phone rang.

'Hello, mate,' said John. 'A container load you say? Okay, I'll take 'em. Five grand, no problem, it's a deal.' With that he put the phone down and immediately started dialling.

'Won't be a minute, Len,' said John as he waited for the person to answer.

'Hello, Stevie, I've got a container of tiles, they're the blue ones; you interested? They're ten grand. Okay, mate, we'll deliver them too, you drive a hard bargain.'

With his deal done we carried on talking but it did amaze me. There was John making £5,000 in less than five minutes. I had no cause for complaint because while I had to tighten my belt on occasions, it was only when things had gone pear-shaped with relationships and because of my business. The dance school and teaching ticked over and gave me a bloody good lifestyle – barring the odd hiccup. Now I see just how very different things can be, how easy it is to make some nice dollops of money when you have a degree of fame. Don't think I have any illusions about myself, I'm just a judge of *Strictly Come Dancing*, but the world is a crazy place. Just before I went off to America in the spring of 2008 they decided to show *Dancing with the Stars* on one of the satellite channels and wanted Bruno and I to do a little promo trailer. They sent a car to pick me up, I spent a couple of hours filming and then they dropped me back home – they paid me three grand! It's truly bizarre. I'm no different now to what I was 30 years ago – why didn't they bloody come along then? I had more hair and I was better looking. Still, better late than never.

I've been known to complain about some of the professional dancers on *Strictly* and their attitude to fame and celebrity. For some it has gone to their heads and they began thinking they were bigger celebrities than the celebrities they dance with. Take Brendan Cole: he was in a TV show called *Celebrity Love Island*, which I never saw, but I gather he was runner-up to somebody's son. A load of young blokes and girls on an island where there's lots of shagging and they film it! He seemed to come off that thinking he was a superstar. You must never forget who you are and I'm always saying to him, 'I don't understand you; we're just lucky to be doing what we're doing. I never forget that I'm just a dance teacher from Dartford – that's what I am – never forget where you come from.'

Recently I was putting some petrol in the car and a woman

standing at the next pump said, 'You're Len Goodman, aren't you?'

'Oh, hello,' I said.

Bloody daft! I'm always saying to family and friends, if you ever see me behaving like I'm up myself, give me a bollocking. I hate all that.

Having a son when you're a slightly older parent probably helps to keep your feet on the ground. It certainly did for me. On one occasion when James was 17 and I was 55, we went to the pictures. I went to pick him up.

'Dad, you can't go out like that!'

'What's wrong?' I said.

'Look at you, your shirt's tucked in.'

'Of course it is, my shirt's always tucked in,' I said.

'Dad, no one goes out with their shirt inside their trousers.'

'Well, I do,' I said

'Dad, it's embarrassing. What if we bump into one of my mates? You look ridiculous.'

'Well, what if we bump into one of my mates?' I suggested.

Anyway, for a quiet life I pulled my shirt out of my trousers and off we went to the pictures. I felt more than a little self-conscious. Just before we went in to watch the film I followed the golden rule of the over-50s. Never trust a fart, never waste an erection and never pass a toilet without having a pee. After five minutes of waiting James came looking for me.

'Dad, hurry up, we're going to miss the film.'

He found me under the hot air hand drier trying to dry the tail of my shirt – I'd peed all over it.

I've talked a lot about my love for golf and should probably say that it was all Cherry's fault that I got involved with the game at all. Someone once said golf is a serious of tragedies with the occasional miracle, but the reason I started playing was a complete fluke. In 1971 Cherry had a female pupil at the dance school that was a member of Dartford Golf Club. Her name was Jan and they became friends and would meet for lunch up at the golf club. Following a bit of cajoling from Jan, Cherry booked six lessons with Peter Mitchell, the assistant professional. He was a 16-year-old lad then, but went on to win many tournaments throughout Europe. After six lessons Cherry had a nine-hole playing lesson on the course and I went along to walk around with her and the Pro. Well Cherry had as much talent for golf as Diarmuid Gavin had for dancing; she actually missed more balls than she hit. As she was playing her last hole I said, 'Give me that club – I can do better than that!'

As I went to hit it, I missed it. I think if I had hit it I wouldn't have bothered, but missing it made me mad so I booked six lessons with Peter Mitchell; from then on I was hooked, although Cherry somehow got unhooked and she never played again.

As the nineties rolled along the school was doing fine, thanks as much as anything to the good staff I had around me. My life, like most people's lives, was not one full of excitement and amazing things. Holidays came and went, judging trips abroad came and went and there was the ever-present fun I derived from golf and the friends that I made through the golf club. In 1995 I joined the London Club – the one that they had to come and pick me up from when I did the pilot for *Strictly Come Dancing*. Naturally, John Knight joined too, but I also made a whole load of new mates through the club, which was brilliant; working at the dance studio makes it harder to keep friends because you work a lot in the evenings. Most of the members of the London Club are self-made business people of one type or another; we had the odd mega-rich and one or two characters with shady pasts. Nick Leeson, the guy who brought down Barings Bank for £800 million, is a member.

One of my regular playing partners is Sir Henry Cooper – one of the loveliest guys you could ever wish to meet. My regular game was with three real characters, Dave, Tony and Harry. Dave is a natural wit and anything he spots about you physically or personally he preys upon. Tony, who is about five foot six, is regularly on the receiving end of his jibes. One day Tony had been practising and walked into the clubhouse saying:

'It's cold enough to freeze your balls off.'

'With your little legs it must be a ground frost,' said Dave.

With Harry and me it's our noses. One day I had a cold and my conk was blocked up.

'Here, Len, let me blow it for you. I'm nearer to it than you are,' said Dave. We had a spate of things going missing from our lockers so Dave put up signs all over the place saying 'Neighbourhood Locker Watch – keep your personal belongings safe.'

However, the real bonus, and a totally unexpected one, from becoming a member of the London Club was that I found myself a new dance teacher – which only goes to prove how important golf really is! One Saturday, after a round with Dave,

Tony and Harry, we headed into the clubhouse to have one of those 'what if', and 'if only', conversations that you do after a game. I ordered a sausage sandwich and as I was standing waiting for it I noticed an attractive girl and a gentleman sitting at a table over by the window; well, attractive girls and golf clubs don't usually go together so it certainly got my attention. I didn't like to stare but I had a feeling I knew her and, sitting with my golfing mates, I kept trying to think where I knew her from. We finished our in-depth analysis of our golf game and on my way out of the clubhouse I had to pass her table.

'Don't I know you from somewhere?' Original or what?

'Yes, Len, you do. I teach dancing in Essex and I've seen you many times at competitions, but possibly you remember seeing me when I also used to come to have lessons at your Gravesend school. My name's Sue.'

'That must be it, thank God we've worked that out.' She then introduced me to the man that she was sitting with.

'This is Jim Lamb from America, I work at Lloyds Insurance Market and he's an attorney for the State of Kentucky.'

'Well, nice to meet you Jim, and nice to put a name to a face, Sue. I tell you, if you're ever looking to change dance schools give me a call, I'm looking for a good teacher.'

A few days later she called.

'Hi Len, were you serious about a job?'

'Yes,' and I said I needed help with both classes and private lessons.

'Well, I fancy a change so maybe I could come to work at your school in the evenings and weekends because I'm still working at Lloyds.'

I agreed we'd give it a go and Sue was brilliant; she worked every Saturday, and three days a week she would drive to Dartford from Southend at seven in the morning, park up, get the train to London and then after work take the train back to Dartford to work in the studio until ten before driving home. Amazingly, after working together for ten years, we discovered all our metronomes were in sync and Sue and I are very happy together. Despite the fact that Sue taught in my school we hardly ever talked to one another – she would come in and teach her classes and then go; it's so very different from the sort of relationships that develop in a more normal office environment. But it's a funny old world and sometimes things come along when you're least expecting it, which is exactly what happened to us – maybe a bit on the late side, but my life is finally complete.

During the second half of the decade I was affected by two sad events. My dad passed away in 1996 and Mum went to live in a home; she died shortly after the millennium. The loss of your parents is awful and as someone once said to me, it's a bit like becoming an orphan – which is true even when you're as old as I was when it happened. Dad was 82 when he died, so he had a pretty good innings. I loved my dad and at the risk of repeating myself I learned a lot from him. The divorce from my mum had long been forgotten; Dad and my stepmum Rene were real soulmates. They had nearly 40 very happy years together and really were a perfect couple. I've often said that I wish I could have found a wife like my stepmum, that's how good they were together. Dad's funeral took place not long after the IRA had bombed Canary Wharf, which in normal circumstances would have been two totally unconnected events, but they gave rise to a close shave with the law.

After my dad's cremation I kept his ashes in an urn, as the plan was to get the headstone where my nan is buried changed, after which my stepmum and I could sprinkle Dad's ashes there. The week or so after his cremation John Knight and I had been up to London for a meal and were on our way home in the early hours, having been to a Casino. We were on our way across Westminster Bridge where we were confronted by an armoured vehicle blocking the road, and standing beside it were soldiers with machine guns. They indicated for us to stop, which I did, and lowered the window. An army corporal said:

'Okay, get out of the car.' Unlike the police there was no politeness involved. John and I both got out of the car and stood on the bridge next to it feeling like a couple of kids caught nicking sweets.

'Get your hands out of your pockets.'

'What?' I couldn't believe the way they spoke to us.

'You heard. And open the boot.'

'Look, mate, I'm a bloody East-End bloke who has been up town for a night out and you're treating me like I'm Paddy McGinty's goat.'

'Just open the boot, do as you're told.' As I opened it, right smack in the middle was the box in which was an urn containing Dad's ashes.

'What's that?'

'That! That's my dad's ashes, he was cremated last week,' I said, not quite believing what was happening.

'Open the box.'

'No! I 'm not bloody opening it! The bloody ashes might fly

out.' From thinking it was all a bit stupid I had now got the right hump.

'Open the box.'

'No!'

'Sarge, we've got a right one here.' With that the sergeant walked around to the back of the car.

'What's going on?' asked the sergeant.

'This bloke is refusing to open this suspicious parcel.'

'Look,' I said, as I picked up the parcel. Well that was it, four guns were trained on me; it was like something out of a film. 'These are my father's remains that we're endeavouring, once the grave is ready, to place next to his mum and I'm not prepared to open this box in case I lose them.'

With that, an officer came over, having seen them raise their weapons. I went through the same rigmarole with him and eventually they let us go. I can't imagine what my old man would have said to it all. I hope he would have been proud of me, because I was always proud of him.

When I finally go, I would love to be taken in the sidecar of a motor bike, sitting up, with a white scarf with a wire frame that makes the scarf flare out behind me. I think someone might object to that; I'm sure Health and Safety or some other department will put the kibosh on it. It would be perfect – they can take me down the crematorium like that and then stick me in the box and have me done. I'd like them to play 'Come on baby, light my fire' as I slip down the runway. Then I'd like my ashes to be put into a very nice tub or a half butt with a rhododendron; I'd like it put in my son's garden. I want to be a constant pain in the arse to James. Even when it's time for him to move house he will have to remember to pick up his old man and put me in the back of the removal van. Not that I'm thinking of popping my clogs anytime soon.

When my mum passed away in 2000 she was 89 years old and had been in a nursing home for quite a few years. Ever since I can remember, Mum would say to me, 'Well at least when I go, Len, you'll have the house, it's all paid for.'

Well, she would have been so bloody cross with what actually happened. The care home that Mum was in was a very nice place that cost £500 a week, so during the time she was in there it used up almost all my inheritance. From my point of view it was no problem at all: it was money well spent and I would have been happy if it had used all of it and more. But Mum would have been livid. I always was the apple of her eye and she would have been furious if she had known how much it was costing. If she had been lucid enough she would have topped herself. She never was any different all her life: she hated banks or anything like that and she hated waste; it would have really made her mad.

Probably my greatest regret is that my mum and dad never got to see what happened a few years later – their little Lenny on the telly; they would have been so proud. However, at this point in my life I had no idea about what was to be my future. I was resigned to continuing to do what I'd been doing for the last ten years or so. Not that this was a problem: as I kept telling Sue, 'It'll give me even more time for golf.'

When the word started to spread around the ballroom and Latin American dance world that the BBC were planning a new television show I didn't think for a minute that it might involve me. In our little world the gossip machine went into overdrive as people tried to second-guess who the BBC might pick to be a judge. Even when people I knew were interviewed about the possibility of appearing I didn't really think I was in the running; I was just miffed that no one had thought to even speak to me about it.

Chapter Twelve

Strictly Unbelievable

Well it is, isn't it? Sixty years old and I get 'discovered'; well, I get a job on the television. Grandad Albert in his flat cap would have been bloody surprised, and so would my nan: she'd have a little rhyme up her sleeve to make sure I didn't get too big for my boots. Having done the pilot on Saturday 24 April I spent the weekend enjoying myself. I was feeling a little fragile on Sunday morning after the night at the Ivy, but had a lovely day on the Sunday, which was my actual birthday. This was the start of a run of celebrations amongst my closest friends – a bit like waiting for a bus and then they all come along at once. There's a few things good about growing old: first it means you haven't died young, and second you appreciate things that when you were young you might have dismissed. When I was younger happiness was normally something I recognised in retrospect, whereas now I always try to be aware of it as it happens, not after it happens. On my sixtieth birthday Richard Gleave, the guy whose records I melted nearly 40 years earlier, gave me an expensive bottle of Dom Perignon. Shortly afterwards he and his wife Ann invited me to his sixtieth at

Chewton Glen, a beautiful hotel near Bournemouth. I gave him a bottle of champagne; I've got a feeling it was the same bottle he gave me. Next up came Michael Barr who with wife Vicky had his sixtieth at Stoke Park, a country house hotel surrounded by a beautiful golf course. Mike organised a golf game for the guests, and an errant tee shot of mine landed in the churchyard beside a plaque saying this was where the poet Gray had written his Elegy:

'Hard by yon wood, now smiling as in scorn,
Muttering his wayward fancies he would rove'

In my case it was my two-wood that struck the wayward tee shot. Later I noticed Richard had given Michael a bottle of Dom Perignon and I suspect it's the same one he'd originally given me; I'm hoping to get it back on my seventieth birthday.

The first ever *Strictly Come Dancing* was scheduled for 15 May 2004, which gave everyone involved with the show plenty to do. There were meetings where we talked over things that had happened on the pilot and how we needed to tweak and change things for the big night. I was, according to the BBC, made head judge because I was the one with the most experience of ballroom and Latin American dancing – I gave it 'technical and professional credibility'. One thing that was clear from the start was that we couldn't just look at the celebrities and judge them purely on technique because, let's face it, they were, for the most part, coming off a standing start. It was important to look at all the qualities that they would bring to their particular dance, even if in some cases the word 'quality' is a long way wide of the mark. It was clear to me that you can only judge it as you see it, what actually happens from dance to dance and from week to week, and it was something that would come home to roost for judges, celebrities and professionals.

One of the biggest challenges when judging individual dances is that you watch them one by one and therefore it's hard to compare them to another couple's performances. To begin with we gave more sixes and sevens as we tried to find our basis for judging people. On my mind, probably more than the other three judges, was a sense of responsibility I felt to the dance world; I was the dance judge's judge. The BBC told us it was their mission to bring in a big Saturday night audience, the Holy Grail, as they called it, of eight-year-olds to eighties. This meant that they had to attract new people to dance, but we also couldn't alienate the serious dance fans and participants. I came away from our production meetings thinking that it was a big gamble. My fears that it might not work were never far from my mind in the three weeks between pilot and premiere. While the production team were very positive about the series no one was sure if it would work or whether it might all just fall a bit flat. What I cared about most was that dancing's image was not tarnished; whether or not it was a hit show was totally out of my hands – it was all a bit of 'suck it and see'. But you have to admire the BBC. They didn't poke it away at 10.35 p.m. on a Tuesday evening: they went for it, big time. It was the glitz and the glamour of a full-scale production. In fact, it wasn't the first time I'd been on the television – I'd been a judge on the BBC's *Come Dancing* during the 1980s with Angela Rippon. A judge on the original show hardly ever said anything, and if you did it was only a sentence: 'I thought you danced well and I award my points to Home Counties North.'

Having committed to be on *Strictly* for eight weeks I was also just a little worried that if it was terrible, and I was crap, then all my mates in dancing would go after me – big time. I could feel the giants of the dance world, past and present, looking down on me.

From the outset I had a problem, one that has reoccurred ever since: there were one or two celebrities that I've heard of, but there's usually more who I wouldn't know from Adam – soap stars in particular, because when they're on TV I'm usually out teaching. The eight celebrities on that first series were a mixed bag and need to be praised as they were the guinea pigs. David Dickinson I'd heard of, Lesley Garrett I knew, likewise Martin Offiah, because I'm keen on sport, and I watch the news so I'd heard of Natasha Kaplinski – the thinking man's crumpet. But Jason Wood, never heard of him, still have no idea what he does, Claire Sweeney I don't think I knew, Verona Joseph, no, and Christopher Parker from *EastEnders* I definitely didn't know.

For the show to succeed it didn't matter how much planning went into it: unless the professional dancers could do their bit then the whole thing would fail. It all boils down to the art of teaching and how to get the best out of your pupil, whether it's at the world championships or on *Strictly Come Dancing*. If you've got a celebrity who is limited in their ability it's the professional's task to disguise it. They need to give them steps that will make them look good, not stupid. On the 2007 series of *Strictly Come Dancing* you couldn't show Kenny Logan, the former rugby union player, the same routine as singer Alesha Dixon was taught; her routines were far more complicated. It's no different for the professionals. Take Anton du Beke: he's a great ballroom dancer but he's not as strong on the Latin

American side, although that's being picky because he's a fine dancer; he brings out in his celebrities a much higher standard in their ballroom than their Latin American, because that is where his strengths lie. On the other hand Karen Hardy, another of the professionals, who partnered the winner of series four, Mark Ramprakash, did really difficult stuff with him, but when she danced with Bill Turnbull on an earlier series she did much simpler things, routines that Bill could cope with, but they made him look pretty good. Darren Bennett, who won series two with Jill Halfpenny, did the most brilliant jive, and they deservedly got four tens. In the next series he did a jive with Gloria Hunniford, which was much simpler: it was nice and easy and it suited his partner's abilities. It's a testament to all the professional dancers on both the UK and the US show that they create routines that show them to the best of their joint abilities. This they do in just a week, which is a fantastic achievement and one that may be somewhat undervalued by the viewers that are not dancing professionals.

For me the most frustrating thing about the first series was the bloody clothes they dressed me in – serves me right, I suppose, for turning up as the eccentric Englishman in my tweeds for the interview with Izzie Pick. They asked me to go into the BBC one day to try on the suits that they wanted me to wear. Because I was green I agreed, but I remember some of the things they put me in – strange colour combinations and styles – I looked like a bloody idiot. They made Bruno, Craig and I look too alike, by colour coding us – it wasn't my scene at all. Being the new boy I agreed, but once I got my foot under the judge's table I said, enough, I want my own clothes.

Not only did I feel like the new boy, I also felt like the odd one out amongst the 'motley crew', as I soon began to call us four judges. I'd vaguely heard of Arlene Phillips from Hot Gossip, but I hadn't heard of either Craig Revel Horwood or Bruno Tonioli. I found out that they all knew each other. Bruno had appeared in a video for Elton John's 'I'm Still Standing', shot in the South of France, which Arlene had choreographed. Bruno was wearing Speedos and sunglasses and not much else. Craig has done many directing and choreography jobs in London's West End. So the three of them were from the world of luvvies. To begin with I wondered why the BBC hadn't got four people from my world of dancing, but I soon realised that they had got it just right. If they had done that, they would have got four very similar critiques, instead of each of us judging through the eyes of our own experience. But I still felt like the old fuddy-duddy ballroom expert amongst the showbiz crew.

Another aspect of being the ballroom and Latin man that came into play before the first show was the fact that they needed my expertise to tell them what to look for in each dance. I got several calls saying, 'What do you look for in the foxtrot?' A day or so later the same question about the cha-cha-cha. I eventually went to meet one of the production team to explain in great detail what judges in professional dancing look for. It had taken me a lifetime to accumulate all this knowledge so I cheekily said to the BBC, why don't you take me on as a consultant as well, because knowledge doesn't come cheap. Despite being a licence payer, I got the bum's rush and they pleaded poverty.

Unusually for me I found myself getting nervous as the days ticked by, not so much about my own performance, but more about whether it was actually going to happen or not; of course it was going to happen because it was in the *Radio Times*. What if I should come over as a bit wooden? I contented myself by remembering what my dad always said to me: 'Be yourself, don't try and be what you're not, don't try and disguise who or what you are or where you come from.' I think I've done pretty well on that score; no one could accuse me of trying to posh myself up.

I suspect the BBC expected me to be fairly dry in my comments, something like I had been on *Come Dancing*, but nobody's telling me what to say: but I just make it up as I go along – there's no script, and I just busk it. Instead of saying, 'Your head should have formed a picture to the left as with your partner,' I come out with all my little sayings, which is the way I've always taught anyway. 'It's lovely rise and fall, up and down like a bride's nightie,' or 'You're just like a trifle, fruity up the top but a little bit spongy down below.' The other judges, especially Bruno who has become a master of analogy, learnt very quickly. I think Jason Wood was probably the first one to be on the receiving end of one of my specials – 'Wood by name, wood by nature.'

One of the most useful things that we got prior to the first show was a briefing sheet from the BBC; we get them for every series. Each one has a photograph of the celebrity; it gives a synopsis of their career, if they went to theatre school and other titbits of information. For me those were invaluable in helping me get to know the people I'd be judging, as well as giving me some background that I might be able to work into some funny quips. While that side of things was all very organised, the one thing that worried me more than anything was how an earth were the professionals going to teach some of these celebrities to dance? It was in some ways less of a problem for the first show, because they had been practising for five weeks, so their first dance was made much easier. It was week two and thereafter where it started to get tricky. Naturally they start to work on subsequent dances so on the first series the people that did the cha-cha-cha on week one, then did a quickstep on week two, a jive on week three and foxtrot on week four. The couples that did a waltz on week one then did a rumba, tango and then a paso doble on the subsequent weeks. For the fifth week the five remaining couples all did the samba and for the last three weeks the dances were mixed up, but they were all dances they had done in the opening weeks. Putting it like that makes things sound very straightforward, but believe me it's asking a lot to have people remember what to do and in the correct order. Every series has had its share of disasters, but a lot less than I thought there would be when we started out.

Apart from raising their profile one thing the show does do for the celebrities is to get them very fit. In that first series Lesley Garrett lost virtually two stone, none too surprising when you consider she was dancing four or five hours a day, for five weeks, and she stayed in until the next-to-last week. Some people come up to my dance classes for an hour's tuition in air-conditioned luxury and cannot understand why they aren't losing pounds and pounds; it helps to keep you fit, but not much more. In the third series Darren Gough lost a heck of a lot of weight. I don't suppose it did his cricket any harm either.

Naturally I had no difficulty with knowing the professionals as I had judged most of them for years, some since they were just kids. Their problem is that it's not just about impressing the judges but also the public sat at home on the sofas; for the most part my fears were unfounded. I really felt sorry for one or two of the professionals, especially Kylie Jones who danced with Jason Wood. He was the worst dancer on the first series and was off on the second week and Kylie has never been asked back. It was a similar story with Hazel Newbury who danced with Quentin Willson – definitely the worst dancer who has ever been on *Strictly*. Hazel is one of the highest-ranked professional dancers to ever be on the show and after a week with Quentin she was never seen again. Anyone who had either of these celebrities as a partner had as much chance of winning as a ham roll at a Jewish wedding.

The first series was a novelty for me, but I also loved it because there was such an eclectic mix of celebrities. I managed to get my 'all sizzle, no sausage' into the first show when I described Verona Joseph and Paul Killick's efforts. It's one of those expressions I've been using for years but now people are forever throwing it back at me. I was surprised that Natasha won, not because she wasn't a good dancer because she turned out to be great, but after the first week she hated the show and wanted to be off it. But gradually her loathing of ballroom turned into an absolute love for it, which was wonderful to see, and a great advertisement for dancing. Not surprisingly the BBC loved it because she was one of their own; it was straight out of the Angela Rippon script. Having read the news for years Angela did a dance sketch on Morecambe and Wise's show; to everyone's surprise she had legs and pretty good ones at that.

With the first series over everyone was just overjoyed by how well it had gone; even those people who always thought it would do well couldn't have begun to imagine just how well it did. There was a very quick decision to put on a second series in the autumn, which was a much better slot than the summer season was for series one. The run up to Christmas, the dark nights drawing in, the fun of a Christmas final, is just the right recipe for success. In fact, the finals have been getting closer to Christmas the longer the series has run on, with the last two being the Saturday before Christmas.

Everyone, from the production people to the professionals and us judges, was excited about the prospect of a second series. We were told that it would this time feature ten couples although it would still only last eight weeks. This was the series when Quentin and Hazel amassed just eight votes and Bruno came up with a corker, 'It's like watching a Reliant Robin with a Ferrari.' What became clear in this series is how sports people have got such a great work ethic and they take being coached very seriously. Series two also had some bizarre pairings and some interesting moments.

Julian Clary's name was the one that jumped out at me when the BBC sent me the biographical notes. Not an obvious choice for a male celebrity, particularly after he announced that he had never touched a woman in his life. 'Tinkerbell', as Bruno christened him, surprised himself and probably us all too. Erin Boag, his partner, was amazing in the performances she pulled from him. He also produced one of the great comebacks when Craig was highly critical of his paso doble in the fourth week. 'Craig, you wouldn't know a paso doble if you sat on one! And you have far too much make-up on.' Brilliant! Julian made it all the way to the final but was well beaten by Denise Lewis and Jill Halfpenny.

It was in the second series that we had our first public spat between a celebrity and a judge. There was Diarmuid Gavin, who I described as 'spotted Dick' – one of the least talented dancers we have ever had on. Others like Roger Black, the athlete, and Aled Jones were really good and perhaps even did better than they or the public imagined they would. I really liked Aled despite describing him as 'All balls and no heels'. However, the spat involved Carol Vorderman, who was knocked out after the second show, and Arlene. Carol hurt her cartilage in the rumba while dancing with Paul Killick. Arlene said of her performance that she didn't see any connection between her and Paul and that Carol lacked emotion. Whether it was losing out so early on or something else that got to Carol, it certainly kicked off between the pair of them. Carol wrote a newspaper article in which she said that Arlene showed, 'undisguised animosity ' towards her. Throughout the shows, both in Britain and the USA, I'm always reminding myself about what Laurence Olivier said when Charlton Heston asked if he read what the critics said. 'I take no notice of bad ones, even less of good ones.'

I'm often asked how they pair celebrities and professionals – it has nothing to do with us judges. We don't know until just before the series starts who is with who, which is how it should be. The first thing they think about is the couple's height; it's no good having a six-foot-four bloke paired with the shortest lady professional. There's also the personalities of the professionals: if you have one of the more abrasive male dancers with one of the gentler female celebrities then they'll spend most of their weeks training with her in tears, although that has happened to some of the toughest of our female celebrities. At the other end of the professional spectrum is Anton du Beke who has stayed friendly with almost all his partners.

By the time we got to series three we'd got into our stride, added to which I think it had the greatest variety of good and bad – so far. From Zoe Ball, who is a very good dancer, to Fiona Phillips who was rubbish. She was the exact opposite to what Walter Laird explained to me about toning. Fiona had absolutely no toning: she was just like a filleted kipper. Poor Brendan Cole, her partner, had no chance – she was so floppy on the dancefloor it was like trying to control a jelly.

Possibly the three surprise packages in this series were James Martin, the TV chef, Colin Jackson, the athlete, and Darren Gough, the big chunky Yorkshire cricketer. They all got down to the last four before James, who worked incredibly hard, was knocked out in the semi-final. Darren Gough went on to win it, despite coming a close third behind the other two finalists on the judges' vote. When I looked at the list of celebrities when we started, I thought, Darren – he's likely to be a Yorkshire pudding, but he turned into a Yorkshire terrier. For my money Colin Jackson should have won, but for the blunder in the final when he and Erin Boag did their speciality exhibition number. Rather than do a traditional dance together Erin decided to try something very different. She used two full-size rag doll puppets, which were attached to their feet; Colin danced with the female doll and Erin with the male doll. It was a brave effort and you never know what will work and what won't, until you've done it, but theirs was a gamble that didn't quite come off.

Quite naturally there's a bit of them and us, them being the celebrities and the dancers. They develop a very strong bond so it's none too surprising that they sometimes react to a caustic comment from a judge. I've rarely said anything I regret, or I didn't honestly mean, about a celebrity's dancing. I admire what they do so much, for having the guts to go out there and put themselves on the line. How many of us would risk making total fools of ourselves in front of the whole nation?

One of my only regrets is what happened with Kelly Brook and Brendan Cole in 2007. For the first seven weeks on the fifth series, they were always in the top two or three and looked certain to make the final. On week eight I gave them both a bit of a bollocking. I was particularly on Brendan's case, saying, 'This girl is so talented, Brendan, I don't think you have given her a routine that was good enough for a girl of her standard.'

I had no doubts that the following week they would come back stronger and it would allow me to say I'd been hard, but was happy to see them come back to be so much better; sadly Kelly's father passed away and she withdrew from the competition. I always felt awkward about what happened and I'm sure Brendan has felt a tad of animosity towards me.

On the fifth series the BBC introduced a new system of judging so that the public were not the only ones to decide on who was in the dance-off each week. It meant that we the judges had to make a choice between two celebrities. It partially came about because in the previous series DJ Spoony and Ray Fearon got voted off; it was wrong that they were eliminated because there were far worse dancers that stayed in. DJ Spoony is a sports journalist and DJ on BBC's Radio 5 Live so he's not one of the best-known celebrities and that counted against him. I've heard since that people have suggested that it was because they were black, but I'm certain the issue was about them being not very well known. So often it's us judges trying to keep people in while the public, who has a mind of its own, want them out. With the new format it put much greater focus on us as the final arbiters, and me in particular as head judge, as I sometimes had to decide who stayed to fight another week. I felt terrible when Penny Lancaster and Gabby Logan were in the bottom two, somewhere neither of them should have been. Kenny Logan, yes, almost any week, but not his missus. Later I had to vote off either Gethin Jones or Matt Di Angelo and whereas Gethin had for me been better over the whole series Matt was better on that night, so Matt stayed. Ironically Matt should have gone the week before, but the public had kept him in. Sitting watching the show were Karen Hardy, who had been voted off in week one, having partnered Brian Capron, and Carol McRail, a teacher and judge I know very well. As the show finished and we were walking off the set, Karen said:

'Len that must have been a really tough call, but you made the right decision, well done.'

Karen gave me a kiss and Carol said pretty much the same, so I felt better as both of them have been dancing all their lives, so they know what's what. Just then Brendan Cole came by.

'You arsehole,' said Brendan.

'What did you say?' He just kept on walking. 'Oi, what the bleedin' hell did you say.' I went after him and as I caught up with him, I said, 'Who the hell are you calling an arsehole?'

'You! You're an arsehole.'

At that moment Claire Callaghan, the producer, along with several other people came along and Brendan walked off. I explained what had happened and Claire said that she was sorry he'd said that and what I did was absolutely right. I was still upset but headed back to my dressing room. In normal circumstances I probably would have laughed and said, 'Bugger off, you silly sod.'

Sue was there, which was a good thing because she calmed me down. 'I can only put it down to the Kelly Brooks business a couple of weeks earlier. Then again it could be because he used to dance with Camilla Dallerup and she was dancing with Gethin and he wanted her to do better. Who knows what it is,' I said to Sue. 'I tell you one thing, I was wrong to go off on one in public, but I was so upset.' At that moment there was a knock on my dressing room door. It was Brendan who apologised to me. One thing my dad always said to me was, 'If someone is big enough to apologise, you be big enough to accept it.'

'Brendan, we all go up in the air over things, it's of no consequence as far as I'm concerned, it's all forgotten. Passions rise in the heat of the dance.'

And it was all forgotten. Everyone takes it very seriously and tensions run high, which of course is why the dancing is often so brilliant. Claire Callaghan then came in to see me and to make sure I was okay. I said, 'Look he probably thought I had made a mistake. He's been in and apologised so as far as I'm concerned it's over. I think Brendan's great because he's a personality, he's spiky, he's got an edge, you never know what he's going to do and he's a great dancer, both in ballroom and Latin, so to me he's an asset on the show.'

It reminds me of an old story about what are the three hardest things in the world to do? Climb a wall that's leaning towards you, kiss a girl leaning away from you and criticise someone who's looking directly at you. Perhaps a strange outcome of the show is that dancers like Anton du Beke or Darren Bennett or Camilla Dallerup and Brendan have become bigger stars than some of the celebrities because more people watch *Strictly Come Dancing* than most other shows on the television.

The highlight of series five was the discovery of an absolutely brilliant dancer in Alesha Dixon. One of the downsides was Gabby Logan being voted off before Kate Garraway, What is it with GMTV? Do they give them some sort of filleting agent to drink every morning to relax them which makes them come over all floppy on the dancefloor? John Barnes was far from the best dancer but I was glad to be able to give him a ten, much to the annoyance of the other judges, for his salsa. In dance you can make a case, good or bad, for almost anyone. I often say to people, judging is like eating Brussels sprouts; I like Brussels sprouts, maybe you don't. You're not wrong, it's your taste, and taste is what it's all about. I've often thought that before anyone is voted off they should all do both a ballroom and a Latin dance. Take Brian Capron who was the first one kicked out in that series. I didn't know him, he danced once, the waltz, and then he was gone. How do we know he wouldn't have been a brilliant Latin American dancer? Maybe he wouldn't, but they should all be given that opportunity. Look at Darren Gough: I bet anyone could have got 100–1 down the bookies against him winning after his first dance.

Soon after we finished the second series of *Strictly* we started to hear rumours that ABC television in America were thinking of taking the series. At first I assumed that it would have little effect on anything we did, as it would be American stars and local judges. In the late winter of 2005 it was finally confirmed that ABC did want to take the format but it was a real will they, won't they kind of deal. Apparently their executives loved it but were less sure about the public's reaction. They decided they would try it out in a period when it could do the least damage; the early summer schedules, and just a six-week run at that. It meant that if it failed it could just be buried and no real harm would be done to anyone's reputation. Besides their uncertainty about the show they also didn't understand the UK title, because they'd never seen *Come Dancing* on their TV. When it finally did air in June 2005, ABC decided to call it *Dancing with the Stars*. It does exactly what it says on the tin.

I heard a whisper that they were considering Bruno for one of their judges, and then he confirmed it. 'You know what, you know what, Len. I've been asked to be judge on American TV. Have you been asked, Len?'

'No, I 'aven't.'

It was like a bloody rerun of getting the *Strictly* gig in the first place. I also thought, bloody great. Arlene's doing a big West End production, Craig had done *Dancing on Ice*, Bruno's been asked to go to America and I'm back in Dartford teaching Mr & Mrs Someone to cha-cha-bloody-cha.

A couple of weeks went by. I was at home getting ready to leave to teach a class when my mobile rang.

'Hi, Len, just thought I'd phone,' said a chirpy-sounding Bruno. 'I'm at the airport waiting to fly first class to Los Angeles. I'm off to do the American show.'

'That's great, Bruno, you have a good time. And good luck.'

'Okay, Len, I see you, bye for now. Ciao.'

Bugger my old boots; lucky sod, was all I could think.

The following week I was in Blackpool at their dance festival. I hadn't been asked to judge but I went as a spectator because it's such a wonderful week. The festival started on Friday 27 May and ran until the following Friday 3 June – it is always held over the May Bank holiday weekend. So there was Bruno living it up in LA and I'm having fish and chips in Blackpool. Not that I honestly gave it much thought because I was with friends I'd known for years, having a great time.

I was staying in the Hilton Hotel on Blackpool's prom and I can tell you the exact time this happened. It was Saturday 28 May, the second night of Blackpool, at ten past six in the evening, when my mobile rang.

'Hello? Hello? Len?' There was an echo on the phone so I knew it was long distance.

'Yes, it's Len, who's this?'

'It's Izzie, Len.'

ABC had booked Izzie Pick to produce their show; BBC Worldwide own the show but ABC could have used whomever they wanted, but they went with Izzie because she had done two British shows already and she knew the format. She'd written what they call 'the bible' for the production, which sets down every last detail of the show for broadcasters around the world who want to stage their own versions.

Izzie had called me in the run-up to the American show to tell me that she had really wanted me to be one of the judges, but ABC didn't think I was quite what they wanted, which is why they had gone with Bruno, who they love, along with two Americans. ABC opted to go for three judges rather than four and the two they picked were Nick Kosovitch a Russian–American ballroom teacher, much like me, and Carrie Ann

Inaba, an American, of Japanese and Chinese descent, who was raised in Hawaii – a dancer and choreographer.

After asking me where I was, Izzie said:

'Len, I know this is short notice, but ABC have done a pilot with Nick Kosovitch and decided he is definitely not who they want for one of the judges. They've decided that they would like you to come over and do it.'

'Oh, right. When?'

'That's the problem. Tomorrow morning. Is there any chance you could? We'll arrange it, but could you get a flight and come out to Hollywood?'

'That's out of the question. I need to drive back from Blackpool, pack and so on, because I assume I'll need to be there a while.'

'Yes, six weeks.'

'I'll be able to catch a flight on Monday.'

So, instead of leaving the hotel to return to the Winter Gardens to watch the remainder of Saturday's competition, I headed up to my room to pack. Sue and I drove home through the night, and being midsummer the sun was well up by the time we reached Kent. Just over 24 hours later I was in a car heading for Heathrow and Hollywood.

Dancing with the Stars was to premiere on Wednesday 1 June so after arriving at Los Angeles Airport on the Monday evening it gave me little more than a day to get to grips with things. Worst of all I had not heard of virtually any of the celebrities. It had been bad enough in England because I'm not an avid TV watcher; in America I had no chance. The only one I'd heard of was Evander Holyfield, the heavyweight boxer. The American production people clued me in as best they could and off I went.

On the flight over I had thought to myself, I wonder why they haven't picked an American dance teacher? When the production team sat me down it became clear that I would need to get myself something of a new personality.

'You see, Len, the problem here is that if we use someone with an American dance background they will never say anything negative. They are so in awe of celebrities that they won't say the bad stuff and so we need you to be the someone who does the telling. I know that in Britain you don't have to be so harsh because you've got Craig, he's harsh enough for everyone.'

It was a case of no more Mr Nice Guy. Having always had that philosophy of trying to be positive prior to being negative this was going to be a challenge. I found myself becoming slightly harsher in America than I am in the UK; of course, Bruno is usually Mr Nice Guy on both sides of the Atlantic.

I was glad that Bruno was doing it because it meant that I had a friend in America. Having accepted the job well before me, Bruno was all sorted with an apartment not far from the studio, which has a gym, a pool and is part of a complex of five buildings. I decided that a hotel was a better bet for me as I'm useless at cooking, but I'd didn't realise how quickly I would tire of room service. From the second series onwards I moved into the same complex as Bruno, although I stay in a separate building. Quite often I go over to Bruno's apartment for a meal, because he's a very good cook – in exchange I would take some wine and do Bruno's ironing, which I'm pretty good at, although I draw the line at doing his underpants. After we've eaten we sit there like a cross between 'Grumpy Old Men' and 'The Odd Couple', moaning about this, that and the other.

Not that I was moaning about the money I was getting for each episode of *Dancing with the Stars*. When they told me how much it was I thought, bugger me, that's bloody good. I then found that because the show goes out across all the US time zones they have to film a separate results show on the following day, not that this was any big deal because as often as not the three judges just sit there and say nothing. Well, at the end of the series when my money came through, I thought, blimey they've made a mistake and paid me twice as much as they should have. What I hadn't realised was what they meant by 'episode', was not each week, but each show, so I got paid the same for the results show as the dance show. What they don't know is I'd have done it for half that!

They do two series of *Dancing with the Stars* each year, one in the spring and another in their fall, our autumn, when I'm also doing *Strictly*. It means that in the autumn I have to commute for weeks between London and Los Angeles. During this period it feels like my body is permanently mid-way across the Atlantic. Bruno and I flew back and forth eight times in 2006, which I'm told is the equivalent of flying five times around the world. In 2007 it got even worse because ABC had changed their transmission days to Monday and Tuesday, so we had to catch the first flight on Sunday morning, which meant we couldn't have a night at home as we went straight from the BBC to stay at Heathrow. In the spring I'm there by myself for weeks and time drags by. I amuse myself by playing golf as often as I can or I drive down to Venice Beach and hire a bike and ride along with the ocean on one side and all the crazy shops and buildings on the other. It's like being thrown into the bar scene out of *Star Wars* because there are so many weird and wacky people on Venice Beach. One day I was there, it must have been close to 100 degrees, and there was a guy walking around in a fur coat and a fur Davy Crockett hat; I'd no idea what he was doing and I didn't like to ask.

In America most of the sports people came from sports I don't watch so I haven't got my love of it to fall back on, except that boxing is truly international and I've been a fight fan for all my life. On series one we had the gentle giant, Evander Holyfield, the man who had had part of his ear bitten off by Mike Tyson during a fight. He seemed to be a lovely man but I didn't get a chance to speak to him as he only lasted one week doing a cha-cha-cha. He later danced on *Strictly Come Dancing* on a Christmas special. He went off time and I was tempted to say you haven't got an ear for music, but under the circumstances decided it was safer not to.

Later on came Floyd Mayweather, who may have been pound for pound the best in the world, but he had a lot of things about him I didn't like; he was always covered in gold chains, diamond watches, and rings on most of his fingers. As a dancer he was a bit of a rough diamond, far from elegant, he lacked style, but he also seemed to lack the correct attitude when he appeared in the autumn 2007 series. Perhaps it was because he had his upcoming fight with Britain's Ricky Hatton on his mind, which was scheduled for two months after he started on the show; the fight would have been two weeks after the final – if he made it. To be honest he had as much chance as I had of beating Tiger Woods at the play-off at the British Open.

My heart was hoping Ricky Hatton would come out the

winner but my head told me it was unlikely. Two weeks into the show I was walking towards the set at CBS Studios when I saw Floyd sitting in a chair surrounded by three enormous minders. As usual he was dripping in diamonds. Not wanting to walk by and ignore him, I said:

'You should be training, Floyd, if you're not careful Ricky Hatton's going to knock your block off.' Before he could answer I walked on. Later in an interview it seemed Pretty Boy Floyd didn't get the joke. He was convinced I had it in for him, because I was such a fan of Ricky. I thought the following week if I was negative towards him the three massive minders were bound to rearrange my boyish good looks. Floyd danced the foxtrot; it was totally lacking in everything you look for, elegance, good posture, smooth effortless motions – in a word it was terrible. I took the bull by the horns and laid into him verbally, as I hoped Ricky might physically. I gave him a five and the following night in the result show he was voted off. He took it very well and I suppose got on with his boxing training, which was perhaps why Ricky got beat; perhaps I should have tried to keep him on the show longer.

Another boxer who appeared on *Dancing with the Stars* was not a man but Muhammad Ali's daughter Laila, who was female world boxing champion. What the other two lacked in dance skills she more than made up for and got to the final of Series Four, to be pipped at the post by Apolo Anton Ohno, an American speed skater. On one of my cycle rides along Venice Beach I went into a shop where I found a great poster of Laila's father. I thought I could get her to sign it so I could give it to my gym as they have lots of sporting stuff on the walls. I asked her the following week at the studio. 'Sure, leave it with me.'

Three weeks went by with no sign of the poster. I didn't like to ask her for it in case she actually didn't want to, so I just let it go. When the semi-final came around, everyone at the studio was excited because it was rumoured that Muhammad Ali himself was to be in the audience. Sure enough, there he was, frail and only a shadow of the former Cassius Clay. His Parkinson's disease made him that way, yet as the Simon and Garfunkel song 'The Boxer' says, 'I am leaving, I am leaving, but the fighter still remains.' He came only to see his daughter and as soon as she had danced he left. Next time I saw Laila she said, 'I have that poster.' She had signed it, and in very shaky, tiny, writing so had her dad. I felt this was too special to give to the gym. I am a member of the Variety Club Golf Society and we provide Sunshine Coaches for charity. We have a dinner at the Royal Lancaster Hotel each year, followed by an auction. We always need memorabilia to auction and I felt that Laila and Muhammad would be happy that the poster went to such a great cause. It made £7,500 thanks to the generosity of one of the patrons of the Society.

Trying to find things to do when I'm in Hollywood in the spring is my biggest challenge, but ABC is great and are always coming up with things. They know how much I like golf and they got me a ticket to La Costa, a golf resort, south of Los Angeles, for the Accenture tournament in which all the best pros were playing. On the first day of the tournament Bruno, Carrie Anne and I had to do a live interview with *Good Morning America*, which is done from New York. With a three-hour time change it meant that for an eight o'clock slot on the East Coast we had to be in the studio, made up and ready to go for 5 a.m. I'd decided with such an early start I wasn't going to drive to La Costa but by five past five we'd done our thing so I thought, bugger it, I might as well go.

I went back to my apartment, got an overnight bag with what I needed and headed down the freeway. Halfway there I got on the phone to see if they had a free room, and somewhat to my surprise they had one. I got there by about eight o'clock and they took me to my room, which was away from the main building and, having been up so early, I got my bearings all muddled when I went to try and find somewhere for breakfast. I saw a big double door; I pushed it open and found myself in a huge corridor. As I walked along it a man came walking towards me.

'Excuse me, I'm lost.'

Before I could finish asking him how I could find reception he said, 'You're the guy on that dance show, aren't you?'

'Guilty,' I said.

'We love that show, my wife and I watch you every week. We think you're great.'

'Oh right.' Despite having so many people talk to me these days it's sometimes difficult to find the right words. As he talked he started dialling on his mobile.

'Honey, let me put someone on the phone.' He covered the mouthpiece and handed me the phone. 'It's my wife, Susan.'

I felt a bit like Tom Cruise at one of those film premieres.

'Hello, who is this?' asks the lady.

'Hello, Susan, you may know me.'

'You're Len Goodman,' she practically shouted.

After some more chat I handed the man back his phone, and he said, 'Sorry, Len, I should have introduced myself. Gary

Beckner, I look after corporate sponsorship for Accenture. Would you come and have breakfast with us in the players' private dining room?'

As we walked through some more double doors into a large room, full of desks and computers, Gary said, 'Look everyone, it's Len Goodman.'

At this, everyone looked up and in true American fashion said, very nearly in unison, whether they knew who I was or not, 'Hi, Len.'

'Bob, get Len a goody bag. And Bob, make it a *big* goody bag,' said my new best friend. 'Come on, Len, breakfast.'

As I walked into an adjoining room, which was full of circular tables set up for eating, the first person I saw was Nick Faldo with the NBC Television commentary team. At the next table, all alone, sat Tiger Woods.

'Follow me,' said Gary as he headed for Tiger's table. 'Tiger, do you watch *Dancing with the Stars*?'

'No, but Elin, my wife, watches it all the time.'

'Well, this is Len Goodman, the head judge from that show.'

'Len, won't you sit down?' asked Tiger. 'Wanna join me for breakfast?'

He didn't need to ask twice and as I chatted with probably the greatest golfer of all time, I keep asking myself: How the hell does this happen to a dance teacher from Dartford?

Doing the American shows gave me the opportunity to talk to my stepsister for only the second time in 30 years. Adrienne married an RAF guy in the sixties, but soon after they married they emigrated to Canada, which was the last time I saw her until 1974. I'd been asked to judge a weekend ballroom dancing competition in Germany. After judging the first night's competition the organiser said, 'We're taking you to the highest mountain in Germany for breakfast. Be ready at eight o'clock – sharp.'

It was the last thing I fancied doing but they wouldn't take no for an answer. Next morning we got to the top of the mountain where there was a café, a typical Bavarian-style wooden building. I sat down on a long wooden bench at a table that could seat about 20 people. There were about ten of us sitting there when up came a bunch of people, who were not with our group, and one of them said in English:

'Do you mind if we join you?'

'No, there's plenty of room,' I said. As I did, I looked up and who should sit down opposite me but my stepsister. It transpired that her husband, who had joined the Canadian Air Force, was based in Germany. One day, and I've no idea how she got my number, Adrienne called me in Los Angeles.

'Hello, Len, we've been watching you on the television, we couldn't believe it! Suddenly there you are. I'd no idea that's what you did now.'

We had a lovely chat and caught up with each other's lives. The next season I was back in Los Angeles and I called her. Gordon, her husband, answered the phone and he told me she'd died. It was an amazing coincidence that we had met in Germany and I'm so glad she was able to find out my number and we had that chat.

Appearing on *Dancing with the Stars* quickly made me realise that what George Bernard Shaw said was absolutely right: 'We're two people divided by a common language.' I got into trouble from almost the first week when I said, 'The tango was full of fire, full of passion, your eyes met, I could feel the blood lifting in your breasts.' Well, they don't do breasts on American television; the mere mention of the word would bring people out in a rash. Mind you, a few weeks later when I said, 'You were a gnat's scrotum away from getting kicked off', this made it on to the East Coast networks because it's live in New York and they couldn't bleep it out. I think they managed to sort it out before it went out across the time zones. One week when I suggested they 'give it a bit more welly', their Brucie, a man named Tom Bergeron, wanted to know who welly was. Once Bruno found out they didn't know what bollocks meant we couldn't shut him up and he used it all the time.

Rarely have we had anyone English on the show, but we did have Heather Mills McCartney. I'm not sure I could quite believe she was doing it – I was probably not alone. The buzz was, how would someone with one leg cope? Well she coped marvellously well on week one, but it was the foxtrot, not the hardest dance because your partner holds you. However, the Latin American was a different matter: everyone kept looking at her leg, wondering perhaps whether it might fly off and land on the balcony; would she manage without falling over? Again she danced very well and as the weeks went on she was equally at home with ballroom and Latin, and everyone just forgot about her leg; most of my critiques were about her arms and her upper body. The few times I talked to her she always cheery, despite it being the start of her divorce proceedings. When you are learning to dance these types of routines it becomes the whole focus of what you do and I imagine practising every day helped keep her mind off what was going on. One week she had to fly to London to do something regarding her divorce, so her partner, Jonathan

Roberts, went with her, so they could keep practising. Because of our distance from the celebrities, words off camera between us were few and I can only say she was a pleasant enough person – who knows what goes on between husband and wife.

One English star that turned out to be absolutely lovely was Melanie Brown, Mel B from the Spice Girls; she was the one they called 'Scary Spice' and she was anything but. Since she appeared on the show in the autumn of 2007 I've seen her in Hollywood a number of times and been to a party at her house. I thought she and her dance partner were brilliant throughout the series, in fact all the judges did. We marked them higher than any other competitors and in the final we gave them a perfect score, but the public yet again disagreed with us and they were the runners-up to the American Indy 500 racing driver, Hélio Castroneves.

Heather's dance partner also partnered Marie Osmond in the fifth season of *Dancing with the Stars* in 2007. Marie was 48 years old and a mother of eight children – she was a revelation. Donny Osmond came along every week, but sometimes the whole Osmond family would be sitting in the front row opposite us judges, it was like the Mormon Tabernacle Choir had turned up, daring us to say anything negative about their sister. Marie danced well for the first four weeks but on week five it was the samba – her first poor dance. I was the first judge to speak and, to ease into what was to be a gobful from Goodman, I said, 'The samba is a very difficult dance, it's got lots of rhythm changes, steps that move across the floor.' I was just about to give her a blast when down she went; she'd fainted on the floor. The whole place gasped: it was as if the Lord was wanting to save her from the wrath of the judges. Tom Bergeron announced a commercial break and so while the viewers were watching a Gatorade commercial, the medics got Marie to her feet and by the time the commercials were over, and we were back live, she had staggered off backstage to where the Tess Daly of the American show, Samantha Harris, pushed a microphone under her nose. Marie said that when she was under stress she sometimes forgot to breathe and lack of oxygen had caused her to faint. All three of us gave her a seven, her lowest mark, so we got plenty of booing from the audience. She was in the bottom two with the judges, but the viewers' vote put her through.

Two weeks later Marie's 90-year-old father died, so we thought she might pull out, but she decided to carry on and dedicate her performance to his memory. The lady with the most infectious smile, who certainly knew how to work an audience, made it to the final where she came third. She did a dance where she imitated a doll – about which Bruno said it was, 'The loopiest thing I have ever seen. It defies critiquing. It's like, Baby Jane.'

I got the opportunity to meet, if not one of my heroes from my youth, at least his wife – Priscilla Presley. Everyone was excited to see the wife of the king of rock and roll. She started off well but was done for by the rumba; perhaps a 63-year-old attempting the dance of love in front of 25 million people wasn't everyone's cup of tea. Jane Seymour, the actress who was in one of the Bond films, must have done ballet as a child because she had beautiful musicality in her arms and, while her body struggled a bit in the Latin, she was a real ballroom queen. She and her husband live in LA, but evidently have a mansion just outside Bath. One evening in conversation I said that I had been to Bath often and what a beautiful city it was. This led to me being invited down next time she and her husband were there. I'm still waiting, but, you never know, she may one day call and say, 'Come on, Len, come down to Bath and stay with us.' Who knows?

One person who did invite me out when he came to London was Jerry Springer. I've watched his show occasionally, mainly to see how long it is until somebody starts knocking the crap out of somebody else. When we were sent the background notes on each of the celebrities I was surprised to read that he had been Mayor of Cincinnati, but most of all I was surprised to see he was born in East Finchley Tube Station. I was also glad to see he's two months older than I am. He and his dance partner Kim Johnston realised he was not the best dancer, and so what he lacked in technique and flair he made up for by putting a different slant on each of the dances. It was over-the-top costumes, anything to make him popular with the viewers. He had a full matador's outfit when he danced the paso doble, to maracas and a frilly shirt when he danced the samba. As much as we lambasted him, the viewers kept having him back because he was great entertainment.

He said he wanted to last until week five to learn the waltz, why was never clear until he made it through. He wanted to learn it because it was soon to be his daughter's wedding and he wanted to dance the waltz with her at the reception. As he danced on the television his daughter was sitting in the front row. On the last few bars of the waltz he released his partner, went over to his daughter and held her as the music finished. It was the most poignant moment: his daughter is blind, and everyone shed a few tears.

After the show I was standing by my trailer at the studio having a cigar and a glass of wine. Despite his waltz Jerry was voted off and he came wandering by.

'Ah, a Cuban.'

'Yes, Jerry, would you like one?'

'I haven't had a Cuban cigar since I was last in Europe.'

Because he'd been voted out there was no bar to my talking to him. We sat in the evening air, chatting, puffing away and laughing.

'Next time I am in London I'll give you a call,' said Jerry. 'We'll go out to lunch or something.'

Months later I was sitting at home when the phone rang.

'Hello, Len, it's Jerry Springer, I'm in town for three days. My evenings are tied up but do you fancy going for lunch?'

'I'd love to.'

He was staying at the Ritz so I suggested Scott's, just around the corner in Berkeley Square. We carried on from where we'd left off in Los Angeles, chatting away as though we'd known each other for many years: we reminisced about him being born in England, me working in East Finchley and him being born in the tube station. Jerry Springer – a proper gent!

What was nice about the whole incident with Jerry was that I found out something about the real man behind the TV persona, which was not something that was very easy with the celebrities on the American show. From the outset we were told not to mix with them and to avoid even talking to them. There was a code of conduct laid down for us judges, which even ran to details such as, 'If a lift stops at your floor and a celebrity is already in it, you must refrain from entering the lift to avoid fraternising with him or her.' It's got much easier now but all this came about as a result of Paula Abdul, one of the judges on *American Idol*, being accused of having an affair with one of the contestants. As it turns out there was 'insufficient evidence' to support the claims but it got all the networks twitchy about the possibility of similar allegations on their shows.

One day in the summer of 2007 I got a call from Michael Summerton, Arlene's agent, to say they were going to do a live tour of *Strictly Come Dancing* and would I be interested in going? I told him I wasn't very keen as it was scheduled for January and February for five weeks and I fancied some time at home. He asked me to reconsider because Bruno couldn't do it as he was going to the USA to do his own dance show on ABC and so that would just leave Arlene and Craig, which meant it wouldn't really work. I was also unsure how the show could be done in huge arenas like the NEC in Birmingham and retain the atmosphere of the TV show. After I mulled it over for a bit, and not wanting to let the show down, I agreed to do it.

I couldn't have been more wrong about it working. Every night the atmosphere was brilliant, with 11,000 people in the bigger venues all going bonkers. It had all the elements of *Strictly Come Dancing* with people able to text and phone in from the venue, the set was brilliant and naturally the professionals and the celebrities danced their socks off. In the group Viennese waltz, chandeliers were lowered from the ceiling to a foot above the floor and they all danced around them and then they slowly went up – it was fabulous.

The nice thing about the live show was that we had celebrities from almost every series: there was Matt Di Angelo, Letitia Dean, Martin Offiah, James Martin, Zoe Ball, Louisa Lytton, Denise

Lewis and Christopher Parker. Kate Thornton was the compère and she did brilliantly well because she had to be Brucie and Tess Daly all rolled into one. We had Darren and Lilia, Vincent and Flavia, Camilla Dallerup and Ian Waite and Matthew and Nicole Cutler. I think overall Matt Di Angelo won the most times: he'd only just come off the TV series so he was hot; Chris Parker was last every time. Nicole danced with Chris and I was so amazed by what she did. It was not easy having to dance with someone who has so little talent for dance, yet Nicole stayed in character the whole time they did a tango or a paso doble. Every time she would give it her all, as though she was dancing with the greatest dancer; that's very hard to do and incredibly professional.

Dancing, as I've tried to say throughout the book, has a lot to do with life. Learning the techniques of dancing, whether it's posture, hold, or whatever else, are like any skills you need to do a job. I know for many people it's not a job, but for me it's turned out to be my life's work, even if I did start a little later than most. When I first started work, my dad said to me, 'Len, work is only something you don't like doing.'

For most of my life I've had a job that I would have done if I hadn't got paid, so I've been extremely lucky. However, for me, whose job it's been, and for those people who just dance for pleasure, dancing teaches you many other things. It's about struggling to overcome difficulties and problems, about being kicked down and standing up, and brushing yourself off and coming back and having another go. Christopher Parker's attitude on the *Strictly Come Dancing* live shows personified that spirit. He knew he was never going to win but still kept coming out and gave it his all and tried his hardest.

You've all heard the expression 'I could have danced for joy' – well, I have and still do. When I watch the celebrities and the professionals on the television show I see their joy; like you, I get great joy from watching them. But I get just as much joy from watching kids and adults at my little dance school. If I could have my life over again what would I change? Nuffink! Of course, there's been lows, but without them there would be no highs. It's a bit like the waltz: we all need a bit of rise and fall. Well, I've been far luckier than most because there's been a lot more rise than fall. Not that I want any of you to think that I think, that's it, I've had me lot – there's still a lot of sizzle left in this ol' sausage.

The Backword

Most books have a foreword, but this isn't most books: it's my book and I never was one for doing things like everybody else. Seeing as just about everything has come to me late in life, I think a foreword might even be a little bit premature. So here it is, my backword.

Many people would be flattered if they found a little bit of celebrity, no matter how small; through *Strictly Come Dancing* I'm having my '15 minutes of fame', as Andy Warhol called it. Having been lucky enough to have had this wonderful opportunity, I hope I've brought a few more people into dancing; helping to introduce them to the pleasure of holding a partner in their arms – it really is a beautiful thing.

I have to thank the BBC for having the idea for *Strictly*. We now know it was a brilliant idea, but they had to have the vision. Through that vision they've brought dancing into millions of homes every Saturday night. I also have to thank them for – eventually – picking me as a judge; there were so many possible candidates, many of whom are probably better qualified than me and might well have done a better job. I'd also like to thank ABC for giving me the chance to be on American television and so become an international superstar – well sort of.

But I also want to say how much I miss going to my little Dartford dance studio to teach what I love so much. As Chuck Berry once said about Elvis, 'He got what he wanted, but he lost what he had.' Having got my little bit of fame and fortune later in life, I can thoroughly recommend it; who knows, it might even be better this way because I'm able to appreciate it even more.

Well, there it is, my life story: from an urchin selling fruit and veg off a barrow in Bethnal Green to criticising celebrities dancing on the television – life's a funny old business. I started dancing in my twenties, met my soulmate in my fifties and arrived on your television screens in my sixties. You certainly couldn't make it up.

My dear old dad used to say to me, 'Len, you walk along life's highway and sometimes you come to some stony bits that are unpleasant and the going gets tough. But there are also some green bits, which are lovely and enjoyable; remember, whatever bits you are going through, you have to keep going. Try to travel slowly through the green bits and go quickly through the rough patches.'

Well, having arrived in the September of my years, I'm at one of the greenest parts of my life – better late than never.

Acknowledgements

When I finally finished the book, I threw away my pencil and got back to doing what I like best – nothing. A day or two later Richard Havers, my ghostwriter called. 'Len, where's the acknowledgements?'

'Richard, no one reads that stuff. It'll sound like an Oscar's speech, but I'll do my best, if I have to.'

So my first thanks goes to Richard for turning my incoherent ramblings into something that people could read.

Appearing on *Strictly Come Dancing* or *Dancing with the Stars* would have been impossible without the fantastic help of Sue Dimmock, Angela Parkinson, Louise Carlier and her team of helpers, Catherine Austin, Sophie Young, Rachael Breeze, Kerry Beinek, Rory Costain, Lindsay Wallace, Alison Dyer, Sue Whiting and my son James, who all work at the dance school. Over the years there have been many other teachers and helpers, but I'd especially like to acknowledge Maureen Saunders, Diane Dunn, Rachelle Bell, Derek & Beryl Brown and Dot. Special thanks also go to Bryan and Lynda Rolf who worked in the school and were like second parents to James when he was young.

They'll never read this but I'd like to thank the Goodmans and Eldridges who formed me into the person I have become, especially my Mum and Dad who I love and miss so much. Rene, my stepmother, reminded me of much about my younger years; thank you for the love, kindness and happiness you've always given to Dad and me.

At Ebury thanks to Andrew Goodfellow for agreeing to publish my book – he's a good man! Ali Nightingale has worked tirelessly and kept me on track. Jackie Gill, who acted as my agent, performed minor miracles; her charm and patience are assets all too often overlooked today. Richard's agent Paul Moreton was very helpful throughout.

Thank you to the BBC for making the title of my book come true; especially Izzie Pick for picking me in the first place. Thanks also to Martin Scott, Sam Donnelly and their team for everything. Huge thanks to Arlene, Bruno and Craig who've put up with my moaning at them, both on and off air. Not forgetting Claudia Winkleman, who is, to quote Brucie – my favourite. A big thank you to Tess and Brucie – finally I met the man who helped get me into trouble all those years ago.

Thanks to ABC Television for letting me appear on America's screens and in particular to Conrad Green, Matilda Zoltowski and Rob Wade, the producers.

I have had many wonderful experiences in my life, but the best was meeting my Sue. She has been a brilliant help at the studio, especially during my recent 'television life'. She's also been wonderful in assisting Richard and myself with the book. Sue,1 I couldn't have done it without you.

If I've forgotten anyone I'm sorry, but what do you expect at my age?